W9-CCH-925

Literary and Military critics rave about Harry Crosby's

A WING AND A PRAYER

A WING AND A PRAYER

The "Bloody 100th" Bomb Group
of the U.S. Eighth Air Force
in Action over Europe
in World War II

★ ★ ★ ★

HARRY H. CROSBY

HarperPaperbacks
A Division of HarperCollins*Publishers*

HarperPaperbacks *A Division of* HarperCollins*Publishers*
                  10 East 53rd Street, New York, N.Y. 10022

A hardcover edition of this book was published in 1993 by
HarperCollins*Publishers*.

Cover photograph courtesy of John E. Schwartz, Combat
Photo Officer of the 100th Bomb Group.

First HarperPaperbacks printing: November 1994

Printed in the United States of America

HarperPaperbacks and colophon are trademarks of
HarperCollins*Publishers*

❖ 10 9 8 7 6 5 4 3 2

To the memory of Jean Crosby,
and to Mary Alice Crosby,
in appreciation for so much of the joy
in my life then and now.

★ ★ ★

★ CONTENTS ★

★ MAPS ★

★ DIAGRAMS ★

★ ACKNOWLEDGMENTS ★

First of all, it is not enough merely to thank the two pilots with whom I flew when I was on a crew. Were it not for John Brady and Ev Blakely I would not be here, and there would be no story.

Secondly, I must thank the men and women of the 100th—not only the flyers, but those who kept us flying. They all made this narrative the grand story to which I hope I have done adequate service. I must thank, especially, the three great leaders of the 100th, Jack Kidd, John Bennett, and Tom Jeffrey, who did so much to make us proud to be members of the group whom history now knows as "The Bloody 100th."

Since the war, I have been indebted to Horace Varian, Bill Carleton, Bob Rosenthal, Ray Miller, Bud Buschmeier, Butch Goodwin, Hong Kong Wilson, and Cowboy Roane. As leaders of our postwar association, they have kept the group together; they have kept the juices flowing, and the stories growing. I am not sure whether our reunions have preserved fact or legend—especially about Frank Valesh and his indomitable crew—but they certainly have strengthened our friendship and respect through the years.

For the opportunity to check my memories and records, I express my appreciation to Roger Freeman, Richard LeStrange, Ed Jablonski, Tom Hatfield, Ian Hawkins, David MacIsaac, and Martin Middlebrook, whose studies have caught not only the history of the 100th Bomb Group and the Eighth Air Force, but their spirit. Roger Freeman is, of course, the one who gave us our name, "The Mighty Eighth."

Much of the credit for the illustrations in this book must go to John Schwarz, who, during those years, was our Photo Lab Officer.

Credit surely must go to the two editors of *The 8th A F News*, John Woolnough and James Hill, and to Lew Lyle, the founder and guiding light of The Mighty Eighth Air Force Heritage Center at Savannah. They, too, have kept the memories alive.

Two people, who did not fly with the 100th, deserve to be honorary members. My agent, Nancy Love, and my editor at HarperCollins, M. S. (Buz) Wyeth, lived the missions and survived the hazards of bringing this book to publication. They were immensely helpful.

And, finally, I want to express my special gratitude and affection to Jim Brown, Ellis Scripture, and Irv Waterbury, an inner circle of confidants. Their friendship alone has, for me, made this whole project a grand adventure.

A WING AND A PRAYER

★★ ✈ ★★

The Battleground of the
U.S. Eighth Air Force, 1942-45

✳ Bombed Targets

FINLAND

Helsinki

Stockholm ● ●Tallinn
ESTONIA

LATVIA
●Riga

Baltic Sea

LITHUANIA
●Kovno

GERMANY
(E. PRUSSIA)

Warsaw● ●POLAND

Moscow ●

RUSSIA

Poltava ● ●Kharkov

Sea of
Azov

CZECHOSLOVAKIA

Vienna ●

●Budapest

HUNGARY

ROMANIA

Black Sea

Belgrade ●

YUGOSLAVIA

BULGARIA

Adriatic Sea

Bari ●

ALBANIA

GREECE

Aegean Sea

TURKEY

0   300 miles
0   500 kilometers

PRACTICE MISSION
TO THE ORKNEYS

"Lieutenant, Lieutenant!"

The orderly from Squadron Ops shook me again.

"Wake up, sir. You are flying."

I squinted at my wrist watch, 1942 G.I. Air Corps issue to all airmen. At four A.M., in England, with Double British Summer Time, it was already light.

"The 418th is stood down today." I turned over and tried to go back to sleep.

"I know, Lieutenant, but you are flying on a practice mission."

Shivering, I got up and started to put on my pants and shirt. My eyes came into focus. The long Nissen hut had two rows of beds with eight beds in each row. Most of the beds were empty. That meant the crews of Crankshaft, Keissling, and Knox were flying. Next to me and across the aisle my own pilot, copilot, and bombardier were still asleep.

"Why aren't you waking Brady, Hoerr, and Ham?

"Captain Blakely doesn't have a navigator. You are flying with him. Lieutenant Payne didn't get back from pass."

Poor round, smiling, butch-haircut, hard luck Bubbles! He hadn't dated much till he met a nice Land Army girl in Norwich. Since then he had spent nearly every night in town. Once again he had missed the motor pool truck back to the base.

I put on my mission gear. Long johns, blue flannel underwear wired for connection to the plane's electrical system, O.D. wool pants and shirt, low-cut brown oxford shoes, black wool tie. Over this, my flying coveralls. Over everything, fleece-lined boots, leather fleece-lined pants, jacket, and a hat. I picked up my navigation kit, two bags, one like a briefcase and one like a zippered notebook. Just to make sure Ernie Warsaw hadn't borrowed anything I looked inside: E6B computer, Weems plotter, two triangles, pencils, eraser, a collection of U.K. maps, plotting charts, my logbook. Check. After checking the clip to make sure it was loaded, I strapped on my .45 revolver. "Carry it always," we were told.

The briefcase. Yep. Five #10 grocery sacks, just about how many I would need when I got airsick and vomited.

Automatically I checked to locate my packet of pictures of Jean. If I got shot down and ended up in a hospital or prison camp, it would be nice to have some pictures of my wife. Although this was a practice mission, for luck I zippered her pictures in the leg pocket of my flying coveralls.

Okay. Ready for the blue.

Usually before a mission we went to Group Ops for a briefing, then to the Flying Officers' Mess for breakfast, and then to Equipment for our oxygen masks, parachutes, and any equipment specially required for the mission. Then we would go to the flight line where our B-17's were moored on concrete pads called "hard stands." This would be done with ten or twelve officers climbing in and out over the back end-gate of a truck personnel carrier.

Now, when the orderly and I went out the door of our hut, he got into a jeep. I sat in the copilot's seat. Instead of stopping at the mess or Group Ops, the corporal drove straight on toward the flight line.

"Hey, Corporal, what about breakfast?" My breath steamed as I spoke.

"Sorry, sir, but they forgot to wake you in time. We thought Lieutenant Payne would be with the crew."

At Blakely's plane, number Zero-Six-One, with the stupid name *Just a-Snappin'*, the officers and crew were getting ready. Ev Blakely, pilot, Charlie Via, copilot, Jim Douglass, bombardier, and the enlisted men. Top turret gunner Monroe Thornton, ball turret Bill McClelland, radio operator Ed Forkner, waist gunners Lester Saunders and Ed Yevich, and tail gunner Lyle Nord. Forky, the radio operator, curly hair, round, eager face, looked about fifteen years old. I remembered him lipping off at meetings. A smart-ass kid.

Ev Blakely and Jim Douglass were about the two skinniest men I ever saw. Blake's face had so little flesh on it that his head looked like a skeleton. Doug had a mustache—Blake called him "Brush"—but his face was almost as thin. They lived in a different barracks, so I didn't know them well.

Charlie Via, the copilot, smiled and said, "I see we've got a new navigator. How about that?" Since he was from Virginia, it came out, "Hoo-a boot that?"

Blake was in the pilot's seat, on the left side, and the ground crew chief was in the right seat. Ev was running up the engines with the crew chief watching the dials. Although it was a practice mission, the gunners were installing their .50-caliber machine guns. On its first practice mission, our bomb group, the 100th, lost a plane to a flight of intruding Messerschmitts.

"I've got your maps, Croz," said Jim Douglass, the bombardier. "The Group Navigator marked in the route."

I looked at the maps. We were going on a Cook's Tour of England and Scotland. Northwest across England to Liverpool—a straight line, yet it cleared all the restricted areas. Then the red line went almost straight north for the whole length of Scotland to the Orkney Islands. I hoped there would be no clouds. It would be nice to see the country.

"You are in charge, Croz," said Douglass, the bombardier. "We are lead crew this morning."

Lead! I wasn't a lead navigator. On all my missions so far, I had been comfortable in a Tail-End Charlie plane. I could, more or less, keep track of where we were. On a practice mission, when engine trouble made Brady's crew drop out of formation and we had to come back alone, I found our way home. The radio beacon at our field, Splasher Six, was R5, read loud and clear, and with the radio compass I zeroed in on that.

But lead? If there were no clouds I could get to Liverpool. I could see the navigator's friend, a train track, the whole way, and when we got to the end of the railroad, Liverpool would be on the coast. On the northern leg of the flight I could follow the Scottish coastline all the way. On the way home I would tune in on Splasher Six, our base homing beacon, and let the radio compass get us back to the base.

But ETAs? Estimated time of arrival. And making a rendezvous with the other squadrons? Leading a formation of eighteen or twenty-one planes? And giving position reports in code to Ground Control and the other crews? Worst of all—what if we went into the overcast and I couldn't see the ground at all?

At that moment, as had happened several times before, I seriously considered turning in my wings and resigning my commission. Admit that I was a failure? Nope. A winner never quits, and a quitter never wins. My father talking.

At that moment a jeep came up and Major Bucky Egan, as usual in his white flying outfit, vaulted out. He was to fly right seat as command pilot. He spoke to Charlie Via warmly and to the rest of the crew. He hardly noticed me. I had always felt that with my regulation campaign hat and my straight-arrow ways, I was not his kind of guy.

Getting into the nose compartment of a B-17 was never easy. I went to the front emergency exit hatch below the pilot's compartment, reached up about two feet, grabbed the edge of the opening, and swung my feet up and into the opening. I made it. Since Blake had already done all the pre-flight procedures, I heard him calling out the ready-to-roll checklist: "Start Three," and so on.

"Roger," said Egan, acting as copilot.

After waving to the crew chief to remove the wheel blocks, Blake cut the inboards, two and three. Running on the outboards, he taxied us out to the end of the runway. Behind us rumbled twenty-three other planes. Me in front of 230 flyers?

At the end of the runway, Ev started two and three and slowly ran up all four engines, with Egan calling off the instrument readings. As a safety precaution on all takeoffs, I stood behind the pilot, the bombardier behind the copilot. Back in the waist, Charlie Via was now sitting down, with his back to the forward bulkhead of the radio compartment. Soon he would go back to the tail gunner's position. There he could see the rest of the formation. Acting as formation control officer, he could tell Major Egan which planes were in tight and which were straggling.

A quarter of a mile away, across the field and off to the right of the perimeter track, two flares from Flying Control arced up and down over the field.

"Green-green," said Egan on intercom. "Let's go."

"Roger, pilot here."

All four engines roared. Blakely released the brakes and we creaked to a start, Egan reading off the air speed as we gathered momentum. As we rolled and then hurtled along the runway, I thrilled, as I always did, to the full roar of the engines. With our rush punctuated by the bumps and cracks of the struts and skin of the plane, the four engines pulled at the tons of aircraft.

When the bumps and grinds stopped and all we heard was the hum of the four Wright 1,000-horsepower engines, we were in the air.

Excitement! Drama! Just like the movies.

"Wheels up."

"Wheels up and locked, Wilco and Roger."

When we were out of the takeoff pattern and climbing, Doug and I crawled to the nose compartment, and I spread out my maps and equipment.

B-17 CREW POSITIONS AND EMERGENCY EXITS

(From the *Comet Connection*, by George Watt. Copyright 1990 by the University Press of Kentucky.)

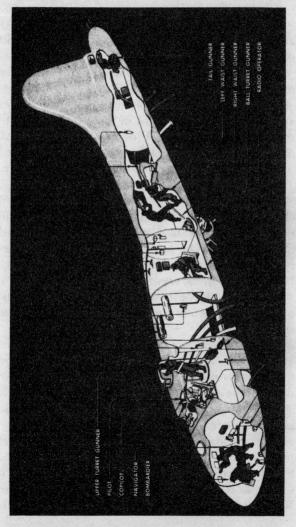

Over intercom, I heard Blakely.

"Pilot to navigator."

"Roger, Pilot."

"Since you have never done a rendezvous, Bucky and I are going to talk the squadron together. Sit back and enjoy it."

"Roger, Pilot." I was so relieved that I took time to notice I had been sweating.

It was an exciting view, watching two planes approach our wings and fit in on each side, just to the rear. Then a second V of three, point forward, drew into position, Egan talking at them over radio.

"Come on, right wing, second element, tuck it in. The Limeys are watching us."

At five thousand feet we could see much of the green checkerboard of East Anglia, the hump of England north of London. It sticks out into the English Channel toward Holland. Our base, Thorpe Abbotts, was ninety-seven miles north of London, on the border of Norfolk and Suffolk, twenty miles south of Norwich.

Behind us, two other squadrons were forming, one of them off right and above us and the other left and slightly below.

"Okay, Downtown Baker and Downtown Charlie, into position." It was Egan, talking to the high and low squadrons, using the code names assigned to them for the day. "Alternate planes, return to base."

A Flying Fortress group formation at that time had either eighteen or twenty-one planes. Our high squadron today was nine planes, a string of three point-forward V-flights of three planes. Sometimes the high squadron flew only six planes. The other two squadrons had six planes, two flights of three in line. With the formation properly in place, we had a barrage of .50-caliber machine guns pointing in every direction, capable of sending out a hail of lead no matter from which direction we were attacked. With one of those planes missing, we had a hole in our defense, and the Luftwaffe could find it. On a mission, to make sure we had full formation, we always started out with two or three extra planes. Just before we left England to penetrate the Continent, if none of the regular formation aborted, the alternates, or "supernumeraries," returned to the base and went back to bed.

"Okay, Croz," from Blake, "how about a heading to Liverpool?"

That was easy. I gave it to him.

"Radio to navigator."

"Go ahead, Radio," I said. What did he want? My own radio operator, Saul Levitt, seldom came on intercom.

"I have the 8:00 A.M. P.R., sir."

P.R.? Position report? What's this?

"Go ahead, Radio."

"Bearing zero-niyun-seven degrees from Splasher Forty-two at Cambridge; bearing two-ay-yut-fow-wer from Buncher Twelve at Norwich."

As quickly as I could, I drew the bearings on the map. Bury St. Edmunds.

I looked out the window. There it was, the forest, the railroad, the stream, the cathedral. Bury St. Edmunds. The kid was right on.

"Thanks, Radio." What was his name? Forkner?

"Radio to navigator. Do you want the P.R.s every quarter hour or every ten minutes?"

What a deal! Back in the radio compartment Forky had a flimsy with pages and pages of radio beacon schedules. Their transmission changed constantly to keep German planes from homing in, but he managed to figure them out and see which could be used at the moment for bearings. He had a remote of my radio compass, and he could get bearings as well as I could. What a stroke of genius for him and Bubbles.

I made a quick decision.

"Navigator to radio. If we are in the clear, every fifteen minutes. If we are in the soup, every ten minutes. Over."

"Roj. Radio, over and out."

On the first leg I could see every railroad, every river, and every town. Forky gave me the bearings, and I checked them visually. He was always exactly right. By comparing our magnetic compass heading and our indicated air speed to the course and speed we were making on the ground, I could calculate what the wind was doing to us. After a little twirling of my E6B computer, which was a circular slide rule adapted for aerial navigation, I came up with the direction and speed of the high winds that would have blown us south of course. Ten minutes later I gave a heading correction and an ETA.

I felt good about knowing where I was. I hit my intercom button.

"Navigator to crew, if you look out the right window you can see The Wash."

"Waist, here. What's The Wash?"

I told him. "It's that huge inlet on the coast."

In a few minutes I hit the button again.

"Now if you look on the port side you can see Robin Hood's hometown, Nottingham. That's Sherwood Forest right by it."

A string of Rogers.

Forky came on again. "Radio to all crew. On

Berlin Radio I've got Vera Lynn singing 'White Cliffs of Dover.' Shall I put it on intercom?"

"Pilot to radio, come on! Don't you know there's a war on? You know crew discipline. Keep the intercom clear."

"Roger, sir. I was just joking."

"Waist here. Jokes are supposed to be funny."

"Radio to the Greek Air Force. Blow it, Saunders. Radio out."

When radio gave me the next position report I plotted it on the map, and measured how far we had gone in the minutes we had been flying. I had my ground speed, and I could anticipate our ETA.

"Navigator to pilot and command."

"Go ahead, Navigator." Egan's voice.

I told him our ETA and added, "I'm turning us twelve miles out of Liverpool. On my map it's shown as restricted."

When we made the turn there was Liverpool, on time, on course.

"Nice, Croz." From Blake.

"Roger." From Egan.

"Pilot to navigator. Heading for Edinburgh?"

I had it for him.

For the next hour I enjoyed myself. For one of the few times since I put on my navigator's wings, I was actually navigating. On most of my previous flights the pilot was either on a radio beam or I was the tail end of a formation, and the lead navigator was doing the work. All I did was follow.

Scratch that. Maybe on today's flight I wasn't navigating, I was keeping books. Forky gave me the bearings, I plotted them on my charts and looked out the window. Since I knew where to look I could always find myself at once. A port? An airbase? A river? One of those blessed railroads, always so valuable to a navigator? Parallel to us they gave us a course line. Crossing our path, they gave us a ground speed line, how fast we were flying.

I tried to keep the crew entertained. I pointed out some places with funny English names, like "Ribble" and "Barrow-in-Furness." I showed them Balmoral Castle, Gretna Green, and Newcastle. Before the war, I had started a master's degree in literature.

North of Edinburgh, for which—thanks to that kid back in the radio compartment—my ETA was perfect, we hit the soup and began to climb. We couldn't see Inverness, which was my next checkpoint.

I didn't panic. As we climbed, the winds changed direction and velocity. Normally I would have had no idea what the changes were. Not so on this trip.

Forky came on. "Your ten-minute P.R." Since we were in the soup, he was stepping up his reports.

For the first time I had ever been in an airplane I knew where we were every minute of the flight. I could be even more efficient in the clouds because I wasn't distracted by having to do pilotage, checking the ground. I just kept the books.

Ten minutes from my ETA for Hoy, which was our I.P., the "Initial Point," Blake asked me if the heading and ETA to the Orkneys that I had given him were still good.

"They're close, Pilot."

I moved the ETA up two minutes and corrected the magnetic heading, two degrees starboard.

Just after I gave him the message the clouds disappeared and we could see all the way to Heaven and to the sea below. Dead ahead were the Orkneys. We were making about 220 mph, ground speed, but from this altitude, we seemed to be floating toward the cluster of islands.

"Good show, Navigator." From Egan.

"Roger, Croz." From Blake.

Hoy, a small village on the west coast of the Orkneys, was the I.P. It would be about six to eight minutes from the practice target. At the I.P., to make a small and exact bombing pattern, the group would tuck into the tightest formation possible. We would make a turn, not too sharp, and head for the target. If the I.P. had been well chosen, we would be going either downwind or upwind, with a minimum of drift correction to complicate the work of the bombardier and his Norden bombsight.

We crossed over the Pentland Firth, within seconds of my ETA. Just before we reached it, I called, "Navigator to pilots and bombardier."

"Roger, Command . . . Roger, Pilot . . . Roger, Bombardier."

"In thirty seconds, right turn to 37 degrees for six minutes, twenty seconds, and bombs away. At Kirkwall, the target, we will swing easy right. Bombardier, from the I.P. to the target expect a drift correction of minus six degrees."

"Wilco." From the pilot and the bombardier.

The B-17 we were flying was an F model, with no two-gunned turret in the nose. In front of me, Doug was hunched over his bombsight. As we turned at the I.P., with his eye still peering at the ground through the refraction of the Norden, he reached out with his left hand and flicked on a panel of switches.

"Bombardier to pilots, I've got it."

"Wilco, it's your baby."

I watched my compass. The bombsight had figured in just six degrees of drift. Good. Was this Crosby who was navigating?

"Bombardier to crew, bomb bay doors going open."

A chorus of Rogers.

"Tail to command, all bomb bay doors coming open."

In the rear, Charlie Via was watching the twenty planes behind us. We didn't have any practice bombs aboard, but we were flying the bomb run as we would over a target in Germany.

The plane felt different. Instead of the smooth corrections that Blake would make, the bombsight was jerking the plane around. The airspeed indicator showed 154 and suddenly dropped back to 150. The compass needle bounced around, with the plane skidding back onto our heading without the usual dip of the ailerons. The Norden bombsight was running the automatic pilot, but Blake was a smoother flyer.

"Bombardier, here. Going pretty, going pretty."

On Doug's panel, lights clicked.

"Bombs away." We didn't have any bombs, but the bomb sight didn't know it. The plane didn't jump up the way it did when we dropped real bombs.

I broke in. "Easy right to 110 degrees. In six minutes, at the Rally Point, you will turn right.

"Command here. Good show, Crosby."

After bombs away, the group headed for the Rally Point.

"Bombardier here, bomb bay doors coming closed."

The grinding noise of gears as the doors rolled up and thumped shut.

"Tail to pilots. All planes with bomb bay doors closed. All planes in position."

Going home was a piece of cake. Almost straight south, CAVU (ceiling and visibility unlimited), the coast of Scotland right below us. Even so, Forkner kept giving me the fifteen-minute P.R.s. My logbook looked like a model back at navigation school. P.R.s every quarter hour, a wind easily computed, a new compass correction, a new ETA. That kid Forkner was making a genius out of me.

When we hit The Wash, in East Anglia, Egan broke in.

"Command to navigator, bring us in with an approach for Runway 28."

I got his point. He wanted to show off. Everyone at the base would be watching us as we came in over the field.

I threw in a dogleg to the west. When we were about over Bury St. Edmunds, I gave a couple of corrections.

"Command to tail, how's the formation?"

"Tail here. Pretty sloppy, sir."

For a few minutes the airwaves were blue, with Egan dressing the pilots down and the formation up. By the time we were three miles from Thorpe Abbotts, Via broke in.

"Tail to pilot, she's tight now."

"Roger, Tail. Command pilot, over and out."

Down below, all eyes were probably looking up, seeing what they were to see all too rarely, all the planes that went out on a mission now coming back, all with four engines and no damage, all in place in the beautiful symmetry of a group formation.

As we passed over the field, the squadrons went into trail, with each plane going past the one ahead of it. One by one, the planes began to peel left and then again left onto the descent leg for a landing. Beautiful, absolutely beautiful.

All of a sudden, I noticed something. I wasn't sick! I hadn't been sick for the whole mission!

I was so busy being a lead navigator that I had not grabbed even once at my supply of vomit bags.

After I crawled down the hatchway and up into the pilots' compartment, I waited for Egan and Blake, as superior officers, to go aft along the fuselage and out the waist door.

Major Egan looked at me. "Crosby, good show. This changes things."

I had no idea what he meant.

CHAPTER
2

TRONDHEIM

Next morning.

Same business as the day before. The corporal waking me and ignoring Brady, Ham, and Hoerr. Everyone else gone. The orderly saying, "Lieutenant Payne got a bellyache and ended up in the infirmary in Norwich."

"Another practice mission?"

"I don't know, sir. We didn't know Lieutenant Bubbles wasn't here, and we didn't call you."

"You mean no breakfast again?"

"Sorry, sir. Please hurry, sir."

Instead of putting on my outer flying clothes I threw them into my A-3 canvas bag. I checked my navigation kit, smiled a little to see that I didn't have to replenish my supply of vomit sacks.

Out to the jeep, my three bags in the back, me in the front right seat, not quite really awake. A fast, careening ride to the flight line. It was cold. I could see the corporal's breath. Dumb of me not to put on my heavy outer clothing.

Already most of the planes parked at the hard stands about two hundred feet apart in the long perimeter row had their fans going.

Blake and his crew were all in the plane, the engines running up in their pre-flight test. The Group Navigator, Lieutenant Omar Gonzales, came up in a jeep and handed me the maps and briefing materials.

"You drew a long one, Harry," he said. "I am sorry we couldn't brief you. I plotted the course on the map and put the coordinates in your logbook."

Then he smiled shyly. "I hope you will make the navigators look good."

To avoid the awkward climb up through the nose hatch I walked around to the waist door. Charlie Via was peering up into sunlight through the barrel of a machine gun.

"You're a gunner today?" I asked.

"Flying Control Officer," he said.

"Who's flying your seat?"

"Colonel Harding."

I was too new at lead to realize what it meant to be flying with a full colonel command pilot.

Tugging at my three bags I stepped into the waist of the Fort and walked, my head lowered to avoid the bulkheads, up through the radio compartment, and the bomb bay. Four 500-pound demolition bombs. Since the load was light that meant a long mission. Through the bulkhead to the pilots' compartment. I saw Colonel Chick Harding in the copilot's seat. He looked over his left shoulder and waved when I went by.

I dropped through the hatchway and crawled up into the nose. Seated before my tiny desk on the left side of the compartment, I unrolled the maps. A long red line ran east to Great Yarmouth and then north by northeast out into the North Sea. I followed the red line to the edge of the map and fumbled to find the next chart.

This one showed our route out over the water.

"Must be keeping to the water before we turn east to Emden or someplace," I thought. Germany!

The next chart kept on going and crossed the coast into Norway. I kept unrolling for hundreds of miles.

Trondheim!

I did a quick computation. Nineteen hundred miles, round trip. Wow! I didn't know a B-17 could fly that far with a bomb load. And me with no breakfast.

What's at Trondheim?

That was Doug's job. All I had to do as navigator was get us there.

I groaned. That was all.

The usual. Pre-flight. Start engines. Taxi out. Run up the engines for the test. Bombardier and navigator leave the nose and go up behind the pilots. Watch Flying Control. Green-green flares. All four throttles forward. Engines roar. Brakes off. The creaking starts. The terrain rushes by. Farmer Draper with his horses. He waves. Funny kind of war.

Lift-off. Wheels grinding up. Flaps up. Level off. Left turn. Climb.

"Command pilot to navigator." I was back in my compartment, my headset connected.

"Go ahead, sir."

"We will assemble the squadron at 2,000 feet over Splasher Six."

"Roger, sir." What was I supposed to do with that information?

According to the log Lieutenant Gonzales had prepared for me, we were supposed to rendezvous with the 350th and 351st Squadrons over Framlingham at H plus 58, or 5:58 A.M. Since I didn't know how to do an assembly procedure I headed our squadron in the general direction, a little ahead of time. As we neared the rendezvous point I had Blake turn slightly and then back again. We lost a minute. Good.

There they were, the other two squadrons. In the lead plane of each squadron, the top turret operators shot flares, yellow-green, to identify themselves.

I directed Blake to S again, watching the squadrons in the air and Framlingham on the ground.

The 350th was lower than we were, the 351st higher. I wished one of them was lead. Now I had to get the group to the wing rendezvous at Great Yarmouth. I began to smell my own sweat. I felt the thud of my heart. Even so I had an instant to be glad that the turbulence in my stomach was gone. I was not airsick. Apparently freedom from airsickness came with being a lead navigator. It's an ill wind that blows nobody good. My father speaking.

I looked to the east and saw two bomb groups circling over the coast. They were shooting red-yellow and green-green flares. The 95th Bomb Group and the 390th.

"Navigator to pilot."

"Roger."

"Heading 90 degrees." No finesse. Just get there.

"Radio to navigator."

"Go ahead, Forkner."

"When do you want P.R.s?"

"Not now. I'm snowed getting the formation together."

"Roger. I'll have them ready when you want them."

I planned to get to the general vicinity of Great Yarmouth and then have Blake tuck on to the lead group.

We sailed to the coast, with Thornton, the top turret, firing yellow-green from the Very pistol, our identification.

About five minutes ahead of our rendezvous time the 100th crossed over Great Yarmouth. I planned to circle back and tack on to the lead.

There they were, the twenty-one planes of the 95th higher than we were, the 390th lower. I suddenly felt very cold. Behind both groups, I could see their supernumeraries, just pulling off. I wished I could go back home with them.

Now both groups slid in behind us.

My God in Heaven, I am the lead navigator. The worst navigator in the group leading the whole 13th Combat Wing. Goddamn Bubbles Payne and goddamn that girl in Norwich.

"Pilot to navigator. Heading please."

I had goofed. I should have given him the heading a moment before, and I still didn't have one.

In pencil the briefing navigator had computed the headings on each leg if the wind was as predicted.

"Sixty-eight degrees," I read.

"Roger." I felt the plane bank to the left, and I followed the turn with my compass. The needle settled. We were on the way.

Twenty-five hundred feet as we left the coast.

We flew and flew. We hit cumulus clouds billowing up thousands of feet. They weren't supposed to be there. My Met flimsy said clear all the way. We climbed, barely able to see our wing planes who tucked in close. We broke out at 18,000 feet, 6,000 higher than planned. Of course our wind would be different. Nothing to check. Forkner called in, "Sorry, Lieutenant, we are out of range of radio bearings."

"Navigator to radio, thanks anyway. Can you get a bearing on Berlin?" That was to show I could still joke.

"I already tried to find Axis Sally, Lieutenant, but she's moved."

"Like my bowels." The Greek Air Force.

"Dammit, Saunders." Blake on intercom. "This is serious."

"Sorry, sir. Waist out."

I could smell cordite, the explosives from past firing of the machine guns. I could smell it so much it stung my eyes. I was conscious of my own sweat. I kept having to turn the volume of my radio down. Were the crew talking louder or was I hearing more? Were they scared, or was I?

Even though I was sweating, I began to climb into my altitude gear. Zipper up my fleece-lined pants, then my boots, and my jacket. I measured it once, thirty-six feet of zipper. Milady's zippers have gone to war. Oxygen mask, connected to hose, hose connected to supply. I should have gone to my mask sooner, but I was too busy thinking of other things. Stupid mistake. Electrical underwear connected to outlet. Flying helmet on, earphones in place and connected; throat mike, connected. Goggles down. Gloves on. Six hoses and wires to keep me alive and in touch with the crew.

By now all the supernumeraries had gone back home. We flew and flew, sixty-three planes alone over all the world. Relaxed formation, droning on. Into the clear, hundreds of miles of a cloud layer beneath us, the sun bright.

Since our flight plan was so much different from what we had been briefed to fly, I had little idea where we were or when we would hit the coast of Norway.

The clouds began to thin out, and we could get glimpses of land. I couldn't have missed the whole country. It must be Norway. Off to port was a coastline, and I bent over my maps to see where we were.

Every fjord in Norway looks just like every other fjord in Norway. Every little village on the Atlantic coast looks like every other village, fishing boats, an inlet for a harbor, a few houses, and a road heading inland. I had no idea which village was below us.

I only had half a problem. As long as I kept the coast off to port I would be on course. But if I couldn't identify one of the fjords, or something, I couldn't get a speed line, and I couldn't get an ETA.

We flew and flew and flew, and not once did I get a pilotage point I could check. I was on course, but where on the course? Norway stopped being a coastline of fjords and became a jumble of islands I could not identify on my maps. What a mess!

About a half hour before my briefed I.P. ETA, I still had no confirmation of my ground speed. Should I call the command pilot and have him ask our high squadron lead for a P.R.?

Not me. I was too proud. A winner never quits and a quitter never wins. Something would come along.

Down below and ahead there was a puff of smoke, and then another puff, and then a lot of smoke.

Smoke screen! In trying to protect our target, the Germans had revealed it!

My heart beating so hard that it hurt, I looked down at Norway. A long inlet from the sea with two smaller, round lakes connected. I tore at my map. In all of Norway there was no other body of water that looked like a penis and two testicles.

"Navigator to pilots, ETA to I.P., eight minutes. Be prepared for a left turn to 285 degrees. Left turn at target to 255. Bombardier, I can't see that there will be any drift correction."

All kinds of Rogers, and bomb run preparation.

Behind us, the 95th swerved slightly starboard; and the 390th took a bigger list, also to the right. When they had an interval they swung back toward course. The three groups slid into bombing formation, in trail.

Smooth. Beautiful.

Doug saw the target, raised his gloved hand with thumb and forefinger in a circle.

"Bombardier, the plane's yours." This from Blakely.

"Roger, and right on. Bomb bay doors going open."

The grinding, the drag in airspeed. My airspeed indicator dipped to 145, the engines filled out, and the arrow went back to 150. We seemed hardly to be moving. Floating into the flak, quite a bit of it.

Endless, endless. Bursts all around us. Flak. Black. Close. A bang, and a jolt as we took a hit.

"Tail here. Biddick just got it."

"Stay off intercom on bomb run."

"Wilco."

Nice guy, Biddick, sweet, gentle. Just before the Officers' Club bar closed he always ordered a double double.

Back to the mission.

The bombs rattled out. A lurch up, wings waggling. Smooth again.

"Pilot, left turn to Rally Point."

"Sorry, Croz, Pilot here. Our low squadron has slid up beside us. I have to throttle down to help Biddick keep up. He's only got two engines."

"Roger, I got it."

Five minutes later we were heading south, and I was breathing hard, recovering from the excitement over the target.

Now to find the way home.

I did not want to go through all those clouds we had encountered on the way north. Maybe somewhere else would be clear and I could keep track of where I was. The strong wind from the south had helped us on the way up, but it would slow us to a crawl on the way home.

"Navigator to command."

"Go ahead, Navigator."

"Sir, I recommend a change in our flight plan. Instead of a head wind on the way up we had a terrific tail wind. That's why we got to the target ahead of our briefing. If we go back as briefed, we will have such a head wind I don't know when we will get home."

"Command pilot here. What do you recommend?"

"That we go southwest till we hit the Shetland Islands. When we are clear of Norway and over the North Sea, we should go down to five thousand and go home under the clouds. When we hit Scotland, we will go directly south to Thorpe Abbotts. Flying visual at 5,000 feet will help Biddick keep up. We will hit land almost two hours sooner and if his Bird won't stay in the air, he crash-lands in Scotland or finds an emergency airport."

"You speak wisdom, Navigator. Give us a heading."

Just at that instant, our gunners broke in, all of them shouting. "Bogeys, bogeys! Two at nine o'clock level!

From our plane and all over the formation our .50s began to chatter. I felt our own rat-tat-tat-tat, almost so fast it was one ratcheting sound.

Thornton in, from the top turret. "Short bursts, short bursts, you guys. Do you want to melt your gun barrels?"

I saw tracers arc toward the oncoming JU-88's. Their 20-millimeter cannons were blinking at us like headlights.

Some gunner got the first German. He blew up and sprayed wreckage all over the high squadron. None of our planes went down as the second enemy aircraft went under us, our tracers after him.

Then the second one got hit, first a trail of smoke and then an explosion, debris in all directions. Neither of the German pilots got out.

An entry in my log: The time, 10:12; the place, 48 n.m. west of Trondheim; two E.A. destroyed. Enemy aircraft. No chutes.

I gave the pilots the heading, southwest, and we began to descend toward the coast of Norway. When I saw the coast up ahead, I gave a heading of 225 degrees magnetic. I wanted to act as though I knew what I was doing.

Just as we crossed the Norway coast, flak rattled at us again. That told me where we were. I looked at the map. The red circles showed where flak was known to be. The only flak installation on the whole west coast of Norway, and I had stumbled right over it.

"Tail to command, close, but no cigars for the Germans."

As we descended I was so rattled that I forgot to go off oxygen. I did not turn off my electric underwear or peel off my line jacket and pants. I began to sweat. I smelt it before I felt it.

We got down to 5,000 right away, still in the clouds. I had the pilots level off. I heard the command pilot call to the 390th and 95th, "Maintain Devils Ten." Our code altitude was 15,000. Every thousand feet higher was Angels One. Angels Five would be 20,000. Every thousand feet lower was Devils One. We were 10,000 feet below our code altitude.

Halfway across the North Sea, I made a correction to 200 degrees. I aimed right at Scotland, a much bigger target than the Shetland Islands.

We hit clouds at about an hour out of Scotland and began a further descent. How would I know when we crossed the Scottish coast? What about the Scottish coast guard? Would they shoot at us?

We knew, because at 3,000 feet we broke out of the clouds and could see—first the water, then some boats, and finally a coast.

"Navigator to pilots, IFF, sir."

"Blake here, Croz. It's on." He had snapped on our Information Friend or Foe identification system. He didn't want to be hit by our own friends any more than I did.

I gave a southerly heading and we floated down along the Scottish coast.

"Navigator to crew, Edinburgh starboard. We couldn't see it yesterday."

"Tail to command, there goes Biddick, sir."

Then I began to worry.

What did they do to a navigator who had screwed up as badly as I had? I never knew where I was. I had forgotten completely that I was to radio back a position report in code every fifteen minutes. I didn't give the groups enough warning before the I.P. If the Germans hadn't sent up the smoke screen we might have gone on to the Arctic Circle.

I had done everything wrong. I messed up the rendezvous. I should have given P.R.s to radio and a strike message, which he was supposed to send in code back to HQ. None of that.

I had left the briefed course. Because I didn't think I could navigate in Norway I took us to Scotland. Instead of being at altitude most of the time I brought us home on the deck.

What did they do for stuff like that? Court-martial? Ground me? That didn't sound so bad. Send me back to the States? Disgrace.

As we headed home, I figured no headings. I computed no ETA's. I made no entries in my logbook. All I did was sit there, ooze sweat, stink, and feel sorry for myself. I grimly realized I was not airsick. I didn't use even one paper bag.

When we hit The Wash I recognized the bulge of East Anglia out into the English Channel. Colonel Harding called the group together and the relaxed formation pulled into tight V's. Twenty of us. Biddick was missing. Maybe he got hit by the flak that I stumbled into over the coast of Norway.

The 95th and 390th each sent up a final flare and headed for Horham and Framlingham.

We flew in perfect formation over the base. No red-red flares, no injured aboard. One plane missing.

After we landed, I decided I could not endure the

debriefing. I got out of the nose, dropped onto the ground. My frozen ankles hurt as I hit. Without speaking to the ground crew I walked off the concrete and into the woods.

It was about a quarter mile to my quarters, but I made it, slinking along to avoid anyone talking to me. When an enlisted man offered me a ride in his jeep, I waved him off.

At the 418th site, no one was around. I went into our Nissen. Empty. I dropped onto my bed. The sweat. The smell of fear and shame. I could not bring myself to take off my fleece-lined flying clothes. I had forgotten to take the radio headset from around my neck. I remembered leaving my parachute in the plane. I should have turned it over to the rigger. What else?

Trouble.

I heard a jeep drive up, stop. A knock at the door.

The court-martial was beginning.

"Come in."

"Lieutenant, I am supposed to take you to Group Ops."

"I know."

No talk on the way. At Ops I opened the door, walked across the huge war room and headed for Major Kidd's office where I could see Colonel Harding, Major Egan, the three other squadron commanders and Blake. Blake was such a good guy. I was sorry I let him down. Doug was there, too.

I walked in, stopped, and threw a weak salute to Colonel Harding.

"Croz," it was Jack Kidd who spoke. "We just got a message from Wide Wing. They were impressed with how far north you went, about even with Iceland and the tip of Alaska. The Royal Navy got a signal from Norway Underground. You hit the target."

Well, at least Doug wasn't in trouble. Just me.

Jack Kidd went on. "We have learned that the other wing got to Bergen okay, but the bombardier couldn't see the target through the clouds. They brought their bombs back."

What a waste! All that time in the air, and no bombs.

"One wing never did get to their rendezvous because of clouds in their area, and they aborted before they ever left England. The other wing went to Heroya and bombed an aluminum plant okay, but their mission was short compared to ours, all the way to Trondheim."

Now Colonel Harding came in.

"Your timing was so perfect that we hit the sub pens or whatever we were after when the workers were off for lunch, but the Germans were changing the guard. We got no Norwegians and twice as many Germans. Norway Underground thinks we planned it that way, and they love the Americans.

"We still haven't really been told what our target was, but it must have been important. Wide Wing says we sunk one U-boat, damaged a Norvic destroyer, and set the shore installations on fire. Judging by the smoke, we may have hit the gasworks. Wide Wing is hush-hush about what else was there. The British are happy with us because we destroyed the pens of the subs that are chasing the American and English cargo ships taking supplies to the Rooskies at Murmansk.

"The Germans were so mad that they vectored half of the Luftwaffe's JU-88's at us. On the way up, they had trouble locating you because you maintained radio silence."

I remembered now the P.R.s I had forgotten to send back to Control.

"And when you hit the deck on the way back you really lost them. The Germans couldn't find you on radar. Only two JU-88's found us, and we got 'em both. You got out of their way in a hurry when you cut across to the Shetlands."

Colonel Harding came in. "Bucky Egan said you were a hot navigator, but this is more than we expected. Eighth Air Force said for us to put me for a Silver Star and the officers of your crew in for the DFC."

"What about Biddick, sir?"

"He's okay, two men wounded, but not bad. He landed with his wheels down on a short RAF runway, but he got slowed down when he went into the Commandant's garden."

"That's Biddick," said Blake.

Then he turned to me. "I guess you are on our crew from now on."

And that was how I got my first medal. That was how I got started on a job that was way over my head. That was how I got involved in the internal warfare of the U.S. Army Air Corps.

CHAPTER 3

THORPE ABBOTTS

On December 7, 1941, Japan bombed Pearl Harbor.

On December 13, along with many other students from the University of Iowa, I joined the U.S. Air Corps, expecting soon to be fighting in the Pacific. It took seventeen months for me to get to the war in Europe.

I said goodbye to my parents and my friends at my hometown in Oskaloosa, Iowa, and at the university. I said goodbye to a girl whom I liked very much but who was not much interested in me. Her name was Jean Boehner—that's pronounced "BAY-ner"—from Chillicothe, Missouri.

In a few weeks I washed out as a pilot. After a few months at Mather Field in Sacramento, California, I became a second lieutenant navigator. Gold bars and wings. At Boise, Idaho, I was assigned to the 418th Squadron of the 100th Bomb Group, which was getting ready to fly missions against the Japanese. The number of my new squadron seemed like a good omen since 4-18, April 18, was my birthday. Our planes were the four-engine Flying Fortress, the B-17. The first time I ever saw a B-17 land, it came in at night and crashed, killing the entire crew.

My crew were John Brady, John Hoerr, and a smiling, round-faced, blond eighteen-year-old with two gold front teeth, Howard Hamilton. Brady's and Hoerr's pilot's wings had a shield in the center. Ham's had a bomb.

Our engineer, who operated the machine-gun turret, was Adolf Blum, who spoke with a thick German accent. Saul Levitt, the oldest of us all, was our radio operator. He had been a reporter in New York where he distinguished himself while covering the investigations of Thomas Dewey. Down in the ball turret was Roland Gangwer, Polish. One of the privileges of flyers in training was that we did not have to stand inspections or march in the Saturday morning review. Gangwer was so good a soldier that he participated in both. Our two waist gunners were Harold Clanton and George Petrohelos. Although Clanton was blond, he was part American Indian. George was a Greek from Chicago. We seemed to have a new tail gunner every week.

When John Brady, short, dark mustache and hair, a round face and a rather round body, first saw us, he smiled and said, "I am not impressed." Then he smiled again, and we liked him on the spot. Before the war he was a saxophone player in one of Bunny Berrigan's bands.

We had a month's training in Boise, Idaho, a month in Wendover, Utah, and a month in Sioux City, Iowa. Either because our training was inade-

quate or because I was not fitted for the job, I had little reason to develop confidence about my ability as a
navigator. On Christmas Eve, 1942, our plane took
off from Wendover, Utah, the weather closed in, our
gas ran out, and we crash-landed in the snowy mountains of western Wyoming. No one was hurt, testimony to the high skill of John Brady.

When a woman saw the smashed plane, she asked,
"Which of you is the Scot?"

"I am Scotch-Irish," I said. "Will that do?"

"Yes," she said. "Scots are lucky. That's why none
of you got killed."

Later she gave me a sprig of Scotch heather and
said, "Keep this and you will always be lucky."

I wish that the woman—her husband was vice
president of the bank of Evanston, Wyoming—gave
the rest of the crew a good luck charm.

During my months as a second lieutenant with
wings, I enjoyed the prerogatives of a soldier in
wartime. Although I still thought of the girl in Iowa
City, I had three romances—one of them serious,
with a girl from Indiana. She was the former college
roommate of the wife of one of my classmates. She
was with us at Sacramento and Boise. When a letter
revealed that my primary interest, the girl I courted
unsuccessfully in Iowa City, was lonely, I went
AWOL, hitchhopped to Dayton where she was a
radio announcer, proposed, and was accepted. On
our honeymoon trip to Boise, Idaho, I missed the
train, grabbed a freight train going in the same direction as Jean's train. In cold April I rode on the back
of a caboose halfway across mountainous Wyoming.

Jean was with us at Boise and Wendover, getting
to know my squadron and some of their wives.

At the end of our training, instead of going to Australia, the 100th was distributed all over the western training command. Apparently there was no place ready for us.

We were supposed to help train new crews in Training Command, but what the 100th did mostly was acquire a reputation as an undisciplined, individualistic outfit. When we reassembled, we messed up a practice mission. We were supposed to fly from Kearney, Nebraska, to San Francisco, but most of the crews landed somewhere else, usually where the pilot's girlfriend lived. One crew landed in Smyrna, Tennessee. Our Group Commander, Colonel Darr H. Alkire, was replaced. Our Air Executive, Bucky Egan, was demoted to squadron commander. Colonel Howard Turner became our new commanding officer.

In the last weeks of May 1943, leaving Jean planning to share a Chicago apartment with Gerry Hamilton and Marge Blakely, two wives of my squadron mates, I navigated our plane to England.

Were we a jinxed crew? We already had crashed once. Because of a navigation error, we missed England and nearly flew into occupied France. When we finally got to England, our wheels would not come down. We crashed again.

On the last week of May 1943, our thirty-six combat crews and five B-17 loads of leaders arrived in England. During the first week of June, forty of the planes and their crews, flying their best formation, flew over a new field in East Anglia and made dramatic landings.

The base was Thorpe Abbotts, twenty miles south of Norwich, ninety air miles north-by-northeast of London.

Crew 32, our crew, was not with the formation. Our plane lay smashed on the runway back in Warton, on the west coast of England. We packed our flying clothes, our parachutes, and our other gear in our A-3 bags, and took out our rumpled Class As from our B-4 bags. I had extra luggage for my navigation equipment, my octant, my celestial tables.

Funny English trains. A trip into and then out of London, our foreheads pressed against the windows. North from London. Two hours or so. It seemed longer.

At Diss, a tall, angular, blue-coated station master and an M.P. corporal were expecting us.

"Lieutenant Brady?" the M.P. said to me, missing my navigator's wings but assuming that the tallest officer would be the pilot.

"No, I'm Brady."

We piled into a personnel carrier, a truck with a canvas cover and two benches front to back along the side. We threw our bags over the end gate into the center and climbed up.

East Anglia.

This part of England is the bulge that sticks out toward Holland. It is primarily two counties, Norfolk and Suffolk, with Norwich and Ipswich the largest towns.

The roads were narrow.

"Get a load of this," said Ham the bombardier. "We are driving on the wrong side of the road. This country sure doesn't look like Kansas."

We went through several little hamlets. The houses were all yellow stucco or clay. The roofs were low, all thatched. The windows were narrow, with brown frames. That's Tudor, I remembered, from the fraternity houses in Iowa City.

"Jolly Old England is as green as they say," said Saul Levitt, our radio operator.

In about a half hour we drove up to a military police station guarding a gate in a fence.

An M.P. came out, saluted, and looked at our papers.

"Site Five," he told the driver and climbed into the truck with us.

We were on a big farm. We saw a farmer out in a field with a team of horses. There were several homes right on the base. At first we didn't see any Americans and then, on the right, a cluster of low, long Nissen huts and a group of G.I.s in fatigues playing catch and hitting fungoes to each other.

Our M.P. escort pointed.

"That's Site Four, the 350th."

After another hundred yards we saw another cluster of huts. They were right in the middle of some farm buildings, with cows going through the squadron yard.

"Site Three, 349th. Already the G.I.s have run up the price of the farmer's eggs."

Adolph Blum asked, "What do we have at the mess?"

"Powdered eggs. That's why the farmer's eggs taste so good."

"Is there a farmer's daughter?" asked Clanton.

"Yes, but she is in the Land Army somewhere. There are plenty of women in town though. You will meet them at the pubs."

"Are they eager?"

"Not like London, but eager enough."

After another hundred yards a left turn, and then another left turn, and a stop.

All of us recognized someone we knew.

"Home, sweet home," said Petrohelos.

One of the other pilots, Crankshaft, was the first to see us. "You are in our hut."

His name really was Charles Cruikshank. The other pilots in the squadron were Ev Blakely, Bob Knox, Ed Woodward, Ernest Keissling, Pete Biddick, and Bill Flesh. Bill was put under house arrest because he buzzed an outdoor war bond rally in Utah, and the charge caught up with him. There had been another pilot, Curtis Green, but he was the one who landed in Tennessee instead of San Francisco, and they made him a copilot in a B-24.

We checked in at Squadron Headquarters. It wasn't marked, but we recognized it from the bulletin board in front. The first sergeant told the enlisted men where they went.

"You are next to the latrine," said our Squadron Adjutant, Lieutenant Tom Toomey, to Brady, Hoerr, Ham, and me. "Hank Ramsey will show you where. You can't check in with Major Egan. He is flying a mission."

"The 100th is up already?"

"No, all the squadron commanders and ops officers are flying with other groups for indoctrination. We lost two crews yesterday on a practice mission."

"Already?

"Yup. The group was practicing over the North Sea and a couple of MEs flew through the formation. Bang! Two planes. Some of the gunners were asleep. They didn't even have their barrels in their machine guns. Air Sea Rescue fished some of them out of the drink."

As we walked past the latrine, constructed by piling up two columns of dirt around two concrete walls, Hank Ramsey, a long, lean, very southern Southerner, pointed to a pole with two bulbs in an electric fixture.

"When the green light is on, it means we are stood down. When it's red, we are alerted for a mission. The bars close and we can't go into the village."

A loud voice came on over a public address system. "At oh-nine-hundred hours, all squadron personnel will meet at Group Ops for a meeting with the new Group Commander."

Ramsey pointed to the loudspeaker. "The Limeys call that dumb thing the Tannoy. Colonel Turner is gone. He's going to head up the new B-24 division."

Crankshaft had come up to us again, and he broke in. "We have a new C.O., name of Harold Q. Huglin. He's even tougher than Turner. The rank up above has declared open season on the 100th, especially since we even lost planes on a practice mission. Everyone thinks we're fuck-ups. We've already given Huglin a bellyache."

The light was red.

"Yeah, but the 418th is stood down for tomorrow," said Crank. "The other squadrons go out to meet the Hun, but not us. The 418th will be on a practice mission. For real missions the squadron orderly will get you up around oh-three-hundred hours, but tomorrow we stay out of the air till the rest of the Air Corps goes out. Then we fly. The Officers' Mess is open all the time, and there's no beer or whiskey now, with the red light on. The Flying Officers' Mess opens at seventeen-hundred hours."

Hank Ramsey made a pained face. "You can eat at the Officers' Mess with us paddlefeet, but your mess is better. You have real eggs, real milk, and fresh vegetables. Everything we ground pounders eat comes out of cans or it's powdered."

Ten days passed as we waited for another plane. We moved around the base, finding out where things were. Station 139 was actually on two farms, not one, each about a thousand acres. One was owned by a Sir Rupert Mann. Once he came and talked testily to the Officers' Club. He looked like a baron or a squire. The other farm was owned by a woman in her eighties. We never saw her. Our two landlords rented to farmers who lived in the huts and worked the fields.

There were at least four tiny villages right in our base. The 100th was a small town, about three thousand men and about twenty women, the Red Cross girls, some British NAAFI, and a few women who worked in the base PX.

The base was so spread out that we bought bicycles for about four pounds, roughly sixteen dollars. English bikes. Instead of American coaster brakes operated by turning the pedals backwards, they had hand brakes, the right hand controlling the rear wheel and the left the front wheel. For the first month we had more men in the infirmary because of bike accidents than we did from enemy action.

The food in the Flying Mess was good, but I preferred to eat in the Officers' Mess, which had tablecloths, and most of the officers were in their blouses instead of A-2 jackets. Then, too, there wasn't as much bluster, the loud talking, the laughing, the coarse jokes, Texas talk.

Our barracks were Quonset huts, like half of a huge tin can, split vertically down the middle, and then resting on the ground with the sides round, and the ends like the lid of the can. There was only one door, in the middle of the front end.

Our barracks, for Brady, John Hoerr, Ham, and me, had eight beds along each side, the foot of each bed pointing toward the center aisle. When we got out of bed we had to be careful not to bump our heads on the sloping side of the wall.

Sixteen officers. Four each from Brady's, Crankshaft's, Knox's and Woodward's crews.

We set up our living quarters. Each officer had a bed and a footlocker, and two or three feet on a wall for pictures.

I got my first letter from Jean. Somehow, even with wartime shortages, she purchased a supply of feminine, tissue-thin, beige stationery. She wrote in brown ink. It was from "Mrs. Harry H. Crosby" to "Lt. Harry H. Crosby." Her penmanship was strong, clear. For the entire war, my letters came like that. The mail orderly spotted them instantly.

In her letters she was less reserved than when we were together. Her letters said what I wanted to hear.

For about three weeks we practiced formation and got used to Thorpe Abbotts.

Then our day came. "You fly tomorrow," Bucky Elton told us. He was Squadron Operations Officer. Both leaders had the same nickname. In the Group we had Bucky Egan, Bucky Elton, and Bucky Cleven. Cleven and Egan were best friends, top flyers, devil-may-care. All the 100th pilots wanted to be like them.

"What plane are we in?"

"Damned if I know. It just arrived this afternoon, and Group Engineering gave it a test flight. It stayed in the air."

"That's something," said Brady.

Brady was like that. Dry humor. By now we liked him very much. We owed him. If it hadn't been for him, we would all have been killed either in the mountains of Wyoming, or on the first runway we saw in England.

CHAPTER
4

FLYING WITH BRADY

 O300 hours, June 28, 1943.

The orderly comes in, turns on the light. "Drop your cocks and grab your socks. You are flying today."

Someone swears at him, and he never cracks a joke like that again. He learns we are tense, close to irritation. Already we see that on mission days the ground people treat the air people with elaborate care. The ground echelon is all business. Air crews can joke, but not the ground echelon.

"Cruikshank's crew, Knox's crew, and Brady's crew are flying. Keissling is supernumerary."

That means that we have a slot in the formation. If anyone aborts, Keissling fills in.

We all get up. It's cold, so we hurry into our pants, shirt, no tie, A-2 jackets. Into the latrine. Brush teeth. No one shaves. We learn later not to put on our sweaty, stinking fleece-lined altitude clothing till we get to the plane. This morning, we put it on. I check my navigation equipment.

Several personnel trucks are outside. We go over the end gate. Down the road past the 349th and some more turns.

"If I had my choice, I'd have breakfast before briefing," says Ernie Warsaw. We are friends, in part because he was with us when we pranged in over Evanston, Wyoming. For some reason all the navigators are on this truck, Frank Murphy for Crankshaft, Ernie Warsaw for Knox, John Dennis for Flesh, Davey Solomon for Keissling. From the other barracks are Manny Cassimatis for Woodward and Bubbles Payne for Blakely. All good guys. We are friends.

On the right we go past the Officers' Mess, then the Flying Officers' Mess. This is a narrow farm road. We see fences and fields, and sheep.

Up ahead we see many trucks with crews piling out and going into a big Quonset. Group Operations.

We stop, jump down. It's cold and our ankles hurt. We join the stream.

What I do not know at the time is that the next ten hours are to be etched into history. Sitting in the back with the enlisted men, our radio operator, Saul Levitt, is taking notes.

Group Ops is big enough to hold the some 250 men who are getting ready for the mission. We herd in and I see what I am to see on every mission. Just inside the door are Glenn Teska, our chaplain, and our three Red Cross girls. It is still not oh-four-hundred hours, but those American girls are there, their hair in place, their lipstick on, their seams straight, their faces fresh, smiling.

"Coffee, Lieutenant? Doughnuts?"

"Thank you." Nothing, nothing ever tasted so good. Dear God, women are wonderful.

Inside, I start to sit down in a back row, but Ham grabs me.

"Come on, Bingo, up front we can see better. We don't want to miss any of this."

We can only go so far forward. An M.P. is saving the front few rows for the brass.

We sit down. All officers in front. Most of them are second or first lieutenants. A few captains. Our gunners are all sergeants of one kind or another. All in flying clothes, all sweating. Their O.D. shirts open at the throat. It's hot. Whether they are in A-2 jackets or the heavier, fleece-lined coats, their zippers are down, revealing their wings over their left shirt pockets.

The room has a man smell: leather from our jackets, tobacco, sweat, a little fear, which has its own distinctive sharpness.

Up front is a stage, a couple of easels, right and left. Across the back is a huge map now covered with a black curtain on a wire.

"Here come the high mucky-mucks," says Ham. Like me, he is tense, but he smiles, his gold teeth gleaming. He actually wanted to come to this war. In training he feared it would be over before he got into it.

From the rear entrance, the Group Adjutant, a heavyset retread from World War I, steps in first. He wears glasses.

"At-ten-HUT," he says, his voice not quite firm enough.

We stand up and pop to.

Down the center aisle stride the group brass, first, Colonel Harold Huglin, our new C.O. He has dark hair; he is tall, thin, ramrod straight, right out of the book. It has been confirmed that he has already been in the infirmary for a stomachache.

Their order as they walk to the front of Ops is strictly G.I. First, the colonel; then our former squadron C.O., Major Bob Flesher, now the Air Executive; then Jack Kidd, formerly 351st C.O., and now Group Ops. His squadron had done well on the San Francisco practice mission, and he got promoted. Then come the four squadron commanders, with Bucky Egan and Bucky Cleven together. They, more than any other of our leaders, had the real Air Corps raunch, their hats cocked on the backs of their heads. Egan's white fleece-lined jacket is his trademark. They both are wearing white scarves.

Egan and Cleven trade quips with their men as they walk forward. I don't normally use the word "debonair," but that's what they are. Bucky Cleven and Bucky Egan are like what their men saw in the movie *I Wanted Wings*. The men wanted leaders like that. Cleven's real first name is Gale, and Egan's is John, but I never heard either name used.

The two Buckys talk like Hollywood. The first time I ever saw Cleven was at the Officers' Club. For some reason he wanted to talk with me, and he said, "Taxi over here, Lootenant."

Bill Veal, C.O. of the 349th, and Ollie Turner, new C.O. of the 351st, walk in, purposefully but unobtrusively.

Clustered around the rank are several ground officers. I had seen them back at Kearney, but I didn't know what they did.

"Seats, men."

It is Major Kidd. I am glad he has been promoted

because "Captain Kidd" sounded too much like Treasure Island. I like him as an officer, a real straight arrow. He has a long pointer in his hand.

Another paddlefoot major stands up. He has a funny name, Major Minor Shaw, another World War I retread. In peacetime he ran an airport in South Dakota somewhere. Here at Thorpe Abbotts he is head of S-2 Intelligence. He takes the pointer from Kidd, walks over to the curtain, pauses dramatically, and pulls it back with a flourish. Cornball stuff.

A red ribbon starting at our base, going through a lot of southern England, then across the channel to a port in France.

An audible sigh of relief from everyone in the audience. France, not Germany.

"Gentleman," says Major Shaw. "Our target is the sub pens at St. Nazaire. If we hit it, there will be fewer losses of the ships coming here from America."

Major Kidd takes over.

"Don't be fooled. This is not a milk run. There are almost a hundred flak guns over the target. There are four German fighter bases within fifty miles."

He pauses.

"Some of you won't be back unless you fly good formation and keep your gunners alert."

In orderly sequence, the whole briefing.

Going to an easel Kidd outlines the formation. With Major Cleven flying command pilot in the right seat, Mark Carnell's crew will lead. Blakely, with Egan in the right seat, will lead the high squadron, about two hundred feet up to the right and a little behind. We on Brady's crew will be flying right wing of the second element off Knox's wing.

The Group Ordnance Officer tells us we have a load of 500-pound bombs to blast through the concrete walls of the pens. The armament officer tells the gunners how many rounds of ammunition they have and warns them again that tracers really don't tell where their bullets are going. The weather officer tells us what the cloud cover will be, and the winds. "Be sure to connect your electrical underwear by fifteen thousand feet. It's cold up there."

A pep talk from Colonel Huglin. "Men, let's show the Hun that the 100th is going to make a difference."

Ham looks at me and shrugs.

The Group Bombardier, Bob Peel, and the Group Navigator, Omar Gonzales, stand up and announce there will be special briefings for navigators and bombardiers. I hadn't come to know either of them yet. I was so intimidated by rank and so unsure of myself as a navigator that I had not introduced myself to them.

The Group Navigator is a first lieutenant from San Antonio, Texas. Because of his skin color and his quiet diffidence, he doesn't belong up there with the boisterous, swaggering Egan and Cleven. Egan calls him "Pancho." Cleven calls him "Omar the Tent Maker." He seems like a nice guy, but I don't envy him his job.

At the navigation briefing, Lieutenant Gonzales carefully lays out our route, the coordinates of every turning point, the distance in nautical miles on each leg. He is businesslike, meticulous, with none of the Hollywood drama so many of our briefers felt necessary. He explains how to use the time and place codes. Every time is based on H-hour. We got up at H minus four hours. We will have our wing rendezvous at H-hour. We will hit the target at H plus

2:40. If all goes well, we will be back over the base at H plus 3:55. Later, when H-hour is announced as oh-five-hundred hours, we can translate H plus twenty-five into 0525, DBST, Double British Summer Time.

Altitude and place are also in code, so we can talk about them by radio, out in the clear. Base altitude this morning is 18,000. We will rendezvous with the rest of the wing, the 95th and the 390th, at Devils Six, that is, 6,000 feet below base altitude, or 12,000 feet. When we hit the French coast, we will be at Angels Four, or 22,000 feet. We will climb in France, to fool the flak, and bomb at Angels Six, 24,000 feet. About four and a half miles up in the blue.

Lieutenant Gonzales shows us four checkpoints. The first one, Checkpoint Able, is Gravesend. To give a position report, we would say "Two-seventy, twenty-eight, Checkpoint Able. That means bearing two-seventy, twenty-eight nautical miles from Able. That would place us about thirty statute miles west of Gravesend.

Tony Gospodor, as Carnell's navigator, and Jim Fitten, the bombardier in the lead plane, get special attention. Tony is briefed about how to get the three squadrons of the 100th together and then in place with the wing. He is tall, slow spoken, easygoing. If he screws up, the 100th is wasted for the day.

Gospodor doesn't seem to be ruffled. Up in front, he gets the head-on fighter attacks. In the last element of the high squadron, we are about as safe as we can be. On this mission, I am strictly a gunner, manning the left gun in the nose. The only navigating I will have to do is make sure I can see Crankshaft's right wing. I wouldn't trade jobs with Tony Gospodor if they made me a bird colonel.

I don't feel real. This is a movie, not me. I am watching. It is not happening to me.

When the navigation briefing is over, we go back outside to the waiting trucks and back to the Flying Officers' Mess.

At the mess hall, I smell bacon, eggs, pancakes, syrup.

The breakfast is good, very good. Real eggs, Canadian bacon, orange juice, oatmeal, pancakes. Not much coffee. In the air it is a long way back from the nose to the relief tube in the bomb bay.

Although I know that up in the air when I get sick I will lose most of it, I eat something of everything the K.P.s put out.

The talk is subdued, nervous, not much laughing. Navigators from my class at Mather Field Navigation School saying, "What position yuh flying?"

I tell them.

"Good," they respond.

Tail End Charlie in the high squadron is considered safe. Up front is where it's bad. The Jerries have learned there are no front guns except the top turret pointing straight forward, so that's where they hit us. Then too, if they knock the lead plane down, they get the command pilot, the lead navigator, the lead bombardier.

Back to the trucks. A longish ride up past, on the right, Group Ops and Group Headquarters with the flag flying, and—on the left—the Tech Site, where most of the repair work is done.

Then out onto the landing field. The main runway is 10 on one end and 28 on the other. Add a zero, and you have their magnetic compass headings, 100 for use when the wind is from the east and 280 when the wind is from the west. There are two N–S runways, 17–35 and 04–22, that cross each other, and then the E–W runway. The north-south runways are shorter and narrower. We will never use them when we have a full bomb load. Around the three runways is a perimeter or taxi strip.

From the air the field looks like a .45 revolver pointing west. E–W runway 10–28 is the barrel and the crossed but nearly parallel 04–22 and 17–35 look like the pistol handle. The perimeter tracks and the series of hard stands trace the outer edge of the revolver. The control tower is on the top, about where the rear sight would be. The 418th hard stands are about where the trigger would be. This morning, when we take off, we will be at the head of Runway 28, about where the hammer of the pistol would be.

At the flight line our truck stops, and Brady, Hoerr, Ham, and I pile out. Our crew is already there. They have the bores of their machine guns out and are cleaning and oiling them. They point a barrel up in the sky, the front pointing to their eye, and they squint through to see if it shines and has smooth rifling. I feel strange about people looking down the front end of a gun barrel. That will be bad enough when we meet the Luftwaffe.

Not much talk.

I go to the front, open the hatch under the pilots' compartment and throw my gear up. I grab the top of the door and swing my whole body up and into the plane. I crawl left and forward into my compartment and stand up. Ham is already there, installing his Norden bombsight. I sit at my desk and arrange my charts, E6B computer, Weems plotter, calipers, and pencils. One of the gunners has already cleaned the machine gun which swings up over my desk and in my way.

Out in front, the ground crew is pushing the props through. This is hard work and takes two men per prop. Revolving a prop 360 degrees twice or so makes an engine fire more easily.

Only today our engines aren't firing. New damn airplane.

The ground crew stand back and watch. Over intercom I hear Brady.

"Start Three."

"Copilot here, starting Three."

I hear the generator push the starter, and a prop grinds slowly and fitfully.

It doesn't catch. The pilots disengage the starter.

"Start Three."

"Copilot here, starting Three."

Nothing.

Normally the pilots start all four engines and run them up to test them. Then they cut the inboards and taxi out to the head of the takeoff strip on the outboards.

Brady tries them all.

Nothing.

At the other hard stands we see the other pilots running up their fans, and we hear the roar. Then we see the inboard props stop whirring, and the crews scurry into the plane and close their hatches.

One by one, lurching and jerky, the planes start to taxi out to the perimeter strip and to the head of Runway 28. They look like huge, ungainly moths. In the air the B-17 is poetry, gull graceful; on the ground, it's clumsy. The noise of twenty-one planes is a steady hum.

Crew 32 is still sitting there.

I hear Brady. "Petrohelos, go out and tell the crew chief I want him to come in."

"Roger, waist here and out."

In a minute I hear Brady again, and I know the crew chief is sitting in the copilot's seat."

"Sergeant, Brady here. This is my first mission, and I am excited. I must be doing something wrong. Will you take me through the start-up procedure, please."

In five minutes all four engines are humming, the crew chief goes out, I feel hatches slam, and I see him standing out there, thumbs up, and a wave.

I am excited and tense, scared, but that incident has lain forever in my mind. Brady was brave enough, and sure of himself enough, to tell the crew chief he was rattled. I am impressed that he had guts enough to admit that he was scared.

We roll out to the end of Runway 28. Everyone else is gone.

We take off. We are really Tail End Charlie now.

At 600 feet we go into the clouds and start our full overcast assembly procedure. Brady turns on Splasher Six, our homing beacon, and starts to corkscrew up around it. He knows how tight to make his turn, what his rate of climb should be. Higher than we are, twenty-one other planes are doing the same. Within ten miles the 95th and 390th are doing the same. If Brady botches it, we smack into another plane.

And he couldn't even get the plane started.

Think of the strain on Brady. For 120 minutes he can see nothing. We could hardly see the inboard engines. All he can do is stare at his instruments. He must keep his air speed at 150 miles per hour. He must keep his turn and bank indicator at a single needle width. His rate of climb indicator must show 150 feet per minute. He must be sure all four engines are exactly synchronized, each showing the correct manifold pressure. He is probably watching fifteen instruments. He must make sure his radio compass needle is about fifteen degrees off center, to make sure the circumference of our climb keeps us out of Horham and Framlingham, where the two other groups are ascending. At 10,000 feet, without permitting any change in anything, he has to put on his oxygen mask.

He calls out to the crew, "Pilot to crew, 10,000 feet, masks on, all check in."

Nine Rogers.

Still thinking about Brady, I find that I am taking stock of myself. On missions, when I don't want to think about what is up ahead of us, I think about funny stuff.

I am Middle West. I was born in 1919. After my sister died, when she was seven and I five, I was an only child. My parents, who are now divorced, were mismatched. My mother was stern, judgmental; my father, a traveling salesman, enjoyed all the sins—drinking, gambling, womanizing. I told my father once that he was the worst husband and the best father I ever knew. Both my parents encouraged me to be a Boy Scout and to go to Sunday School. Somewhere I became obsessed by the Calvinist work ethic. When my father once got a flat tire he drove all across Des Moines, Iowa, on the rim rather than be late for work. I have been brought up to keep a stiff upper lip. I have been taught never to cry nor to question authority. I have never put my arms around a man, not even my father. When I saw an Italian boy kiss his father once I turned my head so I wouldn't have to look. Almost no one, not even my crew members, except for Ham, knows how often I get airsick. I would have died before I admitted that I was scared.

And I have just heard an authority figure admit that he was scared and unable to do his job.

And he did it on intercom.

Maybe it was because I liked and respected Brady so much that I was so impressed by what he did that morning. Maybe I remembered how well he behaved when we hit the mountain in Wyoming. Maybe going to battle was getting to me. Maybe my oxygen mask wasn't working. Whatever.

We don't break out of the clouds until 18,000 feet, which means that we climbed for two hours.

And Crew 32 is now out in the clear, above the counterpane of clouds.

It is very cold. My breath fogs up my goggles. Even in my electric underwear and fleece-lined boots, pants, and coat, I shiver.

Off to the starboard, Square J on the tails, red-green flares, the 390th. Off to port, green-greens, Square B, the 95th. Above us, green-yellow, Square D, the 100th, eighteen planes in place.

So Brady has a problem.

Do we abort and go back home to bed? On this day do we get shot at? On this day, do we get credit for a mission and only have twenty-four more to fly? How do we get Keissling out of our slot? He wants to get a mission in too, especially since it is only to France. The next one might be tougher.

Brady and Hoerr pour on the power and pull up alongside Keissling. We see his copilot, John Stephen, waving us off. In the front the navigator and bombardier, at the top turret the engineer, in the ball the turret operator, in the waist two gunners, in the tail a gunner, all of them waving us away or thumbing their noses at us. Go home!

Over intercom, I hear Lieutenant John D. Brady, quiet-like.

"Keissling, the supers don't get the slots till Checkpoint Able. This is Brady, and I am coming in on top of you. If you don't get out of the way of this expensive part of the U.S. Air Corps, I am going to smash the living shit out of you."

This is a conversation that will be heard by every control tower in the 8AF. This is a conversation that will be heard by every WAAF and WREN monitoring the airwaves. This is a conversation that will be heard by the Luftwaffe.

Keissling also hears—and goes home.

This is my pilot.

I put my head up in the astrodome and look back at Brady. He is smiling. I give him the thumbs-up sign. He and Hoerr do the same to me in response.

And that's the guy who couldn't get the fans started.

I will fly with him anywhere.

The 100th is in behind the 95th. I wonder how Gospodor, the lead navigator, made the rendezvous.

We fly south and the clouds clear. We see London and all of its barrage balloons. Even though they can see our markings and identify us on IFF, the British ack-ack send up a warning puff or two. We fire flares in return.

I always think that France is east of England, and most of it is, but where we are headed, St. Nazaire, is actually southwest of London. Rather than fly over the Normandy peninsula, we are going around it.

England and Scotland on a map look like a skinny triangle, longer north and south than broad east and west at the bottom. To keep from flying over Brest, in France, we fly to the southwest point at the base of the triangle. We fly over Stonehenge, and I point it out to the crew.

When we get to Land's End, we turn south and tighten up our formation.

We hardly get out over the water.

"Bogeys, twelve o'clock! High!"

I hear our guns rattling, and I remember that I have one. When an ME-109 gets in my sights, I pull the trigger, remembering to keep to short bursts. I don't jam my gun, but I don't hit anything.

I see tracers arcing out into the air. Fireworks and sky rockets.

For twenty minutes the Luftwaffe career into us. We see 17's get hit. Holes show in wings. Engines stop and props feather.

Off to the left I see Brest, and we turn left, east. We come over the coast of France, north of St. Nazaire, and prepare for a hard turn to the right.

The I.P. We see St. Nazaire, and the sub pens.

Flak everywhere. It explodes out there, a black puff about the size of a bushel basket. I hear Saul Levitt come on interphone, his voice almost dreamy, "Flak. Great puff balls of hot iron." Debris hits us, and the plane bucks. There's a hole just over my head. Death missed me by fifteen inches. Every time we get hit, and it's often, our plane jumps and bucks. Like a hit horse.

Tight formation. Ham on intercom: "Bombardier to crew, bomb bay doors coming open." The grinding of the gear, the increased drag. Ham watching

NORTH SEA

The Wash

Horsham St. Faith 458 BG
Attlebridge 466 BG
Wendling 392 BG
Shipdham 44 BG
North Pickenham 492 BG
Deopham Green 452 BG
Old Buckenham 453 BG
Snetterton Heath 96 BG
Knettishall 388 BG
Great Ashfield 385 BG
Bury St. Edmunds 94 BG
Rattlesden 447 BG
Lavenham 487 BG

Ludham
Rackheath 467 BG
Great Yarmouth
Norwich
Hethel 389 BG
Seething 448 BG
Lowestoft
Tibenham 445 BG
Hardwick 93 BG
Thorpe Abbotts 100 BG
Bungay 446 BG
Eye 490 BG
Metfield 491 BG
Halesworth 489 BG
Horham 95 BG
Mendlesham 34 BG
Framlingham 390 BG
Debach 493 BG

EAST ANGLIA

Deenethorpe 401 BG
Glatton 457 BG
Polebrook 351 BG
Grafton Underwood 384 BG
Molesworth 303 BG
Chelveston 305 BG
Kimbolton 379 BG
Podington 92 BG
Thurleigh 306 BG
Cambridge
Bassingbourn 91 BG
Nuthampstead 398 BG
Sudbury 486 BG
Ridgewell 381 BG

London

0   20 miles
0   20   40 kilometers

The U.S. Eighth Air Force in England, 1942-45

♦ First Air Division—Flying Fortresses (B-17's)
■ Second Air Division—Liberators (B-24's)
□ Third Air Division—Flying Fortressess (B-17's)

the lead plane. When Jim Fitten in the lead plane drops his bombs, Ham hits a toggle switch and drops ours.

Ham: "Bombs away. Doors coming closed."

Up in front of the squadron, Ev Blakely is in trouble. Red-red flare. He's hit. He is aborting.

Ragged-like, his right wing man slides up and takes over. Blake drops down. Out of sight.

Quiet again. Not a sound, just the droning of the four engines and the swish of the wind.

Doing my job, I call out, "Navigator here, any planes down?"

Gangwer comes in. "Blakely's out there all alone, his number three out."

Petrohelos comes in. "Van Noy got it. He's going down."

"Ball turret here. He's got two engines. He's going back on the deck. The bogeys are really after him."

Ten minutes later.

"Ball here. The Spits are all around Van Noy. They go after the bogeys like hornets. Come on, Little English Friends!"

"Tail here, Blakely's doing okay. The Little Friends are with him."

For the rest of the mission we fly very extended formation. Most of the 100th together, but ragged, Blakely tootling along about five miles behind us and 2,000 feet below us. Van Noy gone somewhere.

Two hours later we are on the ground. Blakely is okay, but he comes in on two engines, with great holes in the vertical fin of his tail. Van Noy is okay when he comes in fifteen minutes behind us. The strike photos show that we have just had our first successful mission. Fitten hit the front doors of the sub pens. Our bombing pattern plopped in like a solid cow pie, small, smooth, and even.

We kid Blakely about flying alone. We call him "The Provisional Group," an outfit that comes to the base to replace missing crews. He responds, "We were behind you, just a-snappin' at your heels." That's where he got the name for his plane.

Two weeks later we read all about our crew on its first mission. Saul Levitt has been transferred to *Yank Magazine* and he gets the story pretty straight. His article appears all over the world. He writes about us often. We are his favorite subject. My navigation classmates in other groups and other theaters read about me. So do my college friends in the army, navy, and air corps.

CURTIS LEMAY
IN ACTION

 Although Colonel Harding got a Silver Star for leading the mission with us to Trondheim, many of us began to sense that the notoriety we had acquired in the States when Darr Alkire was relieved of his command was still with us. Losing two crews when we were on a practice mission didn't help.

We were getting signs that the 100th was in more disfavor even than it was when Alkire got dumped and Egan got demoted. The 100th was losing too many crews on missions. We had too much combat exhaustion, which was what they called it when a crew member was afraid to fly and quit. We had too many midair crashes of our own planes. We had too many cases of our airmen getting into fights at the local pubs.

During the end of June 1943, the Third Air Division commanding officer, Colonel Curtis LeMay, showed up at our station for an inspection, and the 100th treated him in our way. Bucky Cleven was not around when the general inspected his squadron. When Colonel LeMay was in the 350th area, a corporal parachute rigger from Nebraska, Louis Hays, drove wildly past him in a weapons carrier, a group of armorers from the ordnance section hanging on to the sides of the truck. Probably without intending to do it, Hays drove into a huge puddle and threw a wall of mud within a foot of LeMay.

As the story went, the general spoke to Colonel Harding, who told the ground exec, who told Cleven on the next day, who told his adjutant, who told the first sergeant, to "get that man." Louis Hays lost his stripes.

Even though the visit was announced, and we were all supposed to be shaved, polished, and ready, the visit by LeMay was a disaster. Our quarters were a mess. The work sections were deep in grease and disorder. To make matters worse, while LeMay was being driven to the perimeter strip, a 350th crew chief buzzing by in a jeep sideswiped the command car and dented its fender. He instantly went from master sergeant to private.

When we all assembled on the airfield for parade, our lines were straggly and our men out of step. When the squadrons stood by for inspection, Colonel LeMay didn't see Cleven. When he asked where the squadron commander was, the first sergeant responded, "He took to the woods."

This did not surprise LeMay who had heard from our previous commanding officers, Turner and Huglin, that Cleven and Egan were at the root of the 100th's raunchy discipline.

On the next day, Bucky Cleven gathered up the enlisted men who worked at 350th Squadron Headquarters and told them he was going to make up for the indignity they had suffered the day before. He took them out to the flight line and loaded them up in an old stripped-down B-17E, which our group brass used for joyrides and taxi service. Since it had no guns or armaments, it was light and Cleven could fly it like a P-39 fighter plane.

Apparently Cleven had phoned some of his pilot training classmates who were now assigned to P-47's and arranged a surprise. The E was hardly off the runway when it was "attacked" by three American fighters.

For the next twenty minutes, Cleven—whose superb skill as a pilot no one questioned—wrung that old plane out as though it was a Piper Cub. He twisted and turned and plunged, all in a simulated dog fight with his three fighter pilot chums. The three Thunderbolts buzzed the 17 and came within inches of it.

The ground-duty enlisted men in the plane probably never forgot that flight, but it hardly was what the 100th needed at that time. When the fight was reported by the British Home Guard observation team, the report did the 100th no good.

On July 1, Colonel Harold Huglin became the commanding officer of the Thirteenth Wing, the unit which coordinated our operations with the 95th and 390th groups. We knew he had developed stomach ulcers, and the fly-boys exulted about how they had driven him away.

When Colonel Neil "Chick" Harding took over on the second, we looked at him warily. We knew he was old time. We knew he was West Point, a football hero there, the blocking back for Chris Cagle. We heard he was the basketball coach at the Point. We knew he had flown in the early missions in Africa, and we heard that he had participated in somehow storing oil and gas supplies ahead of the drive across North Africa. He was short, a little thick through the middle, and he smiled a lot. Not raunchy, but easy going. The fly-boys instantly preferred him to Huglin, the ramrod.

On the Fourth of July 1943, I flew my second mission, to the sub pens and harbor at La Pallice, on the coast of France. Carrying thousand-pound bombs, we put up twenty-six planes with Colonel Harding as command pilot. About the only festivity that marked Independence Day was that over the target we let go with our Very flare pistols—and we really decorated the sky. Green-green, yellow-yellow, red-green, red-yellow, yellow-green, the works, everything but red-red, the signal of distress.

Same business, Brady's crew on the wing of the second element, me more a gunner than a navigator. I rarely made an entry in my logbook. Up in front was Blake's crew, taking all the frontal attacks from the Luftwaffe. At the Rally Point, with our flares still cascading all over the sky, Blake took a hit and we saw his starboard wing flip up. When he got the plane straight and level, he was short two engines. He feathered One and Three, and he had a big hole in the fuselage.

Bad luck guy. Who was the jinxed crew of the 418th? Not Brady's crew. Blakely's. He got knocked out of formation on his first two missions. Our crew took flak and 20-millimeters on both missions, but we came home tucked into the protective formation.

Blake limped back alone with a Little Friend on each wing till he got out of range of the Luftwaffe. On the second mission, he landed almost thirty minutes after the rest of us.

Blakely's Provisional Group. Always flying home alone.

The 100th lost one crew, over the target. When we saw them last, their bomb bay door was open, and they were dropping. When they turned south, we knew they were heading for Spain. Good luck.

On the mission, Bucky Egan added to his luster. From his seat on the right of the pilot, he noticed that the top turret operator behind him was in trouble. Seeing that the gunner's oxygen hose was dangling, Egan left his own supply and went back to help. Both men collapsed and Egan dropped, tearing his shirt. Somehow they survived and that night Bucky regaled us with his account of how he almost "became a meatball" and "lost his shirt, his Sunday best."

July 24 was Trondheim, and from then on I was on Blakely's crew. The Provisional Group. Ugh! All that responsibility in the front plane? A hard-luck crew. No thanks.

On the Trondheim mission, for me still a nightmare, we believed we had dumped bombs on the pens of the German subs which had been harassing the ships taking supplies to Murmansk. Colonel Harding got his Silver Star and we got our Distinguished Flying Crosses. The long mission began to acquire even more panache as we soon heard rumors about how we had interrupted the German development of something called an atomic bomb.

On July 25, Ops knew I was flying with Blakely, and I got a complete briefing. This time we were high group leader, but someone else was leading the wing. Bucky Egan would be our command pilot.

When we took off, there wasn't a cloud in the sky, and we had the group together by 5,000 feet. All I had to do to make the wing rendezvous was find the 95th Bomb Group with the big Square B on their tails, and tag along behind them. No problem. When we left the English coast and headed out over the North Sea, we were in perfect wing and division formation. Beautiful.

Our target was an aircraft manufacturing plant in Warnemünde, on the north German coast. As we climbed toward bombing altitude, we hit clouds. As we climbed through them on instruments, we doubted whether we would see Germany at all. We had started out with twenty-four planes, three had turned back as supernumeraries, but six had to abort because of the difficult flying conditions.

When we neared Warnemünde, Jim Douglass, the bombardier, and I knew we would not be able to see our primary target. All the other groups were having the same trouble, and the formation began to disintegrate as we wandered around looking for our targets. Just then Bucky Egan called down to us and said that the division leader had advised that we were to head for our secondary target, the shipyards and docks at Kiel.

So we followed the 95th to the secondary and— with fourteen planes dropping with him—Doug hit it dead on.

Another triumph for Blakely's crew, with Crosby as navigator.

Along with my position on a lead crew I had the title of Squadron Navigator. I wasn't sure the pilots would promote a navigator, but the T.O. (Table of Organization) said I would become a captain.

So far, the 418th had done well, no losses, no botched mission. One pilot, Ernie Keissling, turned out to have a vision disability, and he got grounded. When a navigator was needed to replace me on Brady's crew, Keissling's navigator, Davie Solomon, got the job. Their copilot, John Stephens, got the rest of the crew, and a new navigator.

That night John told about how he got checked out as first pilot: "Major Egan called me into his office and asked me if I wanted to take over the crew. When I said that I did, he told me he would have to check me out. We got into his jeep and went to the Officers' Club. We went to the bar, and he asked me to buy him a drink. When we got back into the jeep he brought me back to barracks. He told me I was checked out."

Since Brady's, Blake's, and Crank's crews now shared the same Quonset, I did not even have to move my clothes or my footlocker. Davie moved in, and all was well.

What to do with Bubbles? At first Egan thought of putting him on Bill Flesh's "Bastard Bungalow" crew, which would be disgrace and exile.

Suddenly there was no problem. Bubbles could be kicked upstairs. That was good because he was an affable, roly-poly sort of fellow, and no one wanted to hurt him.

The 100th had not figured out what to do with the Group Navigator, Omar Gonzales. According to the Table of Organization he should have been a major. Although pilots were now regularly being promoted, our squadron commanders had moved up from captain to major, and the Air Exec and Groups Ops were in for light colonel, Omar was still a first lieutenant.

All he did during the main briefings was to call out the signal by which we all synchronized our watches. "Set your watches at oh-four-hundred-zero-seven hours. Five, four, three, two, one, HACK!" At the navigators' briefing, he called out the coordinates and altitudes for the legs of the missions.

Coming across the Atlantic as navigator for Colonel Turner, he split the runway at Presque Isle, Maine; Gander Lake, Newfoundland; Goose Bay, Labrador; Blooie West One, Greenland; Reykjavik, Iceland; and Stornoway, Scotland. Although he was probably the best navigator in the group, instead of flying in the lead plane, he could only fly missions filling in for an injured navigator on a wing crew.

A waste.

One of the 418th pilots, Bill Flesh, continued to get into trouble. He got drunk in the Officers' Club and got into fights. At a local pub he tried to take on every Englishman there. To keep him in check, Bucky Egan assigned an M.P. to go everywhere with him. What this meant was that Bill Flesh had his own jeep.

Since Flesh was grounded so much, his crew was disbanded, and he flew only as a fill-in pilot. On the next mission, Omar filled in on the Flesh crew. Omar knew that Flesh was called the 100th's "fuck-up pilot," but he was anxious to get experience under fire. When the plane went over the target and took a minor flak hit, Bill Flesh rang the "Abandon Ship!" bell. A mistake? Was he so scared he hit the bell by mistake? Who knows?

Out went Omar and all of the crew but the pilot.

Whether he was too frightened to jump, or what, the pilot came home flying solo, no copilot, no navigator, no crew, alone, locked in so tight to his element leader that the lead crew kept waving him off.

With Omar gone, up went Bubbles to Group Navigator.

All this meant that my own tour would take longer. On Brady's crew, I flew every time the 418th flew, which was three out of every four times the 100th flew. All the missions except when the 418th had its turn to be stood down. On Blake's crew I only flew when the 418th had its turn to lead the group. I would be flying only about every twelfth mission. I would not be home by Christmas.

Out in front maybe I wouldn't get home at all.

On both the St. Nazaire and La Pallice missions, I had seen the Luftwaffe frontal attacks take at least one of Blake's engines. With the motionless prop feathered to keep it from windmilling, that is, turned so the leading edge was forward and the prop caused no drag, he still could not fly fast enough to lead the group. On both missions, he had to abort and fly back across France alone. As I looked back at the lonely flight of Blakely's Provisional Group, I was glad I was not on that plane.

Now I was.

I am not certain whether Ev Blakely realized I was not really as good a navigator as I seemed on the practice mission to the Orkneys and the Trondheim and Warnemünde-Kiel mission. What I do know was that Blake spent a lot of time training me. As a lead pilot he could check out a plane whenever he wanted to practice and train. I began to feel that I lived on the flight line or in Zero-Six-One.

Every morning or afternoon when we were stood down, Ev checked out a personnel carrier and rounded up the crew. If we had not got up in time for breakfast that was our tough luck. We flew on an empty stomach—and I dry heaved when my airsickness came. If weather permitted, we went up to 25,000 feet and practiced formation control, navigation, and bombing, pretending that we had seventeen or twenty planes behind us. Doug and I worked out what to do at the I.P., the Initial Point, where we made the turn onto the bombing run. We conditioned ourselves to think of the other planes, gradual turns, exactly maintained airspeed and altitude, smooth, smooth, smooth. Then the abrupt turn to the R.P., the Rally Point, where Blake asked the tail gunner to look around and see what losses we had, and what planes were straggling. Depending on what imaginary report the tail gunner concocted, Blake "helped" the damaged planes to catch up by turning into their side to permit them to catch up.

Practice, practice, practice. Smooth. Beautiful.

He expected me always to give headings two minutes before the turn. He preferred to warn the formation and then ease into the bank. Easy, easy, easy.

Daylight bombing with Flying Fortresses required that all planes in the formation be exactly in place. On an M.E., Maximum Effort, the task force put up by the Eighth Air Force consisted of three divisions, the First, which was the oldest and most experienced, the Second, which flew B-24's, called the Liberators, and the Third, us, the one commanded by Colonel Curtis LeMay.

Flying with B-24's was especially difficult.

You can still start an argument with a WWII Air Corps veteran as to which was better, the B-24 or the B-17. Because of its highly efficient Davis wing, the B-24 carried a heavier load and flew faster. However, because of that same slim, narrow wing, the Lib was vulnerable. Hit that wing and down went the plane. A B-17 could get its crew back on one engine. Even with half its tail torn off or with a huge, gaping hole in the wings, fuselage, or nose, a good pilot could get his Fort and his crew back to the base.

What mattered to me was that the B-24 flew at 180 IAS, but the B-17's indicated air speed was 150. Therefore, Liberators started out after we did and we rendezvoused with them at the last possible minute. Then, to keep from overriding us, they did an occasional dogleg.

As the lead crew of the task force, we had to think about all that.

What was tough for me was the rendezvous. When we hit enemy territory we had to have every group right in place. If there was a straggling group, it got hit, and hit bad.

That meant I had to assemble the squadron, usually as we circled up through the overcast around Splasher Six, our homing beacon. Then, according to our field order, I headed out, upwind, and the other two squadron lead navigators would turn in my general direction and begin a slow, wide 360-degree turn. At about five minutes out I would turn our squadron around, upwind first and then downwind, but quick and hard.

"Rack it around, Blakely, rack it around," I would say as we practiced.

"This is the best I can do, Croz." Patiently. "If I tighten it up, the wing men in the second flight would have to run it up to 220 indicated. It's like cracking a whip."

"Okay, okay." And I would go back to my E6B to try to see when I should have started the turn. I would make it four minutes the next time.

As we headed back to Splasher Six, as neat as could be, we imagined that the other two squadrons would finish their 360 and fit onto our left and right, one high, the other low.

Practice, practice, practice. Strain. Sweat going into my fleece-lined leather jacket. Hard work, like fear, had its own smell.

Now the wing assembly, the other two groups, the 390th and the 95th. Usually we were briefed to meet the rest of the wing over either our splasher or theirs. This meant doing a radius of action, heading for the rendezvous point about ten minutes early and then kicking in a dogleg to use up exactly the ten minutes. The problem was that by this time we were usually up about 18,000 feet and we could have a seventy-mile wind from any direction. If the wind was in the opposite direction from what I thought, we could be off course eighteen miles at the end of the maneuver.

At first, before Blakely went to work on me, I would not know where the wind was. Blake and I worked it out that we could get to 18,000 early and have six minutes extra to do a wind vector problem. If it was clear, which was rare, I did it with pilotage. When there were solid clouds under us, Forky, the boy genius radio operator, would give me fixes to show me what the wind was doing to us. With the crew's help, I knew exactly what the wind was when I started out losing that ten minutes before the wing rendezvous. The fact that the procedure took six minutes meant that I could just add a zero to my answers and get what happened in sixty minutes. I could not make a multiplication error or misread my E6B.

Slowly, I became a navigator. I don't know when I finally began to like Ev Blakely, but I do know that I admired him and respected him almost immediately. I give him a lot of the credit for my later successes as a navigator.

Ev Blakely was a good pilot for a navigator. Instead of jockeying back and forth as John Brady had to do on a wing, Ev, in the lead, could keep his needles and dials fixed. Occasionally on a practice mission, I would leave the nose and go up and watch him and Charlie Via. Ev would be sitting there, beady-eyed, staring at the dials, his muscles tense as he fine-tuned his altimeter, power settings, and airspeed indicator.

As a navigator, I didn't want a hot pilot, a rock. I wanted a truck driver. I wanted a pilot who could keep the needles steady. I got so I could tell by the humming sounds of the airstream outside that Blake had us on heading, on speed, level, all engines in sync. I began to call him "Old Beady Eyes." I could not have paid him a higher compliment.

After the Trondheim and Warnemünde missions, I went with Blake, Via, and Douglass to mission debriefing at Third Air Division Headquarters at Elveden Hall, past Bury St. Edmunds, some thirty miles to the west, inland, of us.

At Elveden Hall, I was in a palace. I learned that it was once the English home of one of the richest maharajas of India.

When we arrived, we were directed to the rear, where we left the car and walked up huge stone stairs.

Along with several quartets of flyers, we walked down a long hall with high, ornate ceilings and into what was probably once the rajah's dining room. The pictures were gone, and the curtains, and the chandeliers, and the oriental rugs were stored—and forgotten—in the basement. Years later, when the heir to the Guinness Brewery fortune purchased Elveden Hall for a summer home, he opened the basement and found seven million dollars' worth of furniture and art, which he had not known would be included in the palace that he bought for two million.

We all sat down and looked around curiously to see who else was there. In the front row were the full bird colonels and the light colonels, the commanders and air executives of all the 3AD groups. Colonel Harding was right in the middle. We could see that everyone knew him.

"At-ten-HUT!"

We popped to, and looked out of the corner of our eyes to see who was entering the room.

Ahead of three other full colonels, a stocky, mid-height colonel walked in. His hair was dark, slicked down, parted in the middle, and his face was square. Clenched in his jaw was a black pipe, unlit.

Wasting no time, Colonel Curtis LeMay said, "Seats, men, at ease," and began to speak.

We were there, LeMay said, because he was trying to find out why the Third Air Division wasn't doing its job any better. Part of the reason was bad formation. Group commanders were instructed to check out all new crews in formation before they flew. There was to be more practice flying in formation.

Another reason for the trouble, LeMay ground out in his gritty, patternless speaking voice, was that lead pilots had not learned to fly with lead navigators and lead bombardiers.

"Wrong, sir," I thought to myself. In the 100th's case, we had a good lead crew in each squadron, but the command pilots messed us up.

"I am a pilot," LeMay said, "but I am the only person in this room who is also a trained navigator and a trained bombardier. When I was a group commander in the First Air Division I flew a mission as a lead pilot, a lead navigator, and a lead bombardier. I learned that a mission goes wrong when all three don't work together.

"Too many times, the command pilot, who is supposed to lead a mission, is the one who causes it to fail. Every time he sees a burst of flak, he takes the wheel and swerves his plane. That causes trouble for the whole group.

"If there is anything that is necessary on a bomb run it is that there be no evasive action.

"Too many command pilots have their own special ways of taking over on the bomb run. Some of you think you can spare your group from the flak if you descend and confuse the anti-aircraft—and you ruin the bombsight computations. Some of you, understandably, want to keep your formation tight so your bomb pattern will be small. That is commendable. But you have to depend on your wing men to keep in place. You can't jockey back into place. The lead plane must fly straight and level. What you must do on the bomb run is to let the bombardier and the Norden take over."

This guy is tough, I thought. I was seeing a group of full colonels getting chewed out.

"We know all this," Doug whispered, "but how is

he going to make the brass keep their hands off the wheel? Egan and Harding take over on the bomb run."

As the briefing continued, LeMay said, "Now I want you here to tell me what went wrong on the St. Nazaire and La Pallice missions."

One by one the colonels or lieutenant colonels who had flown right seat spoke. Yes, my group assembled on time. Yes, we made the wing rendezvous as briefed, but the other groups weren't there. Yes, we flew good formation during the whole mission. Yes, we were at the fighter rendezvous, but the fighters weren't. At the I.P., we tucked in tight, but the bombardier missed the target.

After all the command pilots talked, LeMay said, "Do any of you lead navigators or lead bombardiers want to add anything?"

Of course, we didn't. We were all first and second lieutenants. Not one of the command pilots had described a mission anything like the way it was really flown. Even so, who among the lieutenants wanted to contradict our own brass?

Silence. Uncomfortable silence.

"Lieutenant Shore, Group Navigator of the 390th. Who was the bombardier with you in the nose on the mission of July 18th?"

Marshall Shore pointed to a bombardier.

LeMay turned to the bombardier. "Do you have anything to add?"

"No, sir."

"Were your bubbles level during the bomb run?"

When Colonel LeMay asked that question, I must have gasped. I knew exactly what he had in mind. Maybe because of the sound I made, Colonel LeMay looked directly at me.

He slowly winked. Something was wrong with one side of his face, and it was a grotesque wink, but that was what it was.

I felt my heart speed up. I could hardly breathe. I looked around at the other navigators and bombardiers. How many of them knew what LeMay's question meant? What he was really asking was who was flying the plane. If the bubbles in the bombsight were level, the Norden was flying. If the bubbles were off, a pilot had overpowered the controls—and was probably doing evasive action.

When I looked back at Colonel LeMay, he was still looking at me. I winked back at him, and nodded. That funny smile again. He looked at the bombardier.

"Did your equipment work all right?"

"No malfunction, sir."

One by one LeMay addressed all the lead bombardiers and asked them several irrelevant questions—and the one about the bubbles.

Then he turned to the navigators, me first.

"Lieutenant, give me your story."

"Sorry, sir, I wasn't leading those missions."

"What group are you in?"

"The 100th, sir."

Colonel LeMay turned to Colonel Harding. "Why is he here, Chick, if he isn't a lead navigator?"

"He was the lead on Trondheim and Warnemünde. Before he replaced the navigator on the lead crew, he was on a wing."

Colonel LeMay looked back at me.

"Trondheim? Good show."

"Thank you, sir."

He turned to Lieutenant Marshall Shore of the 390th.

He asked several questions, but I recognized the key one.

"Lieutenant, when you were on the run from the I.P. to the target, what was the maximum deflection of your compass heading?"

"About twenty-five degrees, sir."

By now every lead navigator in the room knew what was going on. If the Norden was in charge, the corrections wouldn't have been more than five or six degrees. Only a pilot could jerk a plane around more than that.

At the end of the debriefing Colonel LeMay knew what every bombardier and navigator in the room knew, and I doubt if any pilots knew he knew.

I realized I was in the presence of a very bright man, and a very skilled leader.

On the way to the mess, Colonel LeMay went in first and then waited as we all filed past him. One by one he asked our group designation and shook hands with us. As I went by him, he said, "Trondheim?" He looked at my name tag. "Your name is Crosby?"

"Yes, sir."

He smiled, that funny grimace of a smile, and turned to the next officer in line.

That was it.

CHAPTER 6

"HOME BY CHRISTMAS"

✈ About a week after my first trip to Elveden Hall, the squadron orderly once again starts me on a very special adventure.

"Captain Blakely, Lieutenant Via, Lieutenant Crosby, and Lieutenant Douglass are to appear tomorrow morning at oh-eight-hundred hours in Class A's at Major Kidd's office in Group Ops. You may expect to be gone for the day."

A chorus of "Now what?"

Next morning. We are there—and so are Jack Swartout, Arch "Bulldog" Drummond, Leonard Bull, and Al Dahlgren, the officers on the 351st lead crew.

In his office before the two crews, Jack Kidd talks. "I don't know why, but we nine are supposed to go to Elveden Hall in two command cars with the blackout curtains fastened shut. No one is to see us, and we are to tell no one we are going. When we return, we are to tell no one what has happened. Don't tell your enlisted men where you are going, but tell them they are confined to the base. I will ride to Elveden Hall with Blakely and come back with Swartout."

"Great!" says Blake. "Our crew have gone so long without a pass they are about to go AWOL—and I wouldn't blame them."

We arrive at 3AD HQ and walk to the auditorium-with-the-chandeliers.

The usual glances around to see who's been invited, and why. All the officers in the front row are bird colonels except Jack Kidd. The Group Commanders. Jack Kidd seems to be the only group leader who is not a C.O.

I am not surprised. More evidence that Chick Harding and the 100th are in trouble.

In contrast to the rest of the 100th leadership, Jack Kidd was acquiring a good reputation. Darr Alkire's replacement, Colonel Turner, had promoted him from squadron commander to Group Ops. The 351st was now under Ollie Turner, a good man, but it still had Kidd's mark on it. It was having the least casualties and compiling the best service record. The 351st lead crew, Swartout's, had one of the best 100th records.

On missions, Jack Kidd let his lead crew fly a steady course, and the wing crews could stack in tight, no whipping around, no burnt-out engines. He let the bombardier do his job from the IP to the target. He was the 100th's best command pilot.

But why were any of us here?

"At-ten-HUT!"

Not LeMay, but another colonel, this one an older man, no wings, a ground officer. He has glasses. Probably a retread.

He goes to the stage, looks around theatrically, wipes his glasses, and clears his throat. Dramatically he reaches into the chest pocket of his blouse and takes out a letter. It takes him a while to get it out of the envelope. He fumbles with it. Dramatic effect lost. Then he tells us the letter is from his wife, and he begins to read.

"Dear Charles, you have been gone for months. Our Susie and Junior say they remember you, but I fear they don't. They know I cry for you almost every night. I have told them you will probably be home by Christmas."

Charles pauses, and looks up at us. "Gentlemen, what we are going to tell you today will send you on a mission that is so important that we will be home by Christmas. We are going to demolish totally the Boche's complete ball bearing manufacturing ability. We are going to destroy the Hun."

Hun? Boche? Come on now. That proves Charles is a retread. In the Eighth we have come to have so much respect for the Luftwaffe fighter pilots who fly through our formation that we never call them "Huns," "Boche," "Krauts," or even "Jerries." Charles is fighting the last war.

He is the A-2 (Intelligence) officer for the division. By whatever means, Air Intelligence has come to believe that all the ball bearings in Germany are manufactured in one place, in Schweinfurt.

"Wow," I say to Blake. "That's in deep."

Then the retread clicks his heels—honest, he does click his heels—and he sits down. Not a flyer in the room believes him.

His face showing that he is pained by the hokey performance of the A-2, LeMay stands up. An aide rolls back a curtain, and we see a red ribbon going on and on and on. Instead of turning around for a return trip, the ribbon goes on east to the Alps, then south into the Mediterranean almost to Italy, and then west.

"Africa!" A hundred voices.

I whisper to Charlie Via, "That's not Schweinfurt. That's Regensburg."

"When I took over the Third," LeMay says, "I insisted that all our crews get Tokyos. Since we have wing tanks and a gas load of 2,780 gallons, we can go where the First Division can't. Now we can go to Regensburg, and keep on going. In part we will be acting as a diversion to split the Luftwaffe and keep them away from the First, who are going to Schweinfurt. But our target is important. We want to destroy the Messerschmitt factory in Regensburg. Instead of coming back through the Luftwaffe again, we will go on to Africa.

"It's a hard target. Bombardiers and navigators will come here every other day and be briefed for the route and target.

"It's a dangerous mission, especially for you lead crews. Tomorrow two new planes will arrive at your base, and you get them. No one but your line crews is even to touch them. Certainly no one is to fly them. Your navigators will swing their compasses and calibrate your drift meters. Your crews will get their guns and turrets into top condition.

"This is top secret. Nine people in each group know about it, and no one else. We're redundant on this. We're training two crews for the lead. We will select the one to go on the day of the mission. Pilots will go up every day to simulate as much of the mission as we can. When you aren't here for training, you will all be in the air. When we call the mission, we want you to be ready."

"The part I don't like," says Blakely as we ride back, "is the raw deal for our enlisted men. They already know they will get their missions in slower than their buddies on other crews. Now if they get grounded and can't even go into the village for the pub, they will really be burned. We've got to do something about that."

In a few days, the plane arrives. The A-4 painters put on the black Square D on the two-story-high tail fin, just over the numbers 23393. The crew fights about what to name it. Blake wants it to be *Just a-Snappin'* again. The enlisted men want names that are either about sexy women, or our threat to Hitler. One of the gunners comes up with a compromise—*Bombs a-Busting*. On the nose he wants a bosomy woman dropping a bomb. He is hooted into silence. I realize I will call it "Three-Nine-Three" and let it go at that, just as I did with "Zero-Six-One," now assigned to a new crew piloted by Bob Wolff. Names are for kids and Hollywood. I don't put bombs on my A-2 jacket to show how many missions I have flown.

Blake gives up. We don't put a name or a picture of a Betty Grable clone on the nose. Years later we still call it by different names.

The plane is a beauty. Obviously Boeing talked to a navigator. My desk is bigger, the chair with more support. The compass is on a gyro; it is not magnetic like the one Christopher Columbus and my previous plane used. My window is bigger for pilotage. The astrodome is higher and bigger, although I don't know what I will do with it. It is no good for pilotage, dead reckoning, or radio, which we use, and we don't use celestial.

During most of the war I was Harry Straight Arrow. I usually followed the rules. Raunch was just not for me.

Ev Blakely was even worse—or better—than I was. No one, absolutely no one, was as G.I. as he was. In the air he demanded straight-down-the-line discipline. If a gunner didn't have his guns clean, Ev was all over him. No matter where we were, or what we were doing, he wanted a P.R. report from me every fifteen minutes. Even when we were on a short flight slow-timing a new engine, he took the whole crew up and insisted that all gunners be at the ready. No other gunner in the squadron wanted to be on our crew.

We chafed a little. Did we have to be that good?

About halfway through its tour every crew got to take a week off for R&R, rest and recuperation. If the crew had serious losses, went on a string of tough missions, or were unusually flakked up, they might get to go early, or oftener. The Eighth set up some rest homes for just that purpose. Usually the flak shacks were in a castle or mansion somewhere. There would be a swimming pool, maybe horses, a steam bath, Ping-Pong, movies, rooms with card tables where flyers could sit alone and write letters home. There would be three or four Red Cross girls who were especially gracious and solicitous. The food was reputedly out of this world.

Word had come in that the best of them all was at Bournemouth, down on the south shore of England. It was set up for infantry and artillery officers, but when they moved out to prepare for D-Day it was transferred to the Eighth and Ninth Air Forces. So far only a few air crews had gone there.

Because we were getting our missions in so slowly we weren't even close to getting our R&R.

So Blakely decided that our crew would have its own private flak shack.

On one of the days when we had our new plane, Three-Nine-Three, checked out for a practice mission, we scheduled an orthodox spit-and-polish three-leg navigation and bombing trip. Over interphone we could hear our gunners bitching at each other. As usual, Blake was making them keep at their stations, simulating a mission.

When we got to Stonehenge, past London, we kept on going south.

Ahead of us was the coast, lots of ships and boats moored in the harbor.

Over intercom: "Croz, is that Bournemouth?"

"That's it, Blake. Up on the hill is the hotel that's the flak shack."

Blake then explains to the crew that he is sorry they have had no passes. We are going to spend the afternoon and evening at a very lovely hotel with Red Cross girls.

"Let's go in," says Blake.

"Go in where?" says Copilot Via. Do you think this bird can land on water?"

"No," says Blake, "there's a landing field down there."

Charlie Via is from Virginia and deeply religious. He never swears. When he gets excited, he says "Shingle nails!" when someone else would say

"Shit!" When he is really excited, he says "White House Mouse!" In his Virginia speech, it comes out "White hoose moose."

Charlie Via is obviously excited.

"White hoose moose," he comes in over intercom. "That's no landing field. It's a postage stamp. Look, there are Avions parked there. It must be somebody's private flying club. There's only one concrete landing strip, and it's too short."

"We will go in slaunch-wise."

"Look at the wind sock. We will have a tail wind crosswise."

"Yeah, I know it. We will go in on the grass. The minute we touch down you tromp on the brakes. I will flatten the props and use them to slow us down."

"If I were Catholic," says Via, "I would be crossing myself."

"I am and I am," says someone on the crew.

"Pilot to crew, take landing stations, we are going in."

Everyone comes on intercom. A hubbub. Something wrong with the plane?

"Pilot to crew, we are going to take French leave. We are landing at RAF station Herndon. Over and out."

A flick of a switch. "U.S. Army 393 to Herndon Control, request permission to land and instructions."

A British voice comes on, a woman, cool, clipped, amused. Dear God, what it does to morale to hear a woman's voice on intercom. "You Yanks are all crazy."

We know she is British. Her a's sound more like i's. "Yah-inks," and "crah-eezy."

The English voice continues. "If you put your bird down on this pasture, how will you get it off?"

Blake, firm: "Army 393 to Herndon, request landing instructions."

The cool woman's voice, resigned: "Come in on Runway 29. You have 1,500 feet for your roll."

Blake: "Not enough. I have to come in on the diagonal."

Cool British voice, giving up. "Okay, Yah-ink, we'll have the Red Cross lorries ready."

Blake brings 393 in, smooth as glass. We don't bounce once. The engines roar as he changes the propeller pitch and the plane noses forward. He is on the brakes, on and off. We roll and then slow down as we almost go over on our nose, then he eases off, and we roll and then he stops us again. When we stop and he turns us around, we aren't ten feet from the fence.

When we get out of our plane, the field's maintenance crew come up to us. Silently they stare at our plane, and us. They ask us to report in at Flying Control.

The trim little WREN, the air traffic control who brought us in, salutes and briskly turns to the telephone. To someone she says, "We have ten Yah-inks here who need transport into town. Can you supply it? . . . Oh, you are a dear chap."

She turns to us. "Is there anything more I can do?"

"You can go out with me tonight." This from one of the gunners.

She laughs, "You Yah-inks are all fresh." Then she smiles again. "I believe in fraternization, but I am already fraternized. I stick to one American at a time."

"Air Corps?"

"No, Nigh-vy."

A groan from our crew. "Oh, well, we are fighting the same war."

The "transport" is ready for us. An RAF corporal comes in, stomps his foot on the floor, and snaps a salute. We respond awkwardly, the way the American Air Corps does.

We pile into the car and careen on the wrong side of the road, British style, along the coast and into a city which seems to be predominantly grass-lined boulevards. We get to the hotel: "USO. Welcome to Members of the American Military Forces. Your home away from home."

A tall, slender Red Cross girl comes up to us. In good military protocol she extends her hand first to Blake.

"Welcome, Air Corps. My name is Louise Harlan. The WREN from the Royal Air Force station called us on trunks and told us you were coming. We don't get many aviators."

In my entire military career, every Red Cross girl I met was top-notch. No matter how pretty they actually were, they always kept themselves up, they were concerned about our welfare, they were cheerful, and they were therefore attractive. Most soldiers, sailors, and flyers fell in love with at least one Red Cross girl during their service.

Along with the girls who served at our base, Betty Hardman, Hilda Kinder, Dorothy Durang, and others, Louise was one of the best of the best. She knew what a navigator did, not just on an airplane, but on a Fort. She soon found out where our homes were.

Telling her as little as possible about why we had

so much freedom, we told Louise we would be there until after dinner.

"I think we can make you glad you dropped by," she said. "I can give you each a room."

Usually Red Cross clubs were either for enlisted men or officers, and the Bournemouth Hotel was for officers, but Louise made us a special case and welcomed our whole crew.

Most of us went to our rooms, either for a nap or the hottest, longest shower we had had for weeks. At four o'clock—Louise wisely did not call it oh-sixteen-hundred hours—we met in the lounge and had tea and, yes, crumpets. All the help were British, and they loved being especially British for their American guests. Since we were in our flying coveralls and A-2 jackets, we made them feel as though they were really helping the war effort.

After tea, we either swam or played croquet on the greenest, flattest court I have ever seen.

At 7:00 P.M., we had the best seafood dinner we had eaten since we got to England. It was some kind of scallops, creamed, breaded, and on a half shell. The wine was white. We had asparagus, not brussels sprouts. The baked potato had been spooned out, mashed, creamed, and put back in. "We call them twice-baked potatoes," Louise said.

It was luxury. Ever since then, when I get hungry, I think of that meal.

The Bournemouth trip became an every-other-day routine. We would be in the air by seven in the morning. Blake put us through simulated climbs around Splasher Six, the breakout over the clouds, the formation of the flight, imagining a plane coming up on the right and left; then the squadron, with another flight of three tacking on; then the group, with the high squadron coming in on our right and the low on the left, all this at 5,000 feet. Then, on oxygen at 12,000 feet, we practiced the rendezvous with the wing, division, and task force, all of them coming in on trail.

At 24,000 feet we simulated bombing, the approach to the I.P., with every possible wind situation factored in. The sudden, racking turn onto the bomb run, everyone quiet, Doug and his Norden bombsight controlling the plane, bomb bay doors grinding open, no one but Doug and Blake on intercom.

We practiced locating approaching E.A., enemy aircraft: "Bogey, eight o'clock, low." No more, no less. The only other thing we could say about the Luftwaffe during a mission was, "I got him." Blake spelled it out. No profanity on intercom. "It doesn't say anything." Because of that edict, our enlisted men lost half of their vocabulary.

Over and over we rehearsed safety procedures, what to do with fire, parachute readiness, crash landing. Blake was a tyrant, but he worked himself harder than he worked us. We knew that when we got hit by flak or fighters, we could lose three engines and he still would get us back.

And every other afternoon and evening we led the life of Riley with Louise Harlan at the Bournemouth flak shack.

Okay, so we broke the rules.

No one else knew about our forays and only Jack Kidd and Swartout's crew knew why we weren't flying missions. Major Egan, our Squadron C.O., was told he was not to question us, and Flying Control was told they were to clear any flight plan we requested. Everyone was told to stay away from our plane. We could tell that Egan was steaming, but he never said anything.

Then one day when we came back from Elveden Hall and went out to the perimeter, we saw that 393 was gone!

When it landed and taxied back to the hard standing, Bucky Egan was at the wheel. He got out.

"That plane is assigned to my squadron, and I had to take it up and wring it out," he said.

"Yes, sir," we said.

THE SCREW-UP

On August 12, 1943, I made a decision which—I can say without fear of being contradicted—changed the world.

On the evening of August 11, I had dinner earlier than usual. I walked through the club, saw the usual flak jobs going on. Since our replacement crews were already pretty well flakked up because of the 100th's reputation as an outfit with heavy losses, our veteran crews delighted in letting them know how bad the missions were. Exaggeration was, of course, acceptable. A red light went on, and the bartenders stopped selling beer or whiskey. Actually, the ground officers could have continued to drink, but out of courtesy, when the flyers could not drink, the paddlefeet volunteered to curb their own imbibing.

Combat had brought the ground echelon and the air echelon closer together. They knew we were the ones who were going out and getting shot down. We knew that for us promotion and ribbons came quickly. We got the girls in London. We got a trip home—if we were lucky and completed a tour. They were here for the duration. They called themselves paddlefeet; we were the fly-boys.

At the bulletin board, I saw that the movie at the base theater did not interest me. I saw also that on the next Saturday night, we would have a dance with the music furnished by the 100th band, "The Century Bombers." It was a Glenn Miller play-alike. Very good. I wished that Jean could go to the dance with me.

Since our crew was grounded for the Regensburg Raid up ahead of us, there was no point to my going to Squadron Ops to see who was flying. I decided to walk back to my barracks.

Back in the States, Jean was writing me every day. Always those feminine envelopes, addressed in brown ink. To "Lt. Harry H. Crosby." From "Mrs. Harry H. Crosby." I had the letters in a neat, growing pile back at my quarters. Even for the third or fourth time they made good reading. I decided to go back, re-read my letters and write again to Jean.

As I walked along, the stars began to come out, and I heard Farmer Draper's cattle lowing. They were guernseys, he told me once, with pride. I was conscious of the smell of new-mown hay, and put it out of my mind that it smelled just a bit like phosgene, poison gas. Up ahead of me I saw some Englishmen cycling along and laughing. I heard one of them say something about a "Yah-ink." More laughter. A small dog from somewhere came up behind me, insisted that it be petted, and then ran off.

When I got to the squadron area, although I was technically off duty and grounded for the next day, I checked in at the orderly room. Only the C.Q., charge of quarters, was there.

"Yes, Lieutenant," he said as he wrote.

In my barracks, I had the whole room to myself. I was thankful because now I could turn up my Victrola as loud as I wished.

When we left Kearney, Nebraska, we were allowed to take very little baggage overseas. Compared to the infantry, it was a moving van, but we did have to make choices. I had an A-3 bag, which was my parachute bag, canvas, collapsible, with most of its space taken by my chute and flying clothes. For all my other clothes, I had a B-4 bag, a Valpack, in which would hang my dress blouse, short coat, a second blouse, and four pairs of pants. I jammed shirts, underwear, shaving equipment, pictures, books, stationery, and all the rest into the B-4.

In addition, we were permitted two footlockers which were sent by sea after us. To fill up one footlocker, we were assigned a bulky set of impregnated clothing, which was supposed to protect us against attack by gas. I reasoned that the Germans might gas infantry but they would hardly drop gas on a formation of B-17's. Besides, the clothing had a vile smell. I reasoned that with all those crews shot down in England, surely there would be some spare impregnated clothing around.

When I left Kearney I therefore shoved my impregnated clothing under the bed, and left it there. In its space I put my small electric Victrola radio and record player and as many records as the space would hold.

When the footlocker caught up with me I had a corporal in the radio shack rig me up a transformer to U.K. current, and I was one of the few who had his own radio and record player.

I took out my collection of records and turned them over slowly. "Ritual Fire Dance?" I'm not in the mood. John Philip Sousa and the pieces I used to play with the Oskaloosa Municipal Band? Not right. Glenn Miller? Usually, but not now. Beethoven? Yes. It was good when I was flying over the Reich.

I took out the *Fifth* and put it on the turntable. When the music began I lay back on my bed and slowly read the notes on the record cover. Ludwig van Beethoven, I read, went to school in Bonn, Germany. I remembered seeing Bonn on my maps.

Six hours later the same business. The orderly wakes us. All four crews flying.

"No," says Blakely, "we are stood down. No flying." He was right. Colonel LeMay had made it clear that with what we knew, we and Swartout's crew must not be shot down and be interrogated in Germany.

The orderly says, firmly, "Yes, you are, sir. You are to go to Group Ops at once for a special briefing with Colonel Harding. You are leading."

A weapons carrier stops before our barracks to take us to briefing. M.E.—Maximum Effort. A new kind of formation. We are leading the wing, first in the division. When we get to the Ruhr, the wings separate and we have different targets.

A few minutes later, hundreds of flying crewmen assemble at Group Ops, all of us, rows and rows, in sheep-lined flying gear, some with headsets around our necks, here and there a hot pilot with a white scarf. The smell of sweat and tobacco.

Squadron Ops saying to me, "Front row for the lead crew, Lieutenant."

Self-consciously I walk down the aisle past all the other crews, many of them my classmates from navigation school. I sit with the Group Commander, the squadron commanders, and some other majors and lieutenant colonels, with Blake, Doug, and Charlie Via near me, perhaps as self-conscious as I was.

I hear Blake talking to Colonel Harding. "You know, sir, that Elveden Hall has us grounded."

"I know," says Harding. "But we are leading the whole task force, and I want you with me."

I suppose I should feel flattered.

Colonel Kidd does the briefing. He stands up and it is suddenly quiet. He nods to a ground officer, Major Minor Shaw. It still seems like a funny name.

I watch S-2 go through the usual corny, dramatic touch of slowly pulling the curtain back as we watch to see where the red ribbon stretches.

I see where the ribbon ends. I say to myself, "Here we go again. I hope I can find the damned place."

I have forgotten where the target was.

It doesn't matter because we never got there.

For me the mission began very well. My training under Blakely helped. It was one of the few rendezvous I made in the clear. We took off and flew around the base a few times at 5,000 feet and the whole group was in place. I set up a radius-of-action problem and gave the heading to Blake. He flew it perfectly, of course, and I gave him the turn back to our heading. Perfect, right on time. Over intercom, I heard Forky gloat as we flew over the beacon of our rendezvous and the radio compass needle reversed at exactly the second we should have been there.

"Good one, Lieutenant," he said.

Off to the right I saw the 390th coming in high; off to the left, low, was the 95th, perfect. At this altitude there were no contrails. Just beautiful planes flying beautiful formation. Only two days before, I learned that my navigation school roommate was the Group Navigator for the 95th. I wondered whether Ellis Scripture was flying in one of their planes. He was my Mather Field roommate who introduced me to Dot, for whom I took such a tumble. Till I realized it was Jean I wanted.

With the sixty-two planes of the Thirteenth Wing behind me, I gave Blake the heading for a spot just south of Lowestoft where I was to fit in with the other wings of the Third Air Division. We had a wind from the west which was rushing us a little, so I threw in a dogleg and said, "Okay, Blake, a slow, rolling turn to 359 degrees. Take your time."

"Roger, Croz." Confidence in Blake's voice. I felt very good.

We floated over Lowestoft's barrage balloons at 12,000 feet. Right on time. Three other wings smoothed in behind us. Couldn't be better. Off to our left was all of East Anglia. I could see much of England, past Cambridge to Oxford. Some of the top turrets in the lead planes were as exhilarated as I was. They fired their Very pistols with their identifying colors, green-yellow, red-green, all the possible combinations. They fired too many, pumped up because the sky was so blue and England was so green.

We had forty-five minutes to climb 6,000 more feet and go over Ipswich on a heading of 90 degrees. Piece of cake. I could see clear across the English Channel. I was on oxygen now. The cool sizzle of air comforted me.

We came in over Ipswich. On time, on course. Since the whole Thirteenth Wing was right in place, I switched to command radio and heard the leaders exchanging compliments.

"Good job, Fireball Able, we're right with you."

"Roger, Mafking Able, I see you." Harding's voice. "Your formation looks good."

So we began to float easterly toward Holland. On my maps, red circles showed where the flak was. My job was to slip in between them. I could see the whole Dutch coast.

I couldn't miss it.

Of course I smiled when I thought this. The British always say that, but it's "You cawnt miss it, Yah-ink."

As we penetrated the coast, I saw black bursts of smoke to our right and left. Good. Let 'em waste their shells. Our escort of clip-wing Spit 9's were ahead and high. I felt protected. We were on time; they would be with us for about ten minutes. Then, their petrol gone, they would buzz off. Then we would have P-47's with us for a while. I called Colonel Harding and told him we would be on time for our rendezvous with the American fighters.

"Good show, Navigator. Out."

I felt good. I was not airsick. Hello, enemy territory; goodbye airsickness. Trade-off.

I looked ahead.

"Oh, dear God, what have You done to me?" I yelled into my oxygen mask.

All of Europe seemed to be clear except for the part of it up ahead of us. Where our target was supposed to be was covered by a fleecy blanket of clouds at about 12,000 feet. We flew on and on, slowly covering the maps of the Netherlands, Belgium, Luxembourg. I could see Denmark to the left and France to the right.

But I would not be able to see our target.

"What can we do, Croz?" It was Blake.

"Keep going. It might blow off before we get there. If not, we will have to go to one of the alternates."

"Wilco, Navigator. I will notify the other groups to prepare to bomb secondary targets. Out." Colonel Harding.

The clouds did not burn off; instead, they got worse, and piled up to our altitude of 25,000 feet.

When it got to the point where our wing left the division I saw the other wings heading for the clear, and we plowed into the clouds.

After warning the other groups, we ascended to 26,000 feet, Blake keeping the rate-of-climb indicator right at 150 feet per minute. Wisps of clouds began to filter into my compartment.

In front of me, Doug hooked his machine gun in its hangar and turned to his Norden bombsight. It was black, shaped like a football and three times as big, with knobs on both sides. He bent over it to test his ground speed. He couldn't see the ground for the check. He looked back at me and shrugged.

No target.

Colonel Harding came on interphone. "Command to navigator."

"Roger, Command."

"Let's go to the secondary."

"It's socked in too."

"What about the third target?"

"Worse."

"Roger. Let's have a T.O."

That meant I was to look for a target of opportunity. We could drop our bombs on any city, any railroad marshaling yards, any airport, anywhere. Since the whole wing was behind us, I had better pick a target that was worthwhile.

I looked frantically at my maps, mindful of where the clouds were.

"Ahah," I said. "Here is a nice big city."

I twirled my E6B computer, set in the wind, and got a heading to a point south of the city. That would be our I.P., and we could go over the city with no crosswind. I was really percolating. I was not airsick.

We floated over the I.P. and headed for the T.O. Doug took over, and I heard the bomb bay door rumbling open.

"Good show, Croz." This from Doug. "No crosswind."

Now to see the name of the city that we were about to blow off the face of the earth. I had to record it in my log.

Bonn!

Bonn, Germany. That's where Beethoven went to school.

Bonn!

According to what I had read on the record cover, Bonn was a university town, one of prettiest places in Germany.

I hit my mike button.

"All positions from navigator. I have another target. We can't bomb Bonn."

"Command to navigator. Why not?"

"That is where Beethoven went to school."

Nine voices from the crew, all of them with variations of "My God!" or "Shit!"

Sixty-three Flying Fortresses floated over Bonn, some of them with their bomb bay doors open.

But no bombs fell.

This time I really did twirl the E6B. If we turned back toward home and flew a little north of course, we could bomb half the railroads in the Ruhr Valley. I gave Colonel Harding the heading and the plan. In code, he relayed the formation behind us.

At this point the Luftwaffe hit us.

Head-on. Same as usual. Lights blinking at us. As one German pilot went by us, he was so close I saw him adjust his goggles with his left hand.

Doug was ready for the next head-on hit by a Messerschmitt, and he knocked it out of the sky.

Miraculously—and maybe God was on my side after all—I saw no B17's become great balls of fire.

Then Doug went back to his job. Bending over the eyepiece and twiddling his knobs, he aimed at a huge Ruhr railroad center.

He creamed it.

The lead bombardiers in the 95th and 390th also did their jobs. From the tail, Charlie Via reported in: "Streaks of fire all over the place. Explosions along the huge railroad yards. Good pattern."

I wrote it down in my log, with the time.

A few years later, when our defeated foe needed a city for its capital, the only large city not leveled by Allied bombs was Bonn. For whatever reason, we stopped having free-choice targets of opportunity, and Bonn, although it was nicked a few times by the

British at night, was never bombed by the Americans. I can confidently say that Bonn became the capital of West Germany because on that night I left the Officers' Club and went to my barracks and listened to a certain record.

But on the way home on that day I did not know all this. All the way home I was thinking the same way I was on the way back from Trondheim. What happened to navigators who screwed up?

After the mission, Colonel LeMay phoned Colonel Harding.

"Good job, Chick," he said. "Our Spruce Goose recon outfit already has the strike photos. You all did a lot of damage."

"Thank you, sir."

"But you made two bomb runs. What went wrong over the first target?"

"Our lead navigator said that Americans don't bomb college towns."

"Who was it?"

"Crosby. Do you want to talk to him?"

"Crosby! He wasn't supposed to be flying. I want to talk to you about this, Chick."

"Do you want to talk to Lieutenant Crosby?"

"No! For Christ's sake. Keep him out of my sight."

CHAPTER
8

NORTH AFRICA VIA REGENSBURG

✈ "This is it."

It is Jack Kidd talking. Because he is flying, he sits beside us instead of being up in front on the stage, as he usually is.

We are in the briefing room, about 250 airmen, fetid in our flying clothes.

Up on the stage, Colonel Harding goes to the easel which has a chart showing the formation. Blake is in front with Kidd as command pilot. Brady is on our left wing. Wolff, a new guy, is on our right, flying our old plane, 061. Cruikshank is leading the second element. I see that Egan is grandstanding. At Elveden Hall we were told not to use more than two command pilots per group. "No point to wasting one of their missions and their leadership skills," LeMay had said.

But Egan knows there is something big and he has put himself in Crank's plane. He's leading the element behind us, with Knox and Biddick on his wing.

In the high squadron, on the right, Sammy Barr is leading, with the 349th Squadron Commander, Bill Veal, in the right seat. That's as it should be, but I wonder why Swartout's crew isn't leading the high. One of our two crews was supposed to be group lead. Since we are in front, he should be flying deputy lead. Now, if we get shot down, there won't be a crew to take over who knows about all that stuff we learned about Regensburg and getting to Africa.

"Swartout's in the infirmary," says Kidd.

"I wish I were," I say.

Cowboy Roane is on Barr's left wing, Hennington on the right. Van Noy is leading the next element, with Justice and Shotland on his wings. In the third high-squadron element Tom Murphy is pilot; Oakes and Fienup are on his wings.

The 350th is flying low, with Norm Scott as the lead pilot. The 351st is stood down, and only three of their crews are flying, the third element in the high squadron.

I see that Bucky Cleven is grandstanding like Egan. He has put himself in Scott's right seat, leading the low squadron. That's a violation of orders. A command pilot only flies twenty-five missions, and he should never be wasted in the low squadron. He should fly on the right seat of the lead crew in the lead or high squadron, or not fly at all.

I realize that three out of four of our squadron commanders are on the same mission. LeMay will have something to say about this. What if they all get shot down? Three-fourths of the squadron commanders gone? Morale? Experience and training?

Hollenback and DeMarco are on Scott's and Cleven's wing. Claytor, Hummel, and Braley are the second element.

Flying with Murphy in the 349th, the high squadron, is a lieutenant colonel, an outsider named Beirne Lay. We don't know it, but he is on the mission for experience before he gets his own group. He will write an article called "I Saw Regensburg Fall" for the *Saturday Evening Post.* After the war, he will write *Twelve O'Clock High,* mostly about the 100th. He was scheduled to fly in a low squadron plane, but Cleven moved him out of his squadron to preserve his position as ranking officer in his unit. In his *Saturday Evening Post* article, Lay credits this change with saving his life, since the plane in which he was originally scheduled to fly was shot down.

I know that we aren't leading the whole task force. Colonel LeMay told us he would be with whatever group and crew were selected to lead. We are the last group. Maybe Harding is in deep trouble. Maybe our whole group is in disfavor. Maybe I hadn't helped the 100th over Bonn.

I am not disappointed. I would rather fly Tail-End Charlie with Kidd than lead with LeMay. I could imagine what Old Iron Pants sounded like on intercom. I had never hankered to lead the whole task force. Up ahead, some navigator in the 96th was doing the real work, staying on course, avoiding the flak, making our rendezvous, finding Regensburg. As lead navigator for Tail End Charlie, I was just a gunner, an observer, a bookkeeper.

The crews in the 100th are pleased to see they are in the last group. The Luftwaffe at this time are concentrating on the front group, to knock out the leadership. We believe we are in the safest position.

We are wrong.

S-2 reads his flimsy. He tells the other crewmen in the briefing room what we on Blakely's crew already know. "Your aiming point is the center of the ME-109G aircraft and engine assembly shops. If you destroy it, you knock out a third of Germany's single-engine aircraft production.

"Another task force is going to Schweinfurt. Their target produces most of the ball bearings in Germany. Three months after they get their target, there won't be an engine operating in the whole country."

I am not happy to see our bombing altitude, 17,000 feet. I like 25,000 feet better, where the flak is thinner. "If you go up higher," says Weather, "you will make contrails, and subsequent groups will have the target obscured."

I can see LeMay's logic. We might as well go in low, hit the target, and not have to return.

S-2 Major Minor Shaw has one final comment: "Today is an anniversary. Just a year ago, an M.E. for the whole 8AF under General Eaker was twelve planes. They bombed Rouen, France, on that day. Today we are putting up thirty times that many planes."

After briefing and breakfast, our guns cleaned and in place, we taxied out to our position of honor at the head of the landing strip. And waited. It was still dark. The sky was full of stars and a bright, full moon.

We waited.

And waited.

I remember committing minor blasphemy as I sat and sat, and sat.

Headquarters
100TH BOMB GROUP (H)

Target - Regensburg   **Date** - August 17, 1943

Lead Squadron - 418th
Blakely - Kidd - Crosby

Brady   Wolff

Cruikshank - Egan

Bi~~dd~~ick   Kn~~ox~~

Low Squadron   ### High Squadron
350th   349th/351st

Scott - Cleven   Barr -Veal

Holl~~e~~nback   DeMarco   Roane   Hennington

Cl~~a~~ytor   Va~~n~~ Noy

H~~u~~mmel   Br~~a~~ley   Justice   Sho~~r~~land

Murphy - Lay

O~~a~~kes   Fienup

At the briefing before every mission we all got a formation
sheet. This sheet (*above*) for the Regensburg–Africa Shuttle
(August 17, 1943) shows which crews started out and what
position they flew. I was the lead navigator in Blakely's plane.
The X's show which planes went down.

The Regensburg Task Force - on August 17, 1943,
with Colonel Curtis E. LeMay as the command pilot

402nd (later 13th) Combat Wing	401st Combat Wing	403rd Combat Wing
95th Bomb Group ⟶ 21 aircraft	94th Bomb Group ⟶ 21 aircraft	390th Bomb Group 21 aircraft ⟶
100th Bomb Group ⟶ 21 aircraft	385th Bomb Group ⟶ 21 aircraft	96th Bomb Group ⟶ 21 aircraft
		388th Bomb Group 21 aircraft ⟶

"God, why is it," I asked, "that You let the skies be so clear till briefing time, but when I get up into the air with a thousand aircraft milling around me, You sock in the clouds and let us crash into each other? Maybe You are not on our side?"

And then the clouds rolled in. The moon and stars disappeared.

A jeep came up and Captain Frye, the weather officer, got out, walked to the waist, and came in. I went up into the pilots' compartment and heard the report.

"Sir, your target is okay, but the target of the second task force is socked in. Both were supposed to fly at the same time, to split fighter opposition. You are waiting for them."

Just then, from Flying Control, a green-green.

"Uh-oh," Captain Frye said, "you are going in alone."

We had no trouble climbing up through the overcast, circling around Splasher Six. At oh-seven-thirty hours, we broke out over the cloud deck.

Colonel LeMay had the whole division together over Lowes-toft, each group a thousand feet above or below the one ahead of it. The task force was strung out more than usual. When we made a right turn I could see the whole division up ahead of us. We were an armada, fifteen miles long. As we left the coast of East Anglia all the supernumeraries left their groups and flew home, waggling their wings and firing their flares when they went past us, Tail-End Charlie.

At 10:08, we crossed the coast of Holland. I knew that the Luftwaffe now had us on their radar and their RDF, radio direction finders. Soon they could vector their bogeys toward us. In contrast to Trondheim, when I took our formation below the radar screen, now at 17,000 we were at their best altitude.

At 10:17 I wrote in my log, "Woensdrecht, flak, inaccurate." At 10:25, I wrote, "2 E.A., 2 o'clock, low." When they got closer, I added, "FW-190's." They came at us, their closing rate over 600 miles per hour. I heard our guns. I felt the plane vibrate. I smelled cordite.

Why were we getting all the attacks?

On that day the Luftwaffe tried a different approach. Instead of hitting the first group, they came after us. Why? I do not know. Maybe their Intelligence had learned that we soon would have the new G-model Forts with the devastating turret gun in the nose. Maybe some of our groups already had the new plane. Maybe the Luftwaffe had increased the speed of its Messerschmitts, Focke-Wulfs, or Heinkels and thought coming at us from behind would be safer for them.

All I know is that on August 17, 1943, the 100th got it.

Tail-End Charlie had changed from the best position to the worst.

Something had happened to our escort. There wasn't a single P-47, the Thunderbolt, in sight.

Three minutes later it seemed that the whole Luftwaffe was buzzing around us. Gaggles of ME-109's and FW-190's came up behind us, paused for an instant, and then slid up and under us. Arcs of our .50-caliber tracers and their 20-mm cannon fire scorched the sky. Beams of horror threaded our formation.

"White hoose moose," said Charlie Via, in the tail. "The whole last element in the low squadron went out."

I wrote in my logbook: "Claytor, Hummel, and Braley to E.A." Thirty of my friends. I forgot to write in the time and place. A mistake for a navigator.

"Kidd to crew. Any chutes?"

"Tail here. The lead ship in the final low element pulled out of formation and blew up. No chutes."

That was the plane in which Beirne Lay was scheduled to fly before Bucky Cleven pulled him out.

I wrote, "No chutes observed."

At ten-forty-one hours, over Eupen, Belgium, the fight really began. We did not know it, but that was to be the worst attack by German fighters that the 8AF had thus far experienced. Since the Schweinfurt task force was still on the ground back in England, the Luftwaffe concentrated on us. We got it bad, but only once, since we did not go back through the fighter sector. While we were on our way over the Mediterranean, the other task force got it twice, once in, and once out. They lost sixty planes—six hundred guys—that day.

Two squadrons of E.A. (enemy aircraft) came up behind and below us, just off to our right, twelve ME-109's and eleven FW-190's. They drew up even with us—and then careened toward us, their guns blinking. Our interphone became a static of voices and the plane shook with the chatter of our guns.

Off to port, the same thing. German fighters were crisscrossing at us.

Ahead of us, flying all alone and slightly off to our right, a single Messerschmitt kept in position with us. Was that their control officer, radioing directions about whom to hit, and how?

The Germans came up parallel, in singles or pairs, made a U-turn to their left and then a hard right and then hit us from the side. Up ahead the other groups were getting it, but not as bad. Then what seemed to be the whole German Air Force came up and began to riddle our whole task force.

Other groups began to lose planes.

Jack Kidd and Blakely tried to fit us in tighter with the groups ahead.

Now we began to have a new problem. As other planes were hit, we had to fly through their debris. I instinctively ducked as we almost hit an escape hatch from a plane ahead. When a plane blew up, we saw their parts all over the sky. We smashed into some of the pieces. One plane hit a body which tumbled out of a plane ahead.

A crewman went out the front hatch of a plane and hit the tail assembly of his own plane. No chute. His body turned over and over like a bean bag tossed into the air.

An unusual hit. In a plane ahead all four engines got smacked at once, all burst into flames, and then the whole plane exploded. "No chutes," I wrote.

Our gunners worried about their friends. No matter how violent the battle, they always looked for parachutes. In the heat of our present violence, McClelland, from the ball, came in on interphone. "Sir, I counted sixty chutes in the air at once."

We were getting some of them. At first, the E.A. had yellow noses—the Abbeville Kids, we called them. Now we saw blue, red, and black planes, other units vectoring toward us. When B-17's blew up, they tended to be black, from oil fires. When the Germans blew up, they were orange. Hits in their gas tanks.

I saw two of them go at once, as they hit us from the front and starboard, their debris shredding us. A German pilot came out of his plane, drew his legs into a ball, his head down. Papers flew out of his pockets. He did a triple somersault through our formation. No chute.

Now they were queuing up on our right and coming in from two o'clock and low, a plane at a time. Our plane shook constantly, and the smell of cordite was almost overpowering. Tat-tat-tat-tat-tat.

It never stopped.

Another plane blew up.

"Biddick," said Charlie Via, in the tail. No more. I wrote the name down, neglecting to tell the position.

The plane and crew we had saved on the Trondheim mission were gone. Curtis Biddick was one of the most popular pilots in the original group. His navigator on this mission, John Dennis, an Irish tenor, sang with Emma Pritchard, the black Amazon back in Sioux City. Biddick was a sweet guy, made even more genial by the Scotch he drank. In the Officers' Club, when he saw the big hand get to five minutes before bar closing time, he always ordered two doubles. The bartender came to expect it. "Are you ready for double doubles, sir?"

Gone. No double doubles tonight.

German fighters hit us for over an hour.

Van Noy was gone. High squadron. Shotland was gone. High squadron. Hollenbeck, off Bucky Cleven's left wing, was gone. Low squadron.

A plane that was really getting it was Zero-Six-One, our old plane, with the new pilot, Bob Wolff. Part of the vertical stabilizer was gone. There was a hole the size of a bushel basket in the fuselage near the waist gunner. Both wings had torn surfaces, with aluminum flapping. One aileron seemed to be disconnected, up and down, loose in the airstream. How could that new kid keep that plane in the air?

Every time Wolff and his crew got a hit and the plane bucked and came back into position, our gunners cheered. They loved that Old Bird.

Our pilots and gunners were exhausted. We had lost seven crews. Several of our planes had lost engines and were straggling behind us, their unfeathered props still windmilling.

Then fresh new squadrons of E.A. hit us. None of us expected to get to Africa. This was the end.

Below us and to our left, the 350th was getting the worst of the Luftwaffe attack—and Bucky Cleven was experiencing what Beirne Lay in his Saturday Evening Post article was to call "the young squadron commander's finest hour." Others were not so sure. Certainly the 100th was experiencing one of the most controversial incidents in its entire history.

The lead ship of the low squadron, with Norman Scott as pilot, had taken a number of blasts, especially when the whole last element went out on one pass. Now, thirty-five minutes before we got to the target, a 20-mm shell came into the pilots' compartment and exploded, smashing the top turret operator's leg. The plane's electrical system went out. Another 20-mm pierced the radio compartment, cutting off both legs of the radio operator, who bled to death.

A third 20-mm ripped into the nose of the plane, leaving a gaping two-foot hole, and smashing the head and shoulder of the bombardier. A fourth shell slammed into the starboard wing, cutting into the hydraulic system. Red hydraulic fluid—it looked like blood—splattered all over both pilots. A fifth shell hit the plane somewhere in the waist and cut the cables to the rudder, which controlled lateral action. A sixth exploded in the inboard starboard engine, the number three, and fire licked out the cowling.

The pilot, Norman Scott, hit the jump bell. Over interphone he ordered the crew to bail out.

What happened next has been endlessly argued by members of the 100th. Basically, what happened is that Bucky Cleven told the crew to stay put—and he took over the plane. Unquestionably one of the most skilled pilots who ever flew a B-17, he got the plane under control and flew the crew to Africa.

The incident was to become important many weeks later.

We flew on.

From the ball turret: "To all positions, I am out of ammo. Anyone got any extras?"

I had two long belts, and I reported in. Soon, his oxygen mask connected to a blue walk-around bottle emergency supply, Forky dropped down from the pilots' compartment and crawled into the nose. He dragged my extra belts away, waving his hand to me as he left.

In a group ahead, a B-17 was hit and slid down and away from the formation, two engines out and a third trailing smoke. It descended three or four hundred feet. Its wheels came down, the sign of surrender. Was that right? I didn't know.

Three Messerschmitts came into formation with it, no firing.

The injured plane's bomb bay doors came open, and bodies dropped from it. Seven chutes.

At 1150 hours, just before the I.P., E.A. fighters, after over 200 separate passes, began to thin out. That was good because in the last hour and a half of battle most of us had used all our ammo.

Visibility was good. Up ahead I could see Regensburg.

"Navigator to all positions, I.P., in three minutes." I gave Blake a heading and told Doug what I thought his drift would be.

Doug was already in position, fiddling with his knobs and switches.

We hit the I.P. at 1154 hours and turned hard to port.

"Tail to navigator, we have eleven planes in position."

I dutifully entered the record.

Ten planes gone. One hundred of our friends. Biddick. In Knox's plane was Ernie Warsaw, who had been with us when we crashed into the mountain in Wyoming.

By the time we got to our target, most of Regensburg was already obliterated.

"Bombs away."

The plane jerked up, suddenly six thousand pounds lighter.

At the R.P., I gave Doug a heading. "Okay," I said, "let's head for the Mediterranean."

From Thornton, top turret: "Sir, our old plane is so smashed up, I don't think it can stick with us."

I looked back past our right wing. Bob Wolff was flying a plane with two engines, a smashed port wing, a huge hole in the waist, and the whole leading edge of the rudder tattered and whipping in the wind. Only the heroic flying of this new guy was keeping the plane in the air. He had a round, smiling face, just a kid. I don't think he had to shave.

Every member of our crew, I am sure, breathed out whatever kind of prayer we used for that new crew.

"Formation lead to all groups."

It was Iron Pants LeMay.

After the Rally Point, he wanted us to come out of our trail formation and bunch up for a better defense.

"Formation lead to Fireball Able." That was us.

"Go ahead, Formation Lead." It was Jack Kidd.

"Pull your formation together."

"Sir, we are together. This is all that's left."

I looked back. After the target our damaged planes were lagging, and all we had in the whole group was two wing men. Three planes in the 100th!

"My God," said Iron Pants.

As we swung on to our new heading we could look out and see the Alps. Switzerland!

Two crews decided they had had it. They knew their gas supply, and they knew the way they were losing airspeed and altitudes. They dropped from the formation and headed for internment.

One plane, flown by Don Oakes, was a permanent advertisement for a well-known beer. Below a picture on the nose of a woman sitting on a moon, the Miller Brewing Company logo, was the name of the plane, High Life.

Oakes and his crew made it. We watched the plane as it plummeted down and headed for a landing strip. We saw it go in with its wheels up, then stop, and figures jump out.

In our group, Woodward's plane was in worse

shape. It got to Switzerland all right, but at about ten thousand feet we saw crewmen coming out all the escape hatches. The ones who delayed pulling their rip cords dropped down and down. At the last minute, their chutes popped, and they landed in Switzerland.

They were there for two years.

The ones who pulled their cords at once floated slowly down. The wind caught them, and they began to drift northward into Germany. The chutists frantically yanked their chute straps and tried to guide themselves back into Switzerland.

One man pulled all the air out of his chute, and it collapsed. His chute became a streaming white ribbon, and he dropped hideously to the ground.

We had been with Woody's crew since Boise. His navigator, Cassimatis, loaned me his poker winnings for Jean and me to get married. Since Dibble, their bombardier, had exploded when a 20-millimeter hit him two days earlier, they had a replacement in the nose. I didn't know him. Gone before I even knew he was there!

No good.

Near the Brenner Pass, Colonel LeMay made another effort to draw his stragglers into a more defensible formation. He began a slow 360-degree circle.

What a mess. Smoke coming from many engines. Most of the planes had battle damage. Every group with a missing element, or several missing planes. Many planes had so little power they were drifting down out of the sky.

We turned south, slowly losing altitude to save gas. We doglegged around Sardinia and Sicily to keep out of the feeble flak sent up at us.

Range was the problem now.

"Two planes ditching, sir." It was the ball.

"I am going off interphone now," said Jack Kidd. "I want our pilots to check their gas supply."

In a few minutes, he was back on. "Croz, we are in trouble. Two of our planes can't make it unless we throttle back. We are going down to the deck and fly for distance."

"Roger."

I began to re-do my calculations as two planes came onto our right and left wings. We dropped below the formation, which began to pull on ahead of us.

Five minutes later our three planes were all alone, just above the water, the sound different because of the way the wind smoothed past us at our new airspeed.

I knew we were on course because occasionally we would see a ditched plane, its crew climbing out on the wings and inflating their dinghies. They waved at us and we waved back. Thorny sent up a flare to wish them well.

We flew and flew, with Ev checking the gas in all four engines.

From our right wing Bob Wolff called in, "I've just checked our supply. It is going to be close."

And then, blessedly, there was Africa.

Now I had a problem.

Curtis LeMay, a trained navigator, knew that navigating in Africa over the desert without radio was almost impossible. There was sand, and it all looked the same. During the Africa campaign many planes had missed their destination and flown out into the desert until they ran out of gas and crashed.

He therefore had briefed us to hit the coast as close to course as we could make it. Then we were supposed to turn to the right and fly along the coast past Bône to Constantine where there was a dent in the coast which we could identify positively. Then we were to turn inland and follow a railroad back to our landing field.

"You can find your route at Constantine because you know the railroad is there. You know," and LeMay smiled that crooked smile, "the pilot's compass." That was an old Air Corps joke. "Since the railroad is no longer used, much of it has been covered by blowing sand. If you try to cross it inland, you may be at a place where it has disappeared. You would fly right over it and never see it. It is clear enough to help you if you see it once in a while."

Great idea, good thinking by Colonel LeMay, but his route would take us at least twenty more minutes.

During my years in combat I led many missions, and did all right. I got some medals.

But in my mind, during all those months of combat, I just did my job. I acted like a hero just once. This was it.

I hit the mike button.

"Navigator to pilot and command."

"Go ahead, Croz, what you got for us?"

"Sir, if we take the dogleg to Bône, our gas is so low I don't think we will make it."

"Keep talking."

"A heading of 254 degrees should take us in direct."

There was no delay. Jack Kidd's voice came on.

"Two-hundred fifty-four degrees it is. Your ETA?"

"Fourteen minutes."

"Let's all start praying."

"I'm already praying," said someone.

"And shitting," said someone else.

Thirteen and a half minutes later, there it was.

We were just off to the right.

"Good show, Croz, you brought us in on the base leg."

We landed. Blake cut engines two and three and pulled us off the runway. We all looked back at our two wing planes.

They came in. One plane kept taxiing and rolled to the perimeter.

Bob Wolff in our beloved Zero-Six-One rolled to the end of the runway and stopped, his props barely windmilling.

Over interphone we heard his report. A kid's voice. "Sir, for the last leg I was flying a rock. We need a tractor to pull this bird off the runway."

CHAPTER

9

NEW JOB:
SQUADRON NAVIGATOR

 As I look back at the months when I was flying
lead navigator on Blakely's crew, my strongest
impression is that the whole thing was unreal.

On the next day, after a night in a tent erected on
the sands of Africa, we surveyed our losses. We
learned that we did better than we feared, since some
of our planes had made forced landings and were
scattered all over the north coast of Africa. The final
total was nine planes. Ninety men.

In the next weeks, after we flew back across the
coast of Spain, dropped bombs on a token target in
France, and landed our damaged planes at Thorpe
Abbotts, we read how the other groups had done.
Newspapers called the mission "The Double Strike,"
the "most ambitious and cleverly conceived strike
plan" of the war to date. It was noted that it took
place on the anniversary of VIII Bomber Command's

first operations out of England. We learned that the force headed for Schweinfurt had been delayed two hours because of mist and clouds and were hit as badly as we were. A mix-up in our fighter rendezvous left the Regensburg groups unprotected, which accounted for some of our losses.

As for results, from the target Colonel LeMay had radioed, "Objective believed totally destroyed." Beyond what we did to stop the manufacture of Messerschmitt fighters, which was considerable, we had—without knowing it—destroyed the plant which was turning out tools to manufacture the secret jet fighter, the ME-262.

Until that mission, the 100th had never been badly hit. It was at this time that our reputation for being a hard-luck outfit began. On the mission, we did see a plane lower its wheels as a token of surrender but, as was later proved, the plane was not in our group. The story grew and it was told that when three German fighter planes came up alongside the stricken Fort, its gunner shot them down. This was like flying a white flag and shooting an enemy who was helping.

The legend developed, the 100th got the blame, and it became gospel that the whole Luftwaffe had a vendetta against the 100th, the Forts with the square D on their tail. From then on, when our group repeatedly lost heavily, the wheels-down story was told again. The German Air Force, it was believed, hated the 100th Bomb Group. We were doomed.

All told, the Double Strike lost 60 planes, 600 men. At first our gunners claimed to have shot down 288 enemy aircraft, a figure which was later reduced to 148, with another hundred badly damaged. These enemy losses, plus what we did to factories on the ground, probably began the demise of the German Luftwaffe. Although the two task forces lost heavily, I had the feeling that we all felt good about the daring and effective attack. We were grim but we felt somehow special that we were being talked about in pubs all over England.

Somehow, we seemed to be living in four different worlds, worlds that did not mix.

One of our worlds involved a distasteful job. We lived, vicariously, in the lives of our enlisted men. We were their censors. We read all their mail.

I accept the idea that in war there must be some control of information that comes from a theater of war. My experience is, however, that less is better than more, that censorship is usually abused, and that it is usually subjective, illogical, and quite unrelated to how best to win the war.

At Thorpe Abbotts, I and every officer in the group under the rank of major were required to act as censors. No one censored the officers' letters, except for an occasional spot check by the Higher Ups Somewhere. We, however, censored every letter written by an enlisted man.

Every squadron had a different way of getting the job done. In the 418th, most of the mail was given to the ground officers, but on the days we were stood down, the combat flyers were given a high stack of the letters—and we went back to our quarters to complete the odious task. Occasionally a twenty-two-year-old second lieutenant, fresh out of junior college, would read the mail of a thirty-six-year-old master sergeant who had been in the army for years. I wondered who knew the regs better.

There were rules—no X's for kisses, for instance (that might be a code for spies)—which were easy to enforce and seldom broken. Nothing about missions, nothing about where we were, or how many of us. After those simple rules, the problems got sticky. Should we, for instance, cut out the news that a corporal in the motor pool was switched to armament and was loading planes?

Several officers objected so strongly to the responsibility that they boasted of dashing off their signatures without even looking at the letter. Others sat on their beds and laughed uproariously at their gleanings, entertaining the rest of us by reading the juicier bits. "Listen to this one, Joe!"

Some enlisted men wrote interesting letters, keeping their wives, sweethearts, chums, and parents informed at least of their morale and yearnings, sometimes in effective but prudent detail telling what they were doing. Some writers were hopelessly inarticulate, resorting to every cliché and banality. During the first weeks I judged that more than half of the letters began with, "Well, here we are in Jolly Old England. Hah!" Another large group, where they could not put their address, wrote "Isle of View," a pun which had appeared in a current issue of Stars and Stripes. Technically that was code, which was forbidden, but I let it go.

Every drama of wartime played itself out before us. Worried husbands awaited news from their pregnant wives. Back and forth went suggestions about names for new babies, covering the possibilities by providing for both boy or girl. Back home, fathers became ill and died, and I read their sons' halting attempts to console their mothers.

At first, our soldiers wrote to their chums about their conquests of females in London and Norwich. A few months later, we began to read love letters, often in almost the same wording, written by the same man to two women, usually one on the Home Front and another in England. Later, when married men began to succumb to their urges, we read letters written by one man to his wife and, with the same fervor and maybe the same words, to a girlfriend in London.

One sergeant's wife apparently was playing around with a 4F who visited her from another city. By mistake she sent to her husband in our squadron a letter addressed to the stateside boyfriend. Her husband responded in a violently angry letter, and I sympathized with him. Then I read his next letter. It was written to his mistress in London.

One paragraph made me feel good. "It's a lot different here," one mechanic wrote to his brother. "Back in the States, the fly-boys treated us like shit. Now that they know we're keeping them in the air, they treat us like kings. One guy gives me his whiskey ration after every mission."

There was another world, equally unreal.

From way up high came the command that we were to have a new reading room. General Dwight David Eisenhower, the commander of the ETO, believed that the best soldier was an informed soldier. He decreed that every unit was to have a reading room to help keep its members informed about the aims and progress of the war. Our S-2 section was put in charge, and soon we had a popular drop-in center. It had the inevitable two maps, one showing progress of the war in the Pacific, and another showing what was happening in our theater. We could drop in any hour of the day or night, pick up reasonably current newspapers and magazines or examine reports about our missions from some higher headquarters. Twice a day, a captain from S-2, Red Bowman, who had been the editor of the Boston American, gave a detailed if sardonic report on what was going on all over the world.

Somewhere Out There a war was going on, and it seemed worse than ours. While we were getting shot at over Regensburg, a combined and freezing force of Navy, Army, and Marines took the last Japanese holding in the Aleutians. They were still fighting in Kiska but we were now back in our warm quarters at Thorpe Abbotts. We would read Stars and Stripes, put pins in our wall map showing where our Pacific and North African forces were digging foxholes and eating K rations. We got shot at, same as they did, but after we landed, we could go in to the pub at Diss and talk to young English girls and old English men.

In July, we knew the Allies had landed in Sicily, the first of the European offensive. On August 18, the day after the shuttle mission to Regensburg and Africa, the American, British, and Canadian land forces completed the defeat of Italy, and someone strung Mussolini upside down like a pig.

I died a little when I read about the B-24's coming in from Africa to bomb the oil fields at Ploesti. It was 2,400 miles round-trip, 200 miles longer than my flight to Trondheim. To avoid the radar screen the way I had when I went back to Scotland, they flew in at thirty feet.

Thirty feet! That was impossible for a navigator. The terrain went by too fast to locate it on the map.

The mission surely was planned by a pilot.

The plan was to go in north of Ploesti. This would take them around the biggest city in Romania, which was a Luftwaffe base. The only E.A. they expected to meet were untrained Romanian pilots. Then they would turn south, bomb the oil fields, and go back south around the Luftwaffe.

Instead, because of what was called "navigation error," the Liberators turned south too soon—and flew right into where the experienced Luftwaffe were based. The Germans came up in swarms and took picks on the low-altitude bombers. Sixty went down, and they missed the target.

On the Trondheim mission I was lucky: my pre-planned computations worked. I never knew where I was, but I just followed my planning. On the Ploesti mission, the lead navigator followed his data, and it was wrong. He had bad luck.

Jean kept me in touch with another world, the one back home. She wrote every day, three or four pages. She, Gerry Hamilton, and Margaret Ann Blakely, who had met under trying circumstances in Wendover, now all moved to Chicago, got jobs, and lived together. Ham, Ev, and I now had three different versions of what was going on.

I wrote to Jean every night. I wished I could tell her more about my missions, because that was the most telling part of my life.

My other world.

It just could not be real that I went out and bombed cities. It just could not be real that Out There men were shooting at me. They wanted to kill me. It could not be real.

But it was.

During the months that I flew with Blakely, before that awful last mission, one of our biggest jobs was to weaken German shipping and aviation—as is shown by the list of trips I made.

On August 23, for my seventh mission, we went to Bordeaux and hit their harbors and docking facilities. We were high group lead, behind the 390th. I did okay on the rendezvous, and from then on, I followed the leader.

Piece of cake.

On August 31, we bombed an airfield at Les Mureaux, in Normandy. We led the wing, and the whole outfit took a pasting from the Luftwaffe. We learned again and again what a beating a B-17 could take and still get home. Looking back along the formation stream I could see a plane with a huge hole in its waist, three or four feet in diameter, and still its pilot kept it in formation. When we saw planes ditch in the Atlantic, we learned how long a B-17 would float, maybe five or six minutes. Crews would scramble out on the wings, wrestle with an orange bag, pop out their rubber dinghy and struggle with the oars. I would radio their position back. More times than not, British Air Sea Rescue would beat the Germans to what we began to call the "100th Group Navy." The Germans would head for our navy, but the Brits would go right in under their guns and pull our men out. In London on the next pass, no matter who he was, we would buy the first English sailor we saw a glass of bitters. "Right, mite," he would say.

On September 6, we were supposed to bomb an instruments and ball bearing plant in Stuttgart, but the weather was impossible. Our rear squadron got into our contrails and, to avoid them, flew too far back. A flight of E.A. got two of our planes. We split up and dropped our bombs wherever we could. We got rid of our load over a German airfield at Conches. Other flights bombed Bernay, St. Martin, and Évreux. A bad mix-up, but we probably did The Cause some good. Bad weather.

The 100th was ready for legends. We were getting hit so badly that stories were getting started. One of the pilots who went down will forever be known as the "Man Who Came to Dinner." According to the story, his crew arrived in the afternoon, didn't unpack, ate dinner, lounged in the Officers' Mess and the Aero Club. They went to bed, were awakened at three.

"But we just got here."

"Sorry, Lieutenant, we need you."

The crew went down at noon.

Actually the crew were there about a week, but the story was better the way it was told. We were the stuff of legends.

One plane left us near Stuttgart and headed for Switzerland. They crash-landed in Lake Constance, the ball turret operator dead. Most of the crew were badly injured.

One of the original 100th crews, who went through the phases with us and was piloted by Victor Fienup, went down that day. My roommate at Tulare primary flying school, Sumner Reeder, now 349th Ops, lost his copilot, his head nearly blown off. Reeder dived down to the deck and played hide and seek in the clouds. His navigator, even though he had lost an eye, filled in as copilot. Sumner got a DSC for that. The copilot, Harry Edeburn, got one too, but he was dead.

Our group was hit so badly that our crews landed at whatever landing strip they saw first.

On September 15, leading the group, we bombed near Paris, carefully picking out the Renault aircraft factories. It was eerie seeing the Eiffel Tower, Notre Dame, and the Arc de Triomphe and blowing up part of the city nearby. We saw one plane just disappear into the clouds, and then the cloud blew up. One of my navigation classmates, Jim Brown, got hit by flak. He would have bled to death if his bombardier, Joe Armanini, had not trussed him up. The crew considered bailing out. Two days later Jim learned that his parachute wouldn't have worked. It was cut up by flak.

On September 16, with Blakely's crew leading the wing, and Colonel Harding in the right seat, we went back to the sub pens in La Pallice. We were supposed to go to the aircraft works at Bordeaux-Merignac, a long trip, but the whole south of France was covered below us. The flak was horrible. Most of our planes came back with engines out, control surfaces gone, or hundreds of holes in their wings, control surfaces, and fuselages. Blake had to feather a prop to keep it from shaking the whole wing off.

Ugh!

Robert Wolff wasn't flying Zero-Six-One that day. He was in Zero-Six-Four, Wild Cargo, which had been Curt Biddick's plane before he got shot down in another plane over Regensburg. Somewhere along the 1,600-mile trip, Wild Cargo got hit and they just disappeared into the clouds. When I got back to our barracks I wrote his parents a letter, telling why our crew were so sorry to see the kid go.

On this mission, one crew, piloted by Glenn Dye, flew their twenty-fifth. They were done. They could go home. They were the only original crew of the 100th's original thirty-five who finished a tour. One out of thirty-five made it through a tour. And even on Dye's crew, one gunner was killed. None of the original crew all made it. That did not encourage us much.

On September 9, my twelfth mission, we hit Luftwaffe airfields at Beauvois Tille and grimly saw a number of German planes blow up on the ground. Apparently a whole squadron of E.A. seemed to pick on the 100th. The Abbeville Kids, with their yellow-nosed planes, flew right through our formation and our gunners missed them. We respected them.

On September 23, we hit airfields at Vannes. This was my thirteenth mission, usually a bad-luck number, but I thought it meant that I was halfway through my tour of twenty-five. Not much flak, but a swarm of bogeys. I was getting tired of losing all my friends. Only sixteen of our planes got there, with seven aborting. We kept flying with heavier and heavier bomb loads. Major Flesher, who flew as our command pilot, said I did "a good job of locating the target."

On the next morning, the 3AD was supposed to go to Stuttgart. When the mission was scrubbed because of weather, Colonel LeMay sent the whole division up for a practice mission. Mostly we were to practice assembling and rendezvous. Since the mission was called so hurriedly, the gunners didn't have time to load their guns. Some pilots couldn't even find all their crews. The Luftwaffe didn't respect the fact that we were only practicing. Over The Wash they hit us with one pass and we lost a plane which ditched in the sea. We saw a British torpedo boat come alongside and pick up the survivors. Flares all over the sky to express our thanks.

The Luftwaffe didn't hit us only when we were in their skies. Now they were visiting us almost every night. For a while there was no damage. When we heard "Red Alert" over the Tannoy, we only turned over and went back to sleep. Then a series of 500-pound bombs hit our base, destroying a runway. No casualties. Even so, from then on, "Red Alert" meant, "Head for the bomb shelter!" We missed a lot of sleep that we needed.

On September 27 and October 2, I felt for the first time that I might finish my tour. We bombed harbor installations at Emden, and our fighter escort went with us all the way. We saw them out there, those sleek, fast P-51 Mustangs with auxiliary gas tanks fixed to their wings. When our Little Friends dropped their wing tanks, we knew they saw bogeys.

This was an important mission, our first with blind bombing apparatus. A few planes stationed at Alconbury had H2X, a radar scanner, slung under the nose. It looked like a bathtub hanging there. The radar operator could look through the clouds and see the outline of the city. When we got to our target, his plane then dropped a flare, and we all dropped on it. Although I flew in the lead plane with the strange crew, I had no idea what was going on. All I knew was that the equipment stunk to high Heaven, which was why it was called Stinky. The system was not accurate. We were satisfied if none of our bombs was more than five miles from the point of desired M.I., the point of maximum impact.

The missions were not getting easier.

They were very hard work. Up at three or four in

the morning after a night's sleep with fifteen other flyers in our Quonset hut quarters.

Even the truck ride to briefing was hazardous. One lead navigator, Big Pete, caught his ring on a hook just as he leaped down from the back of the truck and tore off his whole finger.

We never get accustomed to a mission, but they lose their charm. We try to act bored at briefing. We snigger when A-2 goes up on the stage to pull the curtain. He pulls it a short distance, and stops. For this mission we rendezvous at Lowestoft, and head south in England. Probably heading for France. He pulls the curtain a bit farther. Across the Channel.

Why the cornball drama? The situation is already dramatic enough. We are fighting a war. In a short time German pilots and flak gunners will be shooting at us. In six hours, about forty young men in the room will be dead or prisoners of war. That's about the level of losses we are running.

Cut the crap and get on with it!

La Pallice. The worst flak batteries on the whole coast. Sub pens. Strong Luftwaffe defense. We will lose crews.

Then Assistant Ops pulls the cover off the formation chart. The 100th is leading the wing, with 95th high and 390th low. Blake, in 393, is lead crew with Brady on the right wing, Cruikshank on the left wing. Good men. We have a new guy flying, Moreno, in Ed Woodward's place, now that he is gone. Since Moreno looks like an Indian, they call him "The Chief." He and his crew will be the first 418th to complete a tour. None of the original crews did.

Someone claps when Blakely's name is read. Pilots like to fly behind him. Half of me is proud that I am leading; the other half wishes I were back on Brady's crew and could just follow along. Already I am visualizing the rendezvous and getting the 95th and 390th behind me. Coastlines are easy for navigation.

Usually before a mission I think four things can go wrong: take-off accidents, flak, bogeys, and me messing up the mission. I should be able to manage this one. Now I only have three things to worry about.

I find myself smiling. Where did I get this confidence?

Weather: Wind, 35 knots from 295; temperature, -12F at bombing altitude. Bomb load: six fives, demos. Allocation of machine gun rounds to gunners: a box apiece; two for the turrets. Chick Harding steps up for his encouragement speech. Does anyone listen?

Bubbles Payne, the Group Navigator, calls the navigators for their special briefing. We stand up to move out, all second lieutenants. None of us has been promoted, although the pilots are now first lieutenants and captains. In our special room with desks for plotting our routes, Bubbles shows us pictures of the coast and the target.

Back into the trucks. Air Officers' Mess. Good fried eggs, bacon, oatmeal, orange juice, milk. I take no coffee, but I grab a couple of apples and oranges to take with me. We also have chocolate bars for the trip. The mess hall is warm for us in our fleece-lined flying gear. Most of us are sweating.

We talk little, just, "Sling me that salt shaker." It gets tossed. "Hey, Corporal, more of that poison." He pours some coffee.

"Have you been to La Pallice before?"

"Yeah. You could taxi on the flak. We came back on two engines and our whole rudder missing. To turn I had to skid around with my ailerons."

I eat quietly, thinking of the crosswind on the assembly. I pray for CAVU (ceiling and visibility unlimited) for rendezvous and assembly but I am pessimistic. When we came into the mess hall it was already foggy outside. The clouds are sure to be solid from 200 feet to 16,000.

I have already gone to the toilet three times, but before I leave the Officers' Mess I go again. Using the relief tube, which is back in the bomb bay, is difficult and cold at altitude. I have to fumble with my oxygen walk-around bottle and three layers of zippers. The wind in the bomb bay is freezing and brisk. Usually I get sprayed in the process.

I get myself as drained as I can.

Back into the windy trucks, everything zippered to keep us warm. Our breath is steaming. Out to the hard stands. The truck goes to the other squadrons, the 351st, 350th, in that order, and then the 418th. The 349th is stood down, but their ground crews are working on their planes. They work all night, their tools like ice. As my friends drop over the end-gate onto the hard ground, they wince. They wave, but say little. Before a mission, you never say goodbye.

At our plane, the gunners are cleaning and oiling their machine guns. They have the barrels out, and peer up into the dim light to see if they shine. Forky says, "Hi, Lieutenant," and Thornton asks, "Can I help, Lieutenant?" but the others are silent. When Blake and Kidd come up in a jeep, they get no more attention than I did. No respect for officers. Our waist gunner has been in *Yank* magazine for his raunchiness.

When a colonel, fresh from the States, came to go on a mission with us, a general brought him to our plane. The general looked at the silent, lounging crew.

"Hasn't anyone told you that you are supposed to salute a general?"

Saunders continued to assemble his .50-caliber. He looked up and said two words.

"Shit, General."

His response got around the 418th. When Saul Levitt left the 100th to work on *Stars and Stripes* and *Yank* magazine, he put the story in military literature.

We are not on a real clock. It's all relevant to H-hour. H-hour has been set at five o'clock DBST, Double British Summer Time. It is now H minus forty-five, or 4:15.

For just an instant Blake pauses. The windows are open. We hear what's outside. Birds!

We hear birds chirping at the morning. We hear Farmer Draper's cows. I know what the Christmas song means. The cattle are lowing. It is getting light. We see the sun. We can see the control tower. Colonel Harding and a group of officers are on the flat roof with a railing around it, talking, looking at their watches.

Every time we fly, I tune in on the pilots' pre-flight check.

Charlie Via sits in the right seat with a list of the procedures. The list is on 8½ x 11 paper. Processed by some kind of lamination, it can be read in the dim light. Charlie reads off the list, and he and Blake do

the procedure, touching handles, flicking switches,
reading gauges. Their hands and fingers flick out
along the instrument panel, and their feet shuffle as
they reach for control pedals. Like two men playing a
silent organ.

"Set on pre-flight?"

"Roger, pre-flight."

"Weight and balance?"

"Check."

"Fuel transfer, valves and switches?"

"Right, all of them."

"Intercoolers?"

"Roger."

"Gyros?"

"Check, left and right."

"Fuel shut-off switches?"

"Check."

"Gear switch?"

"Neutral."

"Cowl flaps, open right?"

"Open left, and locked."

"Idle cutoff?"

"Check."

"Throttle?"

"Check."

"High rpm?"

"Roger."

"Autopilot?"

"Off."

"De-icers and anti-icers, wing and prop?"

"Off."

"Cabin heat?"

"Off."

"Generators?"

"Roger."

"All set to fire up?"

At this point, a pause. Blake is looking around. He adjusts his chute straps and his safety belt and moves his headset to hear better.

Major Kidd has been in the back somewhere. Now he comes up and takes Charlie Via's place. Space is cramped. They are both tall, but they get past each other. Via leaves his seat, steps between the seats, brushes past Doug, Thorny, and me. Via gives us thumbs up as he leaves, and we say, "Keep 'em flying, gunner." He makes a sour face. Having to fly formation control officer in the tail gunner position is the price he pays for being copilot on a lead crew.

Kidd straps himself into the copilot's seat, immediately tunes in on the command set. Says something. Listens to something.

He picks up the cadence.

"Command here. All set." Kidd is back on intercom.

"Master switches?"

"Master switches on." Now it's Kidd's voice, cool, firm, sure of himself. Good.

"Battery switches and inverters?"

"On and check."

"Reset?"

"Roger."

"Booster pumps, pressure?"

"On and check."

"Carburetor coolers?"

"Carburetor coolers open."

"Fuel supply and quantity?"

There is a delay, then, "Check."

"Start engines."

"Roger."

"Energize."

"Wilco."

We hear the generators pull, and the starter engine complains.

"Mesh!"

The number one prop begins to move, slowly, then a little faster. Something pops, and a belch of smokes comes out the exhaust flaps. Another, bigger explosion, and the prop catches, and spins. The Wright engine takes over. It roars. Then Blake throttles back. Now for Number Four.

And so we trundle out onto the takeoff point, start Two and Three, get our flare. We go into the blue, get a bunch of aircraft together, get shot at, kill some people, destroy a harbor, and do our part.

Once a month each combat crew was given a three-day pass.

At first, that meant London: three hours on the wonderfully interesting English trains; Paddington Station, huge, noisy, busy, confusing. Here the crew split up, the enlisted men in a group, going I know not where; Ev and Doug off in one direction; Charlie Via and me in another.

Ev and Doug had much in common. They had been together since Walla Walla. They married friends in Sioux City. They continually cracked jokes at each other's expense, Doug calling Ev "The Skeleton" and Ev calling Doug "Brush," a reference to his mustache. Charlie and I were turned off by the put-downs they thought were funny.

A taxi ride to the USO officers' hotel; a haircut and shave with all the trimmings, maybe even a foot treatment by the chiropodist. In English barbershops there was always a foot doctor. I got all the attention I could buy.

Then dinner at the most expensive place we could find, maybe a movie in the huge cinema. Neither Charlie nor I smoked, and we resented the pall of smoke in every English cinema.

Our leaves were quite uninspired. Mostly we wanted to get away from the missions.

Then the collection back at Waterloo Station. Looking for a missing enlisted man. Then a dash for our train, the enlisted men in one compartment, and the officers in another.

And the station at Diss.

Had I possessed the ability to reflect, to distance myself enough from what I was doing to think about what I was doing, I might have come up with some principles that seemed to be working for me.

My father's proverb for this one: "Life," he said, "is what you make of it."

That was probably true, but the hard word to understand was "make." What was I making of it? In a vague sort of way I was groping for the answer. My father never expected me to be perfect. "If you win all your games, you are in the wrong league." His personal goal was eighty-five percent.

"You learn a lot from the fifteen percent you lose, and the other eighty-five is more fun."

"Never bite off more than you can chew."

Putting his apparently contradictory aphorisms together I translated his lessons into the idea that we can construct an okay life by deciding how far out to look. How far into the future should I worry? How far from home to roam for my concerns? In one of our club conversations an S-2 officer said, "Happiness is an impossible goal. How can you be happy when you know there is a baby crying in China?"

I guess I had stopped worrying about the baby in China. I was so busy keeping my house in order that I had no time to worry about people who lived in igloos or teepees. Or in foxholes, or submarines. Perhaps, once again, I was the product of my time. The United States had been isolationist—"America First" was its leftover aphorism, as phrased by my hero, Charles Augustus Lindbergh. In order to maintain my personal equilibrium in the world of Thorpe Abbotts I had to forget about what went on beyond the M.P. at the gate.

For me there was a war on, and I had better concentrate on my part of it.

All the time I was on Brady's and Blakely's crew I did not meet one person outside the base. When I went on pass, which was rarely, I met no English girls. I talked to no British soldiers. I was a poor tourist. I did not visit the Tower of London, the British Museum, or any of the cultural and historical spots.

In contrast to most of the officers and enlisted men on the base, I did not go into Diss or Dickleborough and meet the local farmers and townspeople at the pub. I never once went to the dance hall in Norwich, where Americans met girls who liked to jitterbug. Our enlisted men came back from London full of the stories which I had read about in *Yank*. There was a book on the subject: They Never Had It So Good. I had heard that English girls were really hungry— "Lieutenant, they fuck like mink"—but that there were others. Several in our squadron had met girls—

"They are nice"—and saw them every pass. I got a letter from Jean almost every day.

I was getting my satisfaction in different ways. I was all business. With Blakely the severe taskmaster he was, we worked so hard and practiced so much that I was usually ready to go to bed at night. My life was circumscribed by duty. I was a lead navigator with a great deal of responsibility. I worked hard, did my job, and was content. Since I didn't expect much, I was content with what I got.

Maybe I was pretty stupid.

Along with my job as lead navigator on Blake's crew came the title of Squadron Navigator. On the T.O., Table of Organization, the Squadron Navigator would eventually be a captain, but I had little hope of that. In March 1942 the War Department had decreed the Air Corps the Army Air Forces. Where we used to sing "Nothing can stop the Army Air Corps," we now sang "The Army Air Forces." Our commanding general, Hap Arnold, could get another—and deserved—promotion, but I didn't expect one. He was a pilot and I was a navigator.

It was still the pilots' Air Force, and as a navigator I felt great when I became a first lieutenant. With my Air Medal and cluster, silver bars, and my DFC from Trondheim, I attracted a few more glances in London. For me, the silver bars meant something else—I was supposed to do some officering, some leading.

As veteran crews were shot down and replacement crews arrived, I saw that most of them were as unskilled as I had been when I arrived. As I looked over their logbooks I realized that on missions, they had little idea where they were. They were content to follow the leader and play gunner. Back in the States, the Air Force was stressing celestial navigation and crews were able to make the Atlantic crossing better than I did, but in our supply shop, octants began to pile up as new navigators realized they could not be used on missions and they got in the way in the barracks. In Germany and France the Germans changed their transmitters irregularly, and we could never depend on a radio fix. During much of our flying we were over the clouds and could do little pilotage. With pilots having to jiggle their airspeed and headings to keep in formation, the navigator could not dead reckon, that is, use headings and ground speed, to calculate where he was.

Most navigators were resigned to doing what I did to get home from Trondheim. If they got hit over the target and lost an engine or two, they would leave the formation and come back alone. Hit the deck, get down low so fighters could not dive on you, head west, visually avoid the cities because that's where the flak was. Out over the North Sea and the English Channel, stay away from boats. Even the friendlies shoot at you. When you hit the English coast, turn on your IFF, Information Friend or Foe. Then turn on Splasher Six and follow the radio compass till you see something familiar and know where you are.

Small wonder that navigators didn't get promoted. They were just duplicates of what gunners could do.

They couldn't even be good gunners. The machine gun in their compartment could swing only about ten degrees right or left; usually it was pointed at another B-17.

I smiled grimly when I read in the newspapers that the Eighth Air Force went over Germany or France and "bombed unidentified targets." What Back Home was supposed to believe was that the authorities kept the targets secret; what it really meant was that we didn't know where we bombed.

I was not happy with the situation. Too often a wing plane, that is, a crew who flew on the wing of the leader, would lose two engines or some of the controls, or catch on fire, and the crew knew it could not make it home. If they were near Sweden, Switzerland, or Spain, they could head for there and spend the rest of the war interned with some very beautiful girls. The problem was that too many navigators didn't know how to get to the neutral countries.

I remembered what happened on the Regensburg Raid, when a plane lost two engines and most of its vertical stabilizer. The navigator got confused by winds over Lake Constance, and told his crew to jump. "I'll see you in Switzerland."

The trouble was that before they landed, the high winds blew them back almost to Bavaria, and German soldiers met them and said, "For you, the war is over," and they all went to Stalag Luft III and the stalag at Barth.

Another problem was that when planes were shot out of formation they often had holes in their gas tanks. If they lost an engine or two, or three, they overused their gas supply and had to get home as soon as possible. Crippled planes whose navigators did not know where they were, or did not know what the wind was, took those extra minutes trying to find out, which meant that a plane had to crashland in occupied France or ditch in the Channel.

Yet another problem was that the crippled planes, flying back alone, very often still had their bomb loads and the navigator was supposed to find a justified target where the bombardier could salvo the bombs. Too often, the crew did not find a good target and the bombs were wasted. On one occasion, a navigator picked out a target, but when the plane made the run, the Norden sight did not work, the bombs hung up and did not drop. When the crew got back to the base and its bomb run camera films developed, the navigator learned that the crew had almost bombed Versailles.

So I tried to help the tail-end navigators. Occasionally, when the going wasn't too rough, I asked Blake to call out to the other pilots something in code to announce our position, something like, "H plus thirty-two, on course, two minutes ahead." At that moment, we were on our briefed course but ahead by two minutes.

When Jack Kidd realized what he was doing he called me "Johnny Eager."

The Johnny Eager in me gave me trouble and made me uncomfortable. I still wore my Straight Arrow hat. I never wore my flying clothes in the Officers' Club. Instead of using their first names, I called the Red Cross girls "Miss" and their last names. I never spoke to "Chick," or "Jack," or "Bucky." They were Colonel Harding, Major Kidd, Major Cleven, and Major Egan.

I spent very little time at the Officers' Club because I felt ill at ease with raunch. I could not swap stories with the hot pilots, all of whom imitated the two Buckys. I did not learn to swagger. As gifts I had four different white scarves, but I never wore one once.

Then there was a development that made me feel even more out of step.

Since the Regensburg Raid I had learned more about Lieutenant Colonel Beirne Lay, who later wrote the book and movie *Twelve O'Clock High* and had been a high staff officer at ETO HQ in London. Now he was flying missions with different groups for training before he took over his own group as C.O.

After the Regensburg mission he borrowed my log, copied down the times and P.R.s and E.A. attacks. He wrote out a full narrative of how he saw the mission. In full detail he described what he thought happened in Bucky Cleven's plane just before the I.P. at Regensburg, when the pilot gave the order to abandon ship, and Cleven countermanded the order.

His narrative went all the way past 3AD HQ, 8AF, ETO, and ended up on Hap Arnold's desk. At the end of the reports he put a section, which he called "Recommendations."

He recommended that every single one of the 100th who went on the mission should get a Distinguished Flying Cross. We were praised for our "courage and achievement," for our "tight formation in spite of the re-shuffling of the group from consecutive losses," and for "our cool judgment and self-control exercised under prolonged strain."

We all did get the DFC, which made two for me, along with the one for Trondheim.

Stories of my two DFC's appeared in the *Oskaloosa Daily Herald*, the Iowa City Press *Citizen*, and in the Chillicothe, Missouri, *Constitution Tribune*, the newspapers in my hometown, where Jean and I went to college, and her hometown.

My friends were impressed. I got letters from girls who had turned me down for dates when I was a civilian.

Colonel Lay recommended other medals. He recommended two of our leaders for the Distinguished Service Cross. Major Jack Kidd, the "twenty-four-year-old leader," was recommended for the "heroism and skill in his leadership," which was "above and beyond the call of duty for one of his age and experience." Major Bill Veal, the 349th squadron commander who led the high squadron, was recommended for one. Just before the I.P., a "cannon shell hit his #3 engine, setting it on fire, and oxygen failure occurred. Instead of turning toward the safety of the Swiss border, which was just sixty-five miles distant, Major Veal feathered the number three prop, a sure tip-off to the enemy fighters in the vicinity, in order to retain his position in the formation."

I heartily approved of another recommendation. Colonel Lay thought that Bob Wolff, who flew in our old plane, should get a DSC. Colonel Lay had seen the tremendous smashing of old Zero-Six-One, and he could hardly believe that the kid could keep that heap of scrap metal in the air. If anyone went to Switzerland, it should have been that crew. Lay commended "Lieutenant Wolff for maintaining formation for the rest of the flight, in spite of the worst battle damage inflicted on any plane." For some reason, Lieutenant Wolff was turned down, but he was shot down and couldn't have gotten it anyway.

The final recommendation came as a surprise to me.

We knew that Bucky Cleven's plane had been hit badly just before Regensburg, and we had heard that he and the pilot, Norman Scott, had differed about what to do. When we got on the ground in Africa, there seemed to be no tension between the two of them, and Scott was laughing and joking just like the rest of us.

According to the Lay report, after the hits, the

pilot had pleaded with Cleven to abandon ship. When Cleven refused to ring the bell, Scott had gotten up and started to leave alone. At this point, "although the odds were heavily against him, Major Cleven's reply was as follows: 'You son of a bitch, you sit there and take it.'"

Lay's report continued, "These strong words were heard over interphone and had a magical effect on the rest of the crew, and they stuck to their guns."

For this, Colonel Lay recommended Bucky Cleven for the Congressional Medal of Honor. The citation was scaled down a bit, and he did get the Distinguished Service Cross.

This story electrified the base, a triumph for the group's most admired twosome. Already Cleven and Egan were the 100th Group heroes. New crews almost immediately began to talk like the two squadron commanders. In the Officers' Club or at Group Ops, young flyers circled around them, and watched the two fly missions with their hands. Enlisted men adored them. Pilots wanted to fly the way the two Buckys did. Back in the days before anyone knew what a role model was, Bucky Cleven and Bucky Egan were the role models of the 100th.

When the story appeared in The Saturday Evening Post it made Bucky Cleven a national hero.

It ruined Norman Scott. He flew a few more missions, sat around the Officers' Club alone. Then the medics sent him home. On his record they wrote, "Combat Failure."

I didn't know how to handle all this. During the long evenings, I usually ate late at the Flying Mess, stopped off for the news at the reading room, and then went back to my letters from and to Jean.

CHAPTER 10

BREMEN: LAST MISSION WITH BLAKELY

One of our planes is missing.
It's hours overdue. . . .
And this is what we hear:
Coming in on a wing and a prayer.
Look below, there's a field over there.

— *Song heard at the Officiers' Club*

✈ It began like all the rest.

A hand on my shoulder.

"Lieutenant, Lieutenant. You are flying today."

For some reason I could never explain, this morning I put on my Eisenhower blouse instead of my A-2 leather jacket. My blouse was short, no skirt like a class A blouse. It had all my ribbons and the solid gold insignia Dot had given me.

An hour later, Jack Kidd talked to Blake, Via, Doug, and me. Bucky Cleven, who was flying with Benny DeMarco in the high squadron lead, was in on the conversation.

"Today is a big one. The biggest M.E. so far. We will have seven hundred planes behind us and as many planes as escort."

"Bremen. Saturation. Every military target within miles goes."

The briefing felt different.

For one thing, we got a report on what the Luftwaffe had done to East Anglia the night before. It used to be that the Germans dumped bombs on the big cities. Now they were mad at the Eighth and were visiting us almost every night. Last night we heard fighters who seemed to be over Norwich, and we knew Bungay, a little village down the lane, got a stray bomb or two.

This morning S-2 told us that more than 175 Germans had at us the night before. Twelve marauders were shot down, two in flames, quite a sight to light up the night.

Back to work. We were up too early. It was oh-five-hundred hours, but takeoff wasn't till 1145.

Bombing in the afternoon. That was something different.

Big deal. All three divisions were to assemble over The Wash. Then they would split up. We of the Third, with B-17's, would go northeast out over the North Sea. The Second, in B-24's, would follow us and we both would come in from the northwest and approach Bremen. The First Division, 17's, would go straight ahead, through Holland. In front of all of us, super-fast, high-altitude Mosquitoes would fly over Bremen sprinkling the area with a new invention which the British called "Carpet." Somehow it was supposed to interfere with German radar which was being used to aim their guns. Americans called it "Chaff."

At about noon, after takeoff and formation, when we are at 5,000 feet, the visibility unlimited, the group beautifully in place, Blake calls me.

"Eighteen minutes for formation assembly, Croz. The best we've ever done." Sweet words from a guy I respect.

We climb to 9,000 feet and pick up our two other groups over Lowestoft.

Kidd comes on intercom. "Croz, it's 1246. You were forty seconds off."

That's a joke. Blake and Kidd know how much I sweat out the rendezvous and assembly. They want me to feel good. I couldn't do much better than that.

At 1329, we have the whole division together. I hear Blake, Via, and Kidd talking about it. Blake says, "This is the best job we have ever done." Poetry.

And Kidd comes on, "And the best formation the division has ever flown."

Looking good.

After droning above the clouds out over the North Sea we turn southeast. As we get close to the German coast, we see Emden. Remembering our last attack, its gunners lay out a huge angry cloud of flak. They have our altitude perfectly.

But we aren't going there. Three divisions are converging over Bremen.

Now the city knows we are coming. Flak, a whole, mean sky full of it. Briefing said three hundred guns. At least.

I write it down in my log. Surprisingly, I find myself smiling. I am glad that I can abbreviate it to "flak" instead of having to write out the whole German name, *Fliegerabwehrkanone*.

German fighters are up, but some of them are fighting with our 51's instead of us. Go to it, Little Friends.

Even so, Via from the tail: "Three-Eight-Six just got it. An FW rammed it. Both of them blew up."

I look at my formation sheet, identify the crew. It goes into my log. I don't know Gormley, the pilot.

We can see Bremen clearly. CAVU. Ceiling and visibility unlimited. Doug is hunched over the Norden, his left hand flipping switches on the panel along the side of his compartment.

Two minutes from the I.P. we take our first hit. McClelland, in the ball, says we were sprinkled with flak but it didn't get into his compartment. They've got us in their sights.

The low squadron leader, with Al Barkin in the right seat, goes down. Via reports in, "A burst in the nose compartment, lots of fire. Their number three is out. There goes the plane, four chutes. Bang! Junk all over the sky. Oh, Mona!"

I think, where does that guy get his slang?

Now, another plane. Three-five-eight. Dumb name: Phartsac. Frank Meadows. A new crew, but I know his bombardier, Bill Hubbard. The flak is the worst I have ever seen.

I.P. Bomb run.

We are still seeing planes go down in the 100th. Salvo Sal, McGlinchey. Another. War Eagle, Beckoft. Another, 840, Nash.

We get it. Flak hits our nose, cracks the plastic. A piece comes through. Doug takes off his glove. Blood. He goes back to the Norden.

Bombs away. The sudden jerk up as we lose the weight of twelve 500-pound bombs.

On the way to the R.P. Blake does evasive action.

The flak has us dead-on.

No good. Something smacks into our number four engine. Something else hits our left wing and I see the ailerons flapping, out of control.

Jack Kidd comes on: "Our stabilizer is gone."

From the tail: "High squadron lead gone. There it goes."

It can't be. Bucky Cleven is in that plane. He is indestructible. No German alive could get him.

From the ball: "Our left elevator is smashed. It's just swinging up and down."

Kidd: "Both of the other squadron leads are gone. Can we keep this thing in the air, Blake?"

Nothing from Blake. He is busy.

The number four is on fire.

Jack Kidd speaks again. We are on fire, the plane is beginning to plunge, and he talks to us calm-like, as though we're on the way to a movie. "Sorry, Blake. Electric gone. Fire extinguisher won't work."

There is only one other way to put the fire out. Dive and blow it out.

Down we go. We are out of it. In the tail Via flashes our abort signal. There is no one to take over. The 100th just doesn't exist anymore. I groan as I imagine the remaining planes looking for other formations to tack onto. Luckily, we are in the lead and high. Our cripples can slide back into other formations and go home with them.

We drop 3,000 feet, smoke trailing behind us. Forkner hears someone on VHF saying that the 100th lead blew up and three chutes came out. Not us. Not yet.

While we are a-dropping and our ears are a-popping—back at the club we sang a song like that—

Forkner was still in his seat, dit-ditting out his message back to 8AF: "Bombs, 1525."

Everyone knows how it feels to pull out of a dive. Your stomach tries to drop down into your bowels. You scooch into your seat. The skin under your eyes and your cheeks sags.

We pull out. Blake has the plane under control. He blew out the fire. Blakely!

What to do?

We aren't even sure the plane will keep flying. We are barely over stalling speed. We have three engines, but the number two is sputtering.

I hear Kidd and Blakely reconnoitering.

Kidd comes on: "Okay, Croz, take us home."

I try to be as calm as they are. "Two lamps or one? By land, or by sea?" What am I doing, thinking of Paul Revere at a time like this?

Kidd: "Straight home. It's shorter, and the water out there is cold."

Ten thousand feet. Two hundred miles from home across Luftwaffe land.

So we start out.

And the whole German Air Force begins to take turns on us.

Up ahead is another B-17, a cripple, like us. Three Messerschmitts are smelling around it. Testing the 17's fire. Some shots from the Fort. Nothing. Wasting that precious ammo.

Suddenly, in trail, the three Germans swoop in. The Fort's tracers arc out. "Lead 'em, lead 'em," Thorny yells out." The lone Fort's gunners are not scoring.

Smack. A hit.

The lonely bomber shudders, a fire comes out of

mid fuselage. It swoops, and then flops over.
Explodes. No chutes.

We are alone.

The three Germans turn to us. We do not shoot.

They come at us. Head on. Thornton and Doug
get two of them before we are in their range.

The third veers up and away. He is afraid of us.

That's what happens when you have dead-eye
gunners. Thanks, Blake. Thanks, gunners.

But the fight is not over. The Luftwaffe keeps
coming. More of them.

Two ME-109's. Twelve o'clock. Their cannons
blink. Tracers looping at us. This is what a duck
must feel like in hunting season. There are holes all
over my compartment, but I don't think I've been hit.
No blood.

I smell the cordite from the shells.

Thorton gets one from the top turret.

Doug blasts the other one clear out of the sky.

Still alive.

An FW comes in, two o'clock high. He is not
smart. He shoots too soon. Thorny gets him.

Down below, McClelland is getting hit. His ball
turret is not operating right, and he is bleeding from
a flak wound. He climbs out of his turret, Forky
wraps him up a bit, and he goes back into the ball.
When he shoots, I feel the plane shudder. Short
bursts the way he should.

A flight of two comes up at our belly and Mac, the
wounded kid in the ball, gets them both.

All that gunnery practice that Blake made us do is
saving our lives. Good Old Beady Eyes.

The Luftwaffe are taking us seriously. Back in the
tail, Via reports that two FWs are holding back,

watching us, at maybe a thousand yards. They come into his range, but they don't fire. They are in Charlie's range. Sitting ducks. Stupid. Via gets them both.

Yevich is complaining over intercom. "I hit that guy a hundred times. I saw them smack. But he didn't go down."

Then his bogey slips to its right and blows up. Pieces of the German pilot and his plane splatter all over our plane.

I am not doing much shooting. My gun is hard to sight, and I am busy doing something else. I see a JU-88, teasing us, alongside. He's at our speed. I don't give him any lead. I see my tracers parabola into his belly. He doesn't fall, but he goes away.

I look down. We are going over a small village, and we are so low that a bunch of policemen or soldiers are shooting at us with rifles. They can't hit us, but it's a new feeling, and not a good one.

Everybody wants us out of the sky.

We are getting near the coast.

From Blake, "Forky, send out an SOS. We will be in range of Air Sea Rescue pretty soon."

The shortwave radio is smashed, including his ticker. He puts two open wires together and scratches out the SOS.

"Okay, crew, check in." How on earth can he and Kidd be so calm?

Nose, top turret, pilots, radio, ball, waist, and tail. That's the order, and we wait to hear.

"Come in, Waist and Tail."

Nothing.

"Come in, Radio."

Nothing.

"Little Britches, go back and see what's wrong."

That is what our crew calls Thornton, top turret.
Some clicks on intercom.

"Radio here. Waist and tail radio out. Saunders
and Yevich have been hit. I think Saunders got hit
bad. It's in his stomach. A hole three inches. Quarts
of blood. Yevich says that Saunders got the plane
that hit him. We gave him morphine. I couldn't get to
the tail. Everything back there is all smashed up, but
I think Lieutenant Via really got it."

No smooth ride now. The engines sputter. The plane
bounces and jerks. Come on, Old Bird, stay in the air.

More trouble. The number four prop, which had
been feathered, is windmilling again. Smoke. Fire.

Blake begins to dive and skid, the only way to put
out the fire. It worked over Bremen. Will it work here?

When we get to 3,900 feet, the fire goes out. Close.

We are out over the North Sea. No German fighters around.

What to do?

With two engines giving us trouble, fire is sure to
break out again. So we blow up?

Or should we go down to the water, ditch, and get
into our rubber rafts?

Doug goes back to check all the equipment.

"Bombardier here. The Luftwaffe got our dinghies.
They are full of holes. I don't think Saunders or Via
could get out. Charlie's whole leg is smashed. There is
so much blood I can't see what's wrong."

From Blake: "Okay, we go home. Croz, give me
the shortest way to England."

"Wilco." From me. I give him a heading, just a little south of due west.

From Blake: "I am not sure this crate will fly.
Dump everything out."

Those of us who can walk begin to salvo everything. In our compartment Doug yanks up his bombsight, opens the floor hatch and tosses it. Thousands of dollars and a military secret for the fish. Out go our .45 revolvers. I was never sure I could hit anything with mine anyway. Our woolen flying clothes. Our boots. By now I am so hot that I take off my Eisenhower jacket. There goes my solid gold insignia that Dot gave me. Jean won't be sorry.

I take my machine gun out, and into the drink it goes. We scrape up all the spent cartridges. Out.

Then I do something dumb. Really dumb.

To get stuff out we have been opening the hatch. When I go back to salvo all my navigation equipment, I grab the emergency button instead of the handle.

The whole door flies off.

My God, what have I done? Now we can't ditch. If we hit the water, the whole ocean would come up through the hole at the bottom of the fuselage, and we would break into pieces.

Blake has felt the rush of air. He calls down. "What happened?"

I tell him. I am so ashamed of myself I can hardly talk.

He is all Blake. No complaint, just, "I guess we gotta fly now. Keep us heading for England."

I become a full-time navigator, which isn't easy. We were settling down, but now Blake and Kidd have lifted us up about three hundred feet. It helped to dump the stuff. We are now at about six hundred feet. We can see the waves. High and smooth. Rolling.

I have to do some guessing. My airspeed indicator is out, so I guess 120 mph. We are listing so badly that my aperiodic compass rose is stuck. I look at the sun, figure out where it should be entering our cabin, and watch our direction from then on by where the sun is.

That water is getting close.

"Top turret to crew. Little Friend at three o'clock level. Don't shoot him down."

I switch my radio channel and listen to pilot talk.

"Little Friend to Big Friend. You look like trouble. What's keeping your bird in the air? How can I help?"

Kidd comes on. "Keep the bogeys away, Little Friend, and check our navigation. Is our heading okay for the nearest land?"

"You're on course, Big Friend. I am with you."

Back in the waist, Forkner and Doug drag Charlie out of the tail. When Doug comes back to the nose he is pale. He nods and I go back to see if I can help.

Lying in the waist, Charlie's whole lower body is smashed and bleeding. Forky is giving him, Saunders, and Yevich more morphine. That kid acts like a trained surgeon. We pad the wounded with an open parachute. Saunders is out, his eyes open, his head nodding. His eyes are glazed. Someone drags McClelland out of the ball, but he keeps fighting, trying to get back to his guns. A 20-millimeter half scalped him when it burst in his face. His head is one mass of blood.

Our right aileron is flapping, the stabilizer is shredded. Only two engines are working full time. The plane is riddled with holes, some of them as big as a basket, some of them as small as a half-penny bit. With all that going on, I smile. I am really English. I pronounced it "HAPE-nee-BIT."

All through the waist, many of the control cables have snapped.

I head forward.

Blake and Kidd are fighting the controls. They are flying old 393 with pure strength. Both of them are wet with sweat.

Land!

A flying field! Must be RAF, short runways.

Nothing ever looked so good in my life. No planes. Nothing on the whole field but one tree.

"Prepare for crash landing. All to emergency positions."

Doug and I go back to the waist. Forky and Little Britches have opened all the chutes and padded the wounded. The four who can still operate sit with our backs to the bulkhead. This is my third time. I pat my wallet. That's where the Scotch heather is. I think of that lady back in Evanston, Wyoming.

Straight in. No approach or base leg. Wheels up.

Descending. Crunch!

We slither and yaw. No control surface operating. Even though the wheels are up in their pods, the brakes work at first. Then one of them gives, and we careen off the runway.

That one tree in the whole airfield?

We hit it. The whole nose goes.

In the back we can't see the tree, but the branches and leaves break the window and come into our compartment. We smell fresh air. Cool, almost cold, on our faces.

We are stopped.

No one gets out. We just sit.

Silence. At first. Then, as always in the English countryside, we hear the birds.

MARIENBURG
AND MÜNSTER

✈ My memories cloud.

We lay there for those quiet moments.

A lorry drives up. The chipper voice of an elderly Home Guard: "Why did you hit the tree? Can we help you, mites?" An ambulance comes up. Brisk men put Saunders, McClelland, Via, and Yevich on stretchers and whisk them out.

The lorry takes Kidd, Blake, Doug, Thorny, Forky, and me through Norwich and on past, down a narrow highway. The truck's engine drones on as we ride on for almost an hour, numb, no talk.

At the main gate, an M.P. salutes, and sits down suddenly.

"Major Kidd, we heard you blew up!"

The British lorry drives off with our profuse thanks. Just as we climb into one of the base personnel carriers, Colonel Harding drives up in his sedan, with Bucky Egan behind him in another car. A volley of words.

"We thought you had it!"

"We got reports that four chutes got out."

"Did you see Bucky Cleven get it?"

We take the enlisted men to their quarters. Since we have not eaten since morning, we need food. We look at our watches: 1930 hours. The Flying Mess will be closed. We head for the Officers' Club.

As we enter, officers, ground and air alike, look up. Stunned.

"It's Blakely's crew!"

Pandemonium. Every man in the club, even the enlisted waiters, rush up and pound us on the back. At least half of them offer us their drinks.

"We thought you bought it!"

"They reported four chutes."

"Did you see Major Cleven blow up?"

Things settled down, and we got a partial report of what happened. Walter "The Chief" Moreno was hit twelve different times by E.A., lost his rudder hydraulic system. He came in without brakes. In *Sunny Jim*, piloted by John Griffin, a 20-millimeter blew away the whole top turret. The plane landed with all four props hit. In *Miss Carriage*, Edward Stork came back 400 miles with just one engine, and no oxygen system. The P.R., Red Bowman, reported the loss of seven planes and crews, with three landing at other bases. In all, the group lost seventy-two crewmen and thirteen more were in the hospital with wounds. Until our crew got back, all three squadron leads were missing. The curse of being out in front. Four chutes were reported from our plane, four or five from Bucky Cleven's plane, none from the low squadron lead. Nine planes were badly damaged. The Group claimed sixteen enemy aircraft. Carnage on both sides.

Bucky Cleven, the impervious, the invincible, was gone. If he couldn't make it, who could? His good friend, Bucky Egan, didn't talk much that night.

My memories dim about some of what happened during World War II—not about the missions because they were etched so indelibly. When I walked into my barracks after I had a late dinner at the Officers' Club, something happened that comes back to my mind as though it were yesterday.

During our combat days, our leaders had to decide what to do about the possessions of crews who went down. A similar problem came up when they had to decide what to do about flyers who were afraid to fly.

Both cases caused morale problems among the combat crews.

When a flyer was undone by missions, when he saw too many planes blow up in front of him, when his tail gunner was cut in two on a mission, when too many of his friends were killed, he sometimes quit. We did not call them "cowards," we called them "combat failures."

It happened.

Since "combat fatigue"—the other euphemism we used—was so contagious, the flyer was whisked off the base immediately and sent to the nearest General Hospital. Here in a special ward he was given psychiatric and religious counseling. After that he usually went back to the States, reclassified, and usually demoted. In some cases, he was court-martialed. Some returned to duty.

While he was gone, to preserve our own courage, we never mentioned him, not once.

When a crew went down, they too disappeared. Two hours after a crew failed to show up, the adjutant and first sergeant rushed to the missing crew's quarters, took down the pictures and moved out everything that belonged to them. The adjutant removed anything incriminating like letters to and from the wrong woman, or lewd pictures, or condoms. Then the possessions were sealed for eventual return to the MIA's family. We did not talk about such crews. It just wasn't done.

If a plane crash-landed at another base or ran out of fuel and had to belly in somewhere, its pilot knew he should phone in that his crew was still in action. In our case, there had been no phone at Ludham.

When we walked into the Quonset hut in the 418th site, our beds were stripped. My radio and record player were gone, my picture of Jean was gone, my footlocker was gone. On the bare cot were two clean sheets and two pillowcases, two blankets, one pillow, all neatly folded. Ready for the next crew.

The war went on.

On the next morning, October 9, the 100th took off at 0430 hours. Awful talk about the bomb load, a new kind of incendiary, M-47 A2, "a 100-pound jellied device." Napalm. The target: Marienburg, two hundred miles past Berlin, the second longest mission after Trondheim.

Blakely's crew was stood down. Via, Yevich, Saunders, and McClelland were in the hospital.

The weather around our base was clear, but a few miles west of us, all the RAF and RCAF bases were socked in. As our planes were taking off, five Canadian Halifaxes returning from Hanover and desperately low on petrol requested permission for emergency landing. Traffic jam.

Late that day, very late, our crews returned. Exhausted. No losses to E.A., but red flares. The long flight took out several engines. We saw that the pilots had feathered engines to keep them from windmilling and shaking off a wing.

That night at the Officers' Club Major Egan badgered Chick Harding, demanding to lead the next mission. "I want to avenge my buddy," he said. "He went down swinging."

"Your squadron lead crew is busted up." Colonel Harding was talking about us.

"I'll get another one."

Stories about our crew were growing. The field where we landed, RAF Ludham, had been abandoned, its runways too short even for fighters. Yet Blake and Kidd had brought old 393 in.

A mechanic counted the holes in 393 as it sat there, a pile of junk. More than twelve hundred holes in it. Salvage.

We heard that Jimmy Doolittle, now the C.O. of the Eighth, had called his old friend.

"Chick, you took a beating. We are going to stand you down and give you a chance to train your replacement crews."

"No, Jimmy. The 100th never goes off ops."

Heroics.

Colonel Harding came to where Blake, Doug, and I were eating.

"You guys deserve a rest. Go wherever you want for a week. Take the old E."

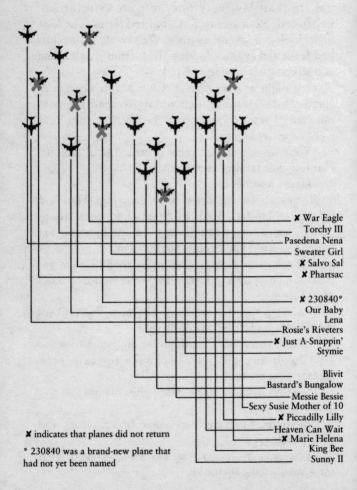

THE MISSION TO BREMEN, OCTOBER 8, 1943

Planes in the 100th Bomb Group shown
in formation after assembly

✘ War Eagle
Torchy III
Pasedena Nena
Sweater Girl
✘ Salvo Sal
✘ Phartsac

✘ 230840*
Our Baby
Lena
Rosie's Riveters
✘ Just A-Snappin'
Stymie

Blivit
Bastard's Bungalow
Messie Bessie
Sexy Susie Mother of 10
✘ Piccadilly Lilly
Heaven Can Wait
✘ Marie Helena
King Bee
Sunny II

✘ indicates that planes did not return

* 230840 was a brand-new plane that
had not yet been named

A long night at the club. I did not write to Jean. What could I say that wouldn't break the rules or frighten her?

The next morning, for the 100th, was the momentous day of October 10, 1943.

For me, it was an anniversary. Just a year ago, most of the navigators in the 100th graduated from Mather Field. They were my classmates. The class of 42-14. They graduated and were commissioned on the same day as most of the bombardiers, also in 42-14. My two bombardiers, Ham and Douglass, graduated on that day, exactly one year ago.

Saunders is dead.

Doug, McClelland, and Forkner are in bandages. Purple Hearts. Yevich and Via are in the hospital. Charlie took a 20-millimeter cannon shell the whole length of his left leg. Miraculously it exploded behind him, the lead back of his seat protecting him.

In the morning, the same old routine. The orderly comes into our quarters. I am not asleep. I sit up.

"Not you, Lieutenant. Just Brady and Cruikshank."

The door opens again. It is Bucky Egan. He goes to John Brady's bed.

"John, I am flying with you. There are no lead crews left. We are going out to get the bastards that got Bucky."

He goes out again. Brady goes over to Ham and Hoerr and Davy Solomon.

He shakes his head. "This is not right. We have never been lead crew before. Ev's crew have worked at it and they know what to do. They are good at it. We are not prepared."

No fear, or uncertainty. Brady is sound, levelhead-ed. It is just that he knows trouble when he sees it.

They leave, and I close my eyes. I actually go back to sleep.

Three hours later, Blake gets a substitute copilot, and they pre-flight the old Model E the group uses to run errands. In spite of what we went through two days before, we would rather fly to Bournemouth than take a train. With the formation on the way to Münster and what with the losses over Bremen, we have the only plane left on the field.

I call my friend, Captain Cliff Frye, the weather-man, and we arrange a code for me to telephone and get a report on what's happening.

We fly south and then west. We see London. We buzz Stonehenge. We land at Bournemouth. The tiny WREN at Flying Control is no longer surprised at what we do. She already has a lorry waiting for us. After a welcome from Louise Harlan, we get rooms and fall into bed.

At sixteen-hundred hours, from Louise's office, I phone the Base. I get Captain Frye.

"Did all my friends get back from pass?" I ask.

No sound. I know something is wrong. He is try-ing to figure out how to break the bad news.

I come in quick. "Did some of them have a perma-nent change of station?"

"Yes, all but one."

All but one! That means that maybe twenty planes got shot down.

The weatherman breaks the code. "Egan's gone. Your old crew is gone. The whole group is gone. The only one who came back was that new crew in the 418th. They call him Rosie."

I drop the phone. I can't believe it. Brady, Ham, Davy and Hoerr, all gone. Cruikshank gone. Old southern-boy Murph, gone. All my friends. Every crew who went through training with me in the States is gone.

I tell Blake and the crew. They say nothing. They just look at each other.

"Okay," says Old Beady Eyes. "R&R is over. Let's go home."

CHAPTER 12

THE MISSION
TO NOWHERE

✈ If Ev, Doug, and I had not already known that the 100th had been wiped out over Münster, we could have seen it when we flew back from Bournemouth to the base and were still five miles out.

At that time there were about thirty-five hard stands around the perimeter of the airfield at Thorpe Abbotts. Usually, except when the group was out on a mission, all the mooring areas had a B-17 in them—and a crew of men would be working around them.

Not so today. There were planes there all right, but each of them showed severe damage. One of them had a whole wing shredded. Two of them had an engine ripped off. On the fourth, most of the vertical stabilizer and rudder were smashed.

"Pilot here. This place is a morgue."

In the Officers' Club that night we heard the whole story.

Since the 100th had lost so many planes over Bremen on October 8 and strained their engines on the long one to Marienburg on October 9, the group only put up two squadrons and the 390th filled in the high. When Rosie came back alone, he was missing two engines and had a hole through his starboard wing.

"You could have dropped a bushel basket through it," said Captain Bill Clift, the 418th Engineering Officer. "What a way for a crew to start, Bremen, Marienburg, and Münster."

"Yeah, when he got out," said Smokey Stover, the SMO, the Squadron Medical Officer, "he looked around kind of dazed-like, and said, 'Are they all like this?'"

Ev, Doug, and I learned that of the 140 pilots, copilots, navigators, and bombardiers who had flown across the Atlantic to England on May 31, just four months and ten days before, we were the only three left on flying status. Dye's crew, with one gunner dead, had gone home. A few of the original flyers were still assigned to the 100th, but the losses of the last weeks had done them in, and they mercifully were sent off on R&R somewhere.

In the last week, the 100th had lost twenty-one aircraft. In that one week, over 200 men were MIA or KIA.

General LeMay—he now had his first star—called Colonel Harding.

"Chick, I say again that the 100th should go off ops until you can get some training. Your replacement pilots will have very few hours on the 17 and almost no formation flying."

Colonel Harding responded as he had before: "The 100th go off ops? Never!"

Just like that.

Years later, in his autobiography, General LeMay, retired as Chief of Staff of the whole U.S. Air Force, wrote that one of the worst mistakes he made in his whole career was not to do something earlier about 100th leadership. "Harding was senior to me. Loved by all the old flyers."

In the morning, we did not go back to our barracks. In our barracks, thirteen of the sixteen beds were empty. We stayed on the flight line and worked on new planes as they came in, or we sat around the Officers' Club to talk to the new crews as they came in.

Our leadership was gone. Colonel Harding became ill and was in and out of the infirmary. In two weeks the 100th had lost two squadron commanders, four lead crews, and three operations officers.

The loss of Bucky Cleven over Bremen and Bucky Egan over Münster seemed to have cut the heart right out of the the 100th.

Without them the 100th was a shadow.

In the 349th, the squadron commander, a good friend of the two Buckys, was just as handsome, just as good a flyer, just as loved, but less of the derring-do. But he was also good at staff work, and he was moved up for the new position as Chief of Staff at Thirteenth Wing. The only squadron which was still at full strength was the 351st. Ollen Turner was steadily in charge, and his lead crew, with Jack Swartout as pilot, had taken some terrific beatings, but it was flying.

A couple of weeks passed. I don't remember much about what happened. A new major named John Bennett came in, and was assigned to the 349th. A new squadron commander? So far he was just looking around. The new crews came in. The new planes arrived. I guess the squadron ops officers took over temporarily in the leaderless squadrons. We flew some missions, mercifully tucked back in the formation somewhere, and didn't get hit.

One morning when he was barely out of the infirmary, Colonel Harding sent a jeep for me. When I got to his office there he was, thin, gray. Bucky Elton, who as 418th Squadron Ops had been filling in for Bucky Egan as C.O., was there. So were Blake and Doug. Jack Kidd came in after I did.

"Bucky, I want you to take over for Cleven in the 350th. Ev, I want you to become squadron commander of the 418th. Doug and Croz, I want you to be Group Bombardier and Group Navigator."

Quiet for the minute it took for the news to sink in.

"What about Bubbles Payne?" I asked.

"He goes to the 349th."

Too bad. Bubbles had hoped that being Group Navigator would make him a major. His father had been a sergeant in World War I.

Jack Kidd stood up.

"Come on, Croz and Doug, I'll show you around. You are now my staff."

As Doug and I walked around after Jack Kidd, I felt as though I were on hallowed ground.

We entered a large central room which had some enlisted men working at their desks. Across the front of the room was a huge wall map of Western Europe, at least twenty feet high and fifty feet wide, from the British Isles east past Berlin and on to Moscow. It went south to Africa. Angry splotches circled all the major cities. Flak. Many of the cities were marked with tiny flags with a Square D. The 100th had been there. Four flags at Bremen—I had been there twice. Flags at Trondheim, in Norway, and at Constantine, in Africa. I had gone as far north and as far south as the Eighth Air Force had gone.

As I faced the map in the huge room, the wall on my right and the wall at my back were all glass. Through the glass walls on the right I saw a sign, "Group Operations." Kidd's office. I turned around and faced the back wall. I saw three smaller offices. Judging from some signs, my office, shared with the Group Bombardier, was on the right, then the duty officer in the center, and on the left, the Air Executive.

"You will get your start tonight," Jack said. "When the red light goes on at the Officers' Club or the movie, come at once to Ops."

At nineteen-thirty hours that night, just as I finished eating, the light went on. On my high English bicycle, I pedaled warily in the dark a quarter of a mile down the lane, past Group Headquarters and on past to Group Ops.

The first person I saw as I entered Ops was Bubbles Payne.

I was embarrassed, but he wasn't. His father and brothers were all professional army, and he knew how it went.

"I wrote a long letter to Jean last night," he said. "I thought she should know that this is an honor for you, and I am not mad at you." Jolly, rotund Bubbles, he couldn't have been nicer. He went on: "Bing, I couldn't handle the job. I hope you can."

We went into the office of the Duty Officer, a different person every night. Just as the ground officers took their turns as Officer of the Day, O.D., so did a group of flying officers take their turn as Duty

Officer, D.O. Mostly they were assistants—the Assistant Group Bombardier, the Assistant Group Navigator, Assistant Group Ops, Assistant Squadron Ops, and so on.

The D.O. got the field order from the decoding section and began to parcel out the information, carefully following an elaborate checklist, marking off each task with a red china marking pencil.

Squadron Commanders alerted. What squadron is stood down? Number of crews? Time for meeting at Ops to set up formation? Check.

Plane requirements to Group Engineering. Check.

Bomb load to Ordnance. Check.

Machine gun rounds necessary to Armaments. Check.

Target information to S-2. Check.

Alert the Group Navigator. Check.

Alert the Group Bombardier. Check.

Weather data to Met Officer. Check.

Number of crews flying to the flying mess sergeant. Time for breakfast. Check.

Motor pool. How many trucks where. And when. Check.

Oxygen requirements to Tech Supply. Check.

Number of flyers to be awakened at what time to Squadron Orderly Rooms.

And much more. This was just half of the list.

During most of that night about three thousand men would work at top speed to fulfill the requirements set up by the field order. Three thousand men to get two hundred and ten flyers and twenty-one planes into the air.

The D.O. tore off the navigation section of the field order and handed it to Bubbles. We took it into the S-2 map room, which was down a hall, and told the map clerk how many packets to prepare. Maps, blank mercator charts, blank log pages.

On the next day's mission, the 100th was high group behind the 390th. The other group in the Thirteenth Wing, the 95th, was scheduled to be low group. The 351st Squadron would lead, with Jack Swartout as pilot. On a blank log sheet I wrote the name of his navigator, Leonard Bull. Good man.

It was about twenty-three-hundred hours, eleven o'clock. The crews would show for their briefing at oh-four-hundred hours.

Bubbles headed back for his quarters. "I will see you at oh-three-hundred."

I decided I had so much to learn I had better stick around.

Oh-three-hundred hours. I am sitting at my new office. The phone rings. The D.O. answers, gets excited just listening. He puts the phone down and yells out, "There's a big change coming in on the field order."

Sergeant Rex Baker, who plays bull fiddle in the group's swing band, gets up from his desk and heads for the crypto section. He comes back soon waving the yellow pages.

Jack Kidd reads it.

"This is new," he says, "We are going to be led by a Pathfinder crew."

A few weeks before, all the B-17 and B-24 groups in the Eighth Air Force, some forty of them, were ordered to send one crew and one plane to an RAF station near Nottingham. It was called Alconbury.

COMING IN ON A WING AND A PRAYER

This painting of my plane, *Just a-Snappin'*, shortly before we crashed, is by Mike Deibel and hangs in the Western Reserve Hall of Fame in Cleveland, Ohio. A copy is also exhibited in David Tallichet's 100th Bomb Group Restaurant near the Cleveland airport. Along the bottom of the picture are the names of all the crew members.

We had been to Bremen that day, October 8, 1943. Leading a large formation of B-17's, we were hit hard over the target by enemy flak, spun out of control and saved from crashing by the superb efforts of our pilot and command pilot. With two engines knocked out, we were forced to head home alone at low altitude, our plane riddled by over 1,200 shell holes by actual count, one crewman mortally wounded and five severely injured. When we were attacked repeatedly by Luftwaffe fighters along the way, our gunners shot down ten of them. Unable to ditch in the North Sea because of our wounded or to make it to our own field, *Just a-Snappin'* crash-landed at a "dummy" airfield on the English coast.

Deibel's painting shows the feathered propellors of the two dead starboard engines and the square D on the tail that was the designation of the 100th Bomb Group.

IT ALL BEGAN IN IOWA IN THE 1930s

My mother, Eva McClellan Crosby

My father, Guy Crosby

IT ALL BEGAN IN IOWA IN THE 1930s

Two pictures of me with Jean Boehner while we were under-graduates at the University of Iowa: (*left*) in the University cafeteria; (*right*) while double-dating with Joe Parkin and Winnie Coningham. Following a long courtship, Jean became Mrs. Crosby after I enlisted. Joe also became a navigator, was shot down over Yugoslavia, and escaped to the Tito under-ground.

Cadet Harry Crosby

IT ALL BEGAN IN IOWA IN THE 1930s

As a new second lieutenant, I went to Illinois to visit my father who was working at Woodward Governor Company.

My navigation class at Mather Field in Sacramento, California.

It wasn't all work; having fun while on a pass at Balboa Beach, California.

MY FIRST CREWS WITH THE
100TH BOMB GROUP

My first crew, in a picture taken after I left it. *Back row*: radio operator Joe Hafer; tail gunner Jim McCusker; top turret Adolph Blum; left waist gunner George Petrohelos; ball turret Roland Gangwar; right waist gunner Harold Clanton. *Front row*: co-pilot John Hoerr; pilot John Brady; bombardier Howard Hamilton (eighteen years old); and navigator "Good ole boy" Frank Murphy, who was usually the navigator on Charlie Cruikshank's crew. They all went down over Münster on October 10, 1943.

MY FIRST CREWS WITH THE
100TH BOMB GROUP

After my third mission I became a lead navigator on Blakely's crew. *Back row*: ball turret Bill McClelland; navigator Harry Crosby; co-pilot Charlie Via; pilot Ev Blakely; bombardier Jim Douglass. *Front row*: left waist gunner Lester Saunders; top turret Monroe Thornton; right waist gunner Ed Yevich; tail gunner Lyle Nordstrom; radio operator Ed Forkner. Saunders and Nordstrom were KIA.

GROUP NAVIGATORS AND EARLY
COMMANDERS OF THE 100TH

Omar Gonzales and me. Gonzales was the original Group Navigator of the 100th. Later shot down, he was captured and became a POW.

The group commander during the early period of the war, Neil Harding. He received the Silver Star for our mission to Trondheim, Norway.

The first commander of the 100th, Darr Alkire.

In this picture I am flanked on the left by Jack Edwards, Ev Blakely's first co-pilot, and on the right by Joe "Bubbles" Payne, who preceded me as lead navigator on Blakely's crew and then as Group Navigator. Payne was KIA.

FLYING FORTRESSES IN ACTION

B-17's, built by Boeing in Seattle, were loved by the men who flew them because they were so hard to knock down. To some of the people in occupied Europe the throaty roar of their engines passing over was "the music of angels." Here they are seen in pictures taken by crew members flying through anti-aircraft bursts (note the big square D of the 100th Bomb Group on their tails); dropping their loads of bombs from open bomb bays; and leaving a mosaic of contrails at high altitudes.

We could not have survived without the support of our loved ones back home whose frequent—sometimes daily—letters helped keep our spirits up; nor without the support of the superb ground crews who kept our planes flying with their skill, dedication, and long hours.

When I went overseas my wife Jean shared an apartment in Chicago with the wives of two members of my crew, and an enterprising *Herald American* reporter took a picture of them. Gerry Hamilton (*left*) was married to Howard Hamilton, our bombardier; Margaret Ann Blakely (*center*) was married to Ev Blakely, our pilot. Jean is on the right.

SUPPORT GROUPS

Often working through the night when it was so cold their tools chilled in their hands, the ground crews earned the unlimited respect and gratitude of the men in the air. They were the unsung heroes of the Eighth Air Force, and the tragedy is that so many of them were nameless; often an aircrew would be shot down before its members even learned the names of their ground crew.

THE GROUND OFFICERS

Ground officers were called "paddlefeet," which sounds derogatory but was actually high praise. They, along with the ground crews, kept the aircrews flying. Their support was crucial. We got the medals, the quick promotions, the flying pay, and we got to go home at the end of a tour—if we were alive. But they kept us going.

Clockwise from lower left: Marvin Bowman, public relations officer, and later the group intelligence officer; Karl Standish, the first group adjutant; Minor Shaw, the first S-2 (intelligence) officer.

Left to right: Armament officer Leonard Rosenfeld and ordnance officer Robert Major.

THE GROUND OFFICERS

The engineering officers. *Front*: Bill Carleton (351st); Eugene Rovegno (chief engineering officer); Don Blazer (350th). *Back*: Jack Herlihy (349th); Bill Clift (418th).

The medics. C. J. McCarthy (349th); John W. Hardy (350th); Lawrence Jennings (Group); Wendell Stover (418th); E. C. Kinder (351st and Group).

Flying over the Alps during the Regensburg Mission, the big D on the tail clearly visible.

THE REGENSBURG — NORTH AFRICA (SHUTTLE) MISSION, AUGUST 17, 1943

Some of the crew of *Just a-Snappin'* pose below a Mediterranean sign. *Back row, left to right*: Crosby, Via, Blakely, an officer stationed in North Africa, and Douglass. *Foreground*: Saunders, Thornton, McClelland.

Remnants of the 100th Bomb Group on the barren airfield in North Africa after the raid. We thought the barrels on the field contained gasoline and filled our tanks from them. Then we learned that it was kerosene, not gas, and had to pump it all out.

These four people were in charge of training navigators and
bombardiers and briefing them before a mission. They were
also responsible for training lead crews. *Left to right*: Assistant
Group Bombardier C. J. Milburn; Group Bombardier Don
Ventriss, who replaced James Douglass; Assistant Group
Navigator Ed King, who replaced me after VE when I headed
for Japan; and me.

NAVIGATORS AND OTHERS AT
THORPE ABBOTTS

At my desk in the nose of a B-17.

Bill Abbey, the Assistant Group Navigator;
Clifton Frye, our weather officer; me; and
Sumner Reeder, 349th Squadron Commander.

NAVIGATORS AND OTHERS AT
THORPE ABBOTTS

The squadron navigators. *Left to right*: Capt. Carl Roesel (418th); Capt. Joe Anderson (349th); Capt. Lee Raden (350th); Maj. Harry Crosby (Group Navigator); and Capt. Ed King (351st).

A newspaper photo of me in the Rockford, Illinois, *Star*.

THE BREMEN MISSION

The end of the Bremen raid for us and *Just a-Snappin'* was recreated in a drawing by Jack Coggins for the December 1943 *Yank* magazine. With our wheels up, Blakely and Kidd landed on a dummy airfield. Our controls snapped and we veered into a large tree at 50 mph.

The end of the old bird. On the next day, ground crews tried to salvage part of *Just a-Snappin'*, but there was little to save.

The fate of the nose demonstrates why the bombardier and navigator never rode in their compartment during a landing.

THE BREMEN MISSION

Jim Douglass, our bombardier.

There was one tree on the field but, out of control, we smashed into it.

Lieutenant General Jack Kidd, in a picture taken after the war, was originally commander of the 351st Squadron. He became Group Operations Officer in 1943 after a command shakeup over poor air discipline. He led some of the outstanding missions of the 100th, including the Regensburg Shuttle and Bremen raids, and was considered one of the best air leaders in the Eighth Air Force.

THE END OF AN ERA

The "Two Buckys," John Egan, commander of the 418th
Squadron, and Gale Cleven, of the 350th, were the heart of
the original 100th—dashing, undisciplined, superb pilots,
exactly what Hollywood expected them to be. When they
were shot down, Cleven over Bremen (October 8, 1943), and
Egan over Münster (October 10), the 100th was devastated—
and a new era began.

It didn't help our morale or our reputation that we had many accidents on our own field. Once seven of our planes piled into each other at the end of the runway after returning from a mission. No one was killed, but all seven planes had to be scrapped. Another time we added extra bombs to all the planes taking off on a mission to see how many they could carry. Three planes crashed just after takeoff, killing thirty men.

"SWEATING IT OUT"

The vigil at the control tower. *Left to right*: Sammy Barr, Bob Flesher, Roland Knight, Sumner Reeder, and Marvin Bowman. *Above*: Chick Harding and Jack Kidd.

The indispensable ground crews waiting, waiting, waiting . . .

A squadron comes over, and the left lead plane peels off to land.

THE DAMAGE WE DID

Coblenz

Cologne

Frankfurt

At the end of the war almost every city in Germany looked like Coblenz and Frankfurt—except for Bonn. The fact that the cathedral at Frankfurt seems to be spared is more a tribute to Gothic construction than to our pinpoint bombing.

ROSIE, THE SOUL OF THE 100TH

Bob Rosenthal was one of the outstanding heroes of the Eighth Air Force and one of the most decorated. Besides the Distinguished Service Cross, Silver Stars, many Distinguished Flying Crosses, and innumerable Air Medals, he was cited by several governments. He was shot down three times and managed to evade capture. Once he went east and ended up in Russia, where he had dinner with the U.S. Ambassador to Russia, Averell Harriman. He completed two tours —fifty missions—and was starting on a third when the war ended. Because of his good nature and concern for his men, he was one of the most popular officers in the 100th.

ON LEAVE WITH JEAN

The only chance to be with Jean since I left for England in the spring of 1943 came in September 1944, when I flew back home for a month's leave. It was a tremendous morale booster. In the picture to the right I am wearing the Air Force's new forest green dress uniform. The photo on the upper right was taken by a photographer with my hometown paper, the *Oskaloosa* (Iowa) *Daily Herald*.

SOME TOP BRASS
COMMANDING OFFICERS OF THE 100TH

Frederick Sutterlin had been a staff officer for General Spaatz before he became C.O. of the 100th, following Robert Kelly, John Bennett, and Tom Jeffrey. After the war he became a brigadier general.

Before he took command of the 100th, Harry Cruver was the 351st Squadron Commander, a squadron frequently cited for excellent maintenance and safe flying.

Jack Wallace was a squadron commander (418th), group operations officer, and air executive before he became group commander. Like Fred Sutterlin, he became a brigadier general after the war.

SOME TOP BRASS

The two leaders who get the most credit for the excellent record of the 100th Bomb Group are John Bennett (*above*) and Tom Jeffery, shown behind his desk with Air Exec. Fred Price (*left*) and his Ground Exec. Bill Utley. After the war both became major generals.

Jimmy Doolittle (*on the left*), talking with Tom Jeffery during a visit with the 100th, was commanding officer of the Eighth Air Force. Before that, in 1942, he led the retaliatory raid against Tokyo of B-25 bombers that took off from aircraft carriers in the Pacific.

We had our share of visiting generals, including Curtis LeMay, who was commanding officer of the Third Air Division and then of the B-29's in the Pacific. After the war he directed the Berlin airlift, was commander of the Strategic Air Command, and became Chief of Staff of the U.S. Air Force. When he autographed this picture for me he must have forgotten about Bonn.

My family at the wedding of my son Jeff and Marjie. *Back row*: Jeff, his brother Steve, and sister April. *Front*: me, Marjie, daughter Rebecca, and Jean.

Jean Boehner Crosby shortly before her death in 1980.

Mary Alice and me.

Mary Alice Crosby and me at our wedding with three of my children and three of hers. *Left to right*: Jeff, Rebecca, Maura, Haley, Mary Alice, me, John, and Steve. My other daughter, April, was in Alaska.

Because the project was so hush-hush we were given no specifications about the crew. Just send a plane and a crew.

Many groups had the same idea: Dump your worst crew. Get rid of your jinxed or most damaged plane.

At the time, the 100th had a crew, piloted by one Frank Valesh, who were recognized as the "number one, highly specialized, complete fuck-up crew." The crew flew in a plane called *Hang the Expense*. When they crashed that plane, and then another, and then another, they persisted in using the same name. They were now on *Hang the Expense IV*. Valesh's most recent escapade was that he invited a nurse from a nearby field hospital to join the Mile-High Club.

"What's the Mile-High Club?" she asked.

Using whatever circumlocutions were popular those days, Valesh told her they would get a B-17, take off, go to 5,280 feet, put the plane on autopilot, and then lie down in the waist of the plane and do what young men and young women have done since the world began. This would be her initiation to the Mile-High Club.

The nurse agreed.

So out they went to the flight line. What lies Valesh told or what rank he pulled to get that plane we will never know, but within a few minutes he and the nurse, she in the copilot's seat, were at the head of the runway in *Hang the Expense IV*, all four engines roaring. He ran up the engines, put on his headlights, and released the brakes. The nurse was on her way to her initiation.

When a B-17 was moored, to keep the huge verti-cal rudder from flapping in the wind, it was locked in place. There were also two more locks on the tail surfaces which made the plane go up and down. Usually the copilot, during the pre-flight routine, would have discovered the problem, but the nurse in the right seat was not up to that. Frank had taxied out on the outboard engines, made his turns with the brakes, and had not used the rudders. Then, too, maybe he had been drinking just a little.

So off they went. When they got up to takeoff speed, Frank pulled back on the elevators, and they moved just a little. The plane went up about a hundred feet, cleared the fences, and that was all. They had no place to go.

Instantly Frank cut the power and tried to settle into Farmer Draper's meadow, just ahead.

No such luck. He, the nurse, and *Hang the Expense IV* slammed into Farmer Draper's barn and landed softly in three hundred bales of hay.

"That is the man," Colonel Harding said, "that we will send to Alconbury."

So Frank Valesh and his crew and our worst plane joined thirty-nine other crews of the 8AF at Alconbury—along with some of the worst planes we all had.

We did not know it, but Alconbury was the 8AF's new base to train lead crews.

When they got there, and the story finally leaked out, they learned they were being trained to be Pathfinders. Their planes would be fitted with the most recent version of Mickey, the radar equipment whose operator could peer down through clouds and find targets even in the very worst weather.

This would have been great if we all had sent good crews.

The news that Sergeant Baker had brought in on the addition to the field order was that weather over the targets had worsened, and the Eighth, for the first time, was going out on a foul-weather mission. The task force would go to Germany with the wings in trail. When we got near Bremen, Bremerhaven, Kiel, and other ports, the wings would split off and bomb separate cities. The 100th would lead the wing with one of the Pathfinder crews, not our own but one that was flying in at 0330.

Harding will be the command pilot. He is sick. Both Flesher and Kidd tell him he should not fly, but he insists.

So back to bed for Swartout, Drummond, Dahlgren, and Bull.

Colonel Harding calls me in. I am shocked at how bad he looks. "Croz, I have never flown with this crew, and we can be sure they will be awful. I want you to fly with me. This will give you a chance to get back at Bremen."

Bremen again. Big deal!

I should have told him that I had been up all night, but I didn't. The 100th never aborts. A winner never quits and a quitter never wins. My father would have been proud of me.

So I fly.

Instead of learning how to conduct a briefing, I am being briefed.

I am one of the first at the briefing room, but I do not enter. In the vestibule, with a potbelly gleaming red and making the room too hot, the chaplain and the Red Cross girls are there, the girls with dough-nuts and coffee. To my dying day, when I smell

Worth's Je Reviens or Bellodgia by Caron I will think of Hilda Kinder and Betty Hardman. They always wore those perfumes.

With Hilda and Betty, officers and enlisted men get the same treatment. Special attention to the crews flying that day. They smile at me. I yearn for them, just a little.

It is not yet five, but the two Red Cross girls are just right, lipstick, straight nylon seams, white blouses pressed, crisp, fresh. They may be the last American women seen by some of the crews. The crews who are shot down, if they live, will think of them during the stay in Stalag Luft III.

The briefing is routine. I am so exhausted I hardly hear it.

I nod off. Someone shakes my shoulder, impressed that I am so at ease. "Nerves of steel," he says.

Colonel Harding is so sick his face is green. When he talks, we can hardly hear him.

"We are going to Bremen, men, and we will make them wish they never got Bucky Cleven. And we are carrying an extra bomb this morning for Bucky Egan."

Silence.

In the history of failed missions of the Eighth Air Force, November 7, 1943, will always remain one of the worst. A real botcheroo.

The plane in which Colonel Harding and I were to fly arrived just before takeoff, and no one on our base gave it a pre-flight. Harding and I went out to the end of the takeoff strip and saw it. It was patches from one end to the other. Dropping down from its radio compartment was a white bowl that looked like a big bathtub. It had a strange, fecal odor.

That was Mickey.

There were two Pathfinders. In one of the planes was the Valesh *Hang the Expense* crew we had sent to Alconbury to get rid of. I had come to know Jack Johnson, the Mickey operator, and Al Franklin, the navigator, and had learned to respect them. Even Valesh had settled down and taken his job seriously. Thus far their planes were so decrepit that they had to abort on every mission.

I wished I were flying with them.

The other Pathfinder pilot, navigator, and bombardier came out, and we talked briefly. They all were smoking cigars. Real smart-ass raunch. They had been briefed at Alconbury. Clearly the navigator was not happy that I was flying with him.

"I'll make the rendezvous," he said.

We were both first lieutenants. Standoff.

"Suit yourself," I said.

The four of us walked toward the waist door. I noticed that the pilot got in first instead of, with military courtesy, hanging back for Colonel Harding, the ranking officer.

So we were ready to lead the mission. A stinking plane some group had dumped. No pre-flight. A crew that was deliberately raunchy. The command pilot was sick. I had been up all night.

The weather didn't help. We hit solid clouds at 800 feet. We were supposed to assemble at 12,000 feet but at 20,000 feet I could still barely see our number two and number three engines, let alone the rest of the group. Winds usually change with altitude, swiveling around rather slowly. On that day the winds completely reversed between the altitudes of 8,000 to 15,000 feet and increased in velocity by fifty knots. Since only the lead planes had radar operators to tell them where they were, none of the rest of the planes caught the wind shift. The British had just put in a new system of medium frequency splasher beacons, but our code flimsies were in a jargon or code we couldn't read. Out of sight of any land reference and his radio jammed, a navigator would think he had an eighty-knot tail wind when he actually had a 120-knot head wind. In fifteen minutes he, 200 planes, and the 2,000 souls in them could be off course twenty-five miles—in an area where forty groups of twenty or so planes each were trying to find each other. Five thousand feet below, a navigator in front of an equally large formation could be off fifty miles in the other direction.

It was a unique and very special Hell.

Down on the ground, 8AF HQ knew we were in trouble. A Mosquito pilot on an observation flight landed and reported in. The Eighth sent out a signal that our division rendezvous would be at Angels Five, 60 degrees, twenty nautical miles from Checkpoint Able.

I looked at my maps. Our new rendezvous was out over The Wash, with no visual pilotage checks. There was absolutely no way on God's Earth that any navigator but the leads could locate that spot.

Some of us got the message, some of us did not. The Luftwaffe did, and guessed where we were.

Just then, at 15,000 feet, with visibility at zero, the plane jumped and bounced violently. The pilot and Colonel Harding fought the controls to get back on steady heading and rate of climb.

Everyone in the plane knew what had happened.

We had flown through the prop wash of another group. We had narrowly missed colliding with twenty-one planes.

When we got to 22,000 feet, the clouds began to thin momentarily. We flew alternately in cotton batting and thin, wispy feathers. We could usually see ahead, maybe two hundred feet.

"Two o'clock!"

Suddenly, from the front and starboard, a squadron of Liberators flew right through our formation. I saw B-24 navigators and bombardiers, their mouths open—they must have been yelling—and their arms up around their heads, instinctively trying for protection.

Swooooosh! Gone. Violent turbulence. Prop wash again.

"Command to tail. Anyone smash into anyone?"

"Formation control to command. I can see most of the high and all of the low, and our squadron. You won't believe this, but they all got through. I bet a lot of pants got filled."

On VHF radio we heard that the other divisions were having trouble. The Luftwaffe had come over the Channel to hit the straggling task force. We could hear "Mayday" signals filling the air as our planes went down. The main fight seemed to be about fifty miles north of us.

When we broke out into the clear, there were B-17's and a few B-24's all over the sky.

Maelstrom.

By firing yellow-yellow, our signal, we got three squadrons together, two from the 100th and a Baker squadron from the 390's, which fitted into our formation on the high right. That meant that we had no

100th deputy lead, and no other command pilot to take over if our plane aborted or got hit.

We headed out over the North Sea. The radar operator kept calling in position reports, and the navigator plotted them. This was really great. We couldn't see the ground but we knew where we were.

None of the other planes did.

Off to the right and left, behind and ahead, straggled clusters of planes were going in every direction, some of them turning back.

Our oxygen equipment had meters, and we should have been able to tell that we weren't getting enough oxygen, but in this messed-up plane nothing worked.

Anoxia, oxygen lack, affects people differently.

About the time we hit the Continent, I began to have an excruciating headache. Everything was black. I would blink my eyes, clear up my sight, squint at a map, and then look out and below. Nothing. The crew navigator and bombardier were just sitting on the floor, slumped over. The radar operator stopped giving me fixes.

Even though we had ten-tenths clouds below us, I knew when we crossed the enemy coast. Flak came up and two planes went down. Twenty of my friends. As lead navigator I was supposed to keep us out of range of those guns. My head was hurting so badly that it didn't occur to me to care.

Colonel Harding was gradually losing consciousness. His intercom made little sense; mostly he just mumbled. I had no idea what was wrong.

Making rendezvous with our fighter escort was completely out of the question. We were at least forty-five minutes behind schedule, and I had little idea where we were.

Over intercom I heard the pilot suggesting that maybe we should abort.

"Command here." Colonel Harding revived a little, slurring the words. "The 100th never aborts."

The Luftwaffe were at us. We saw them pop up through the clouds, climb up above, and then slide down at us, their guns blinking.

The 100th got it first and worst.

"Bogeys, twelve o'clock."

Wham. They careened through us, between us and the low squadron.

"Formation control here. They got two out of the low squadron." He was talking strangely.

We flew and flew, just straight ahead.

After what seemed hours of flying I thought we should be in Germany.

When the clouds broke, instead of land, I saw water.

Islands? The Frisians?

Below me I saw a skinny triangular island. Sylt. The Island of Sylt. We were miles from Bremen.

"Radio to command."

Nothing.

"Okay, Radio, what's up?" It was the Pathfinder pilot.

"Sir, we just got the recall."

"Okay, men, let's go home."

"Sir, Radio here, something's funny."

"Okay, Radio."

"The waist gunners are acting strange. They seem to think they are drinking beer. They keep holding up their relief cans and toasting each other."

"Anoxia." It was Colonel Harding, barely audible.

"That's what's wrong."

"Walk-around bottles, all stations."

A few Rogers, but not all.

"Radio, go to all stations, and get 'em on emergency oxygen."

"Roger."

Five minutes later.

"Pilot to all positions. Okay, men, we're taking the formation home."

No one objected.

Two hours later we were on the ground, exhausted, dejected.

A bad beginning for Harry Crosby as Group Navigator of the 100th Bomb Group.

13

NEW JOB: GROUP NAVIGATOR

As Group Navigator of the 100th Bomb Group I was assigned an office, a telephone, an assistant who was a second lieutenant, an enlisted man who was a corporal, half of a double room in the WAAF site with the Group Bombardier, and a jeep.

The perk I enjoyed most was the jeep.

During World War II there were a few physical objects that soldiers, sailors, airmen and airwomen came to love. I am told that G.I.'s became genuinely fond of their mess kits and came to think of them as good luck talismans. I am told that pilots and crews who flew the C-46 Dakota over The Hump in the CBI—when the British flew it they called it the "Hudson"—swore by them. I wouldn't know.

What I do know is that we in the 8AF loved the B-17. We call it "the Big Gas Bird." We gave our planes tender, sexual, vulgar, or humorous names.

Our Baby. Angel's Tit. Marie Helena. Stud Duck. Laden Maiden. Janie. Alice from Dallas. Torchy. Sweater Girl. Raunchy. El Pisstoffo. Phartsac. Mismalovin. Miss Carriage. Our Gal Sal. Miss Chief. Dodie. Ain't Misbehavin'. High Life. The All American Girl. Katie. Lay or Bust. Faithful Forever. Miss Conduct. She Has Ta. Sweet Nancy.

Because of the many times a Fort got our crews back when it could have dropped them into the drink, we were grateful to it—and emotional about it. The sound of a B-17 engine brought tears to the eyes of anyone who ever flew one.

That I know.

I also know that anyone who drove a jeep thought he had a special dispensation from Heaven. Just as a cowboy felt a strong and abiding affection for Old Paint, so did a G.I. care for his steed.

My jeep widened my horizons.

On the next day after the thoroughly botched mission to Sylt, I felt like getting off alone.

At about 1230 hours, I went out to my jeep, put the top down, and began my first tour of the area.

Technically I was not supposed to take the jeep past the M.P. gate, but when I drove up the guard saluted me, said "Laundry run, sir?" and waved me past.

Out I went into the verdant English countryside.

Our base was in lovely East Anglia, and I saw it now as something other than a point on a map. Narrow roads, very green grass on the side. Tiny bridges, only one car wide. Thatched roofs on small cottages. A man walking along the road with a huge scythe. He waved.

I drove up to a pub and stopped. I went in, looked around. There was a huge Square D on the wall just above a dart board. Apparently my friends came here. No one there now.

A head came out through a narrow door.

"Can I help you, mite?"

"A glass of bitters, please."

I had no idea what bitters was, and since the pub-keeper seemed surprised, I decided I had made a mistake.

"Not many Yah-inks tike bitters," he said.

He went to the bar, and pulled down a long handle over a spigot.

At least bitters was something to drink. The mug was at least a quart. "That'll be a bob, mite."

I fumbled with the English coins, paid him, and sat down on a bench beside a long table.

"I guess the plines kime back early t'day."

I said nothing. Loose lips sink ships.

The pubkeeper nodded understandingly and went away.

I drank about a fifth of the bitters, having trouble with it. It was warm. I saw a sign that said "W.C." and went to it. I poured the rest of the beer into the water closet and pulled the chain. English toilets had a very noisy flush.

Back to the jeep, and slowly back to the base, feeling a little heady from the warm beer.

Back on to base, and on a systematic tour of Tech Site. The 100th had several support units, and I resolved to visit them all. At some of the Quonsets or permanent buildings I only put my head in the door and looked around. At most of the places I stopped a moment and talked with whoever was around. I tried to act as though I knew what they did. The 1776th Ordnance Company. 18th Weather Detachment.

869th Chemical Company. 216th Finance Section. 592nd Postal Unit. 1285th Military Police. 2110th Fire Fighting Platooon. 1141st Quartermaster Company. 83rd Service Group. 456th Subdepot. 412th Air Service Group. 838th Air Engineering Squadron. 662nd Air Materiel Squadron. American Red Cross. Royal Air Force.

Everywhere I went the men—or women—were busy. They treated me respectfully, pleased to have the visit. It took all those hundreds of people to get me in the air yesterday when I went to Sylt. I wasted their effort.

I next went along the perimeter where planes taxied from their hard stands to the takeoff strip. Next stop, Flying Control, on the north side of the field.

A square building, like a box. Windows clear across the front. Enlisted men at their desks.

A second lieutenant whom I recognized as the Flying Control officer came up to me.

"Lieutenant Crosby, this is your first visit. Tell me what the new Group Navigator would like to know."

"Just show me around, beginning with the toilet." The beer was getting to me.

After I left Flying Control, I visited places I hardly knew existed. The parachute shop, radio shack, ordnance vault, bomb dump. Then I drove along the perimeter strip and to each hard stand where a group crew was working.

Nearly every hard stand had a pyramidal tent pitched beside it. I thought this was where our ground crews kept their equipment. Now I learned they slept there. They were on duty twenty-four hours a day. They had beds back in their squadron sites, but most of them went back to the squadron only for clean clothes and their mail. They worked, and worked, and worked. Keep 'em flying.

Flyers liked them, respected them, and appreciated them.

During the next few days, I mostly got acquainted with my job.

Nearly every night I went to a movie. Two rows about one third of the way from the front were reserved for the officers who set up the mission. We sauntered in at 1930 hours, watched about two thirds of the movie, and then groaned when a tiny red light went on. Even if the rest of the audience didn't see the red light, when our two rows got up and filed out, everyone in the theater knew we would be flying the next day.

In the course of my time as Group Navigator I must have missed the last reels of some fifty movies. Years later I was still picking up the endings on late-late television programs.

Since I no longer had my close squadron friends I spent more time alone, much of it in the group reading room.

Much of the news was inexact. Stateside reports of our missions were wildly inaccurate. I listened to Axis Sally from Berlin every night and got a better idea from her of whether we hit our targets or not. But I read the news anyway.

Italy had surrendered. Ernie Pyle was writing about it. Germans were still in Milan, but the Italians were now our allies. The Red Army was beginning to push the Germans back, moving slowly along the Dnieper River. In the Pacific and in the China-Burma-India theater our troops and sailors were pushing, pushing, pushing. Chiang Kai-shek was

Supreme Commander in the China-Burma-India the-
ater, the CBI. Workers were constructing the Ledo
Road across North Burma to India. Our C-46's were
flying The Hump. Out in the Pacific, Americans were
fighting for Guadalcanal. General and Madame
Chiang Kai-shek had met with Churchill and
President Roosevelt in Cairo. In Alaska, Attu and
Kiska were names I had not known before. In
England, nine civilians paraded in anger to demand
the opening of a second front.

On the Home Front, the U.S. was continuing to
transfer some 100,000 Japanese-Americans from the
West Coast to inland camps. Robert Frost got a
Pulitzer Prize.

The S-2 officer tried to help our morale. He suggested that we read Robert Scott's *God Is My Co-
Pilot*, Ernie Pyle's *Here Is Your War*, and Ted
Lawson's *Thirty Seconds over Tokyo*. He told us
which movies to see. *Desert Victory* and *Casablanca*.

Except for the reading room, the abortive movies,
and my letters to and from Jean, for the first few
weeks that I was the Group Navigator for the 100th
all I did was work all night preparing the briefings. I
picked up sleep at odd hours, too little of it.

In the last months of 1943 I flew a few missions,
and I did not do very well. Neither did the 100th
during those months, and we lost many planes and
crews.

On December 13, I flew my eighteenth mission.

Faced with the failure of so many missions, 8AF
and 3AD Headquarters were trying to improve the
work of the lead crews. The Pathfinder crews,
castoffs of every group as they were, and flying
planes with bad battle damage, had spotty records.

They had a rough life. They lived in Alconbury, about eighty air miles west of us, and were not permitted to leave the station. Their crews did not have passes because of the secrets they knew. When they were alerted for a mission they got up at 0100 hours, dressed, skipped breakfast, went out to their planes. They never had time to get warm. They took off and flew in the dark, low-level to avoid the German radar screen, to the group with whom they would be flying. That late at night they were in danger of midair collision with RAF Halifaxes and Lancasters threading the area like shuttlecocks. Almost every night some trigger-happy English antiaircraft took a shot at them. As they came into our base, our guards threw a few rounds of .50-calibers at them.

One of the Pathfinders with whom Colonel Harding and I were to fly took off from Alconbury and landed at our base, only to learn the mission had been canceled. They took off, planning to return to Alconbury. Apparently something went wrong with their plane because they barely got off the runway when they crashed near Eye, a village just down the road from us. Since their bomb load was incendiaries, the plane caught fire and exploded. Thirteen men were cremated, along with three farmers and a horse who were in the path of the plane. Bad business.

The Eighth was having enough trouble making rendezvous and flying formation. When a group flew a mission with these crews who were unfamiliar to them, the problem was compounded.

Jack Kidd called me into his office.

"We're going to Kiel with a Pathfinder crew, and I want you to fly with me. I will make the assembly, and you can handle the rendezvous. It's supposed to be CAVU all the way. We go out across the North Sea with the Frisians on our right. We make landfall at the coast, fly across Denmark and then turn south to Kiel. The Pathfinder crew will be backup, but you and I will be doing most of the work."

When Jack and I went out to the takeoff strip to meet the Pathfinder crew, it turned out to be Valesh's crew, now in *Hang the Expense V.*

Almost from the moment Valesh and Kidd started the warm-up procedure I knew that Frank now had a superb crew. They had, as the expression goes, "grown to fit their responsibility." Valesh, as pilot, Al Franklin, as navigator, Jack Johnson, as radar operator worked very well together. Franklin and I cooperated in getting the Thirteenth Wing together and shook hands elaborately when the parts fitted together smoothly.

On the way in, everything went elaborately well. The problem was that just before we hit the I.P., smoke, flak, and clouds drifted over the target, and the bombardier never did see what was supposed to be the P.M.I., the point of maximum impact.

Before Pathfinder, we would have brought our bombs home, and landed with them. Bad.

Now with the help of the Mickey operator, the bombardier dropped his bombs, aiming generally at the whole city.

By the time we got back to the base, the Mosquitoes had landed and developed their strike photos.

Bombing results: Fair. Better than landing with the load.

Seven more missions to go.

On December 24, we were supposed to have something special.

I had little enthusiasm for flying on that day. I remembered that exactly a year before, Brady, Ham, Saul and the rest of the gunners, Ernie Warsaw, and I had pranged into a mountain near Evanston, Wyoming. Now they were all gone. I didn't know whether they were KIA, POW, or what. All I knew was that they were gone.

I still had the sprig of Scottish heather the woman had given me, but I wasn't sure how much longer the spell would hold.

This time, leading the whole task force, I flew with Chick Harding, still a sick man. General LeMay called him on the scrambler. "Chick, you've got to get this one. You are going after the labs where the Germans are plotting a lot of trouble for us." That's all we knew. The target was labeled "Secret."

We were in the overcast all the way, with the Pathfinder radar operator feeding the crew navigator and me fixes that seemed to make sense. I was increasingly impressed at how well the crew on *Hang the Expense V* worked together. I felt strange about bombing a target I never saw.

At 1600 hours the next day, Christmas, we had turkey and ham, mashed potatoes, gravy, sweet potatoes, corn, peas, cranberry sauce, rolls, pickles, cake, ice cream, and three kinds of pie. We invited 150 kids from the surrounding villages, and they ate as though they had never seen such food.

On December 31, we were alerted for a mission. I left the movie, put the kits together, and went to my quarters. Planning to get up at 11:30 to go to the New Year's Eve festivities at the Officers' Club, I lay down, put out the light.

I slept through, missing the party.

At 0300, the phone rang. "Captain Crosby, it's time for you to come to Ops."

New Year's Day. The mission was scrubbed.

On January 4, 1944, for my twentieth mission, we went back to Kiel. Since it was not the 100th's turn to lead, neither Jack Kidd, Chick Harding, nor I had to fly. We were low group, Tail-End Charlie. Because I felt I had failed when we were there before and now we had to go back, I put myself in the 100th lead plane.

The Germans expected us. There weren't many fighters, but the flak was a black, angry carpet. Almost every plane lost an engine or two, and our planes looked like sieves.

We hit the target, dead on, and I felt vindicated.

As we came in over the field, most of the planes sent up red-reds. Wounded aboard.

On February 3, my twenty-first, this time to Wilhelmshaven, it was the same. The Germans had some new antiaircraft or their gunners had improved with practice. We even saw our fighter escort get hit with flak.

At this time we had another shake-up in our leadership and John Bennett, the new guy from Texas who had done a good job leading several missions, became Squadron Commander of the 349th. Word was out that he was a terror.

Now I had to deal with him.

Bennett had been floating around the base for about a month. He was older than most of us, uptight, stern. We heard he was from Texas but he talked funny. When he told me he went to Princeton, I decided that was where he got it.

He was everywhere. I never saw him at the

Officers' Club, but I saw him plenty at Group Ops. I would be working at my desk, and I would hear something—and realize he had been standing there watching me. He sat down beside the clerk who typed the report of each mission and corrected his spelling, especially his own name.

"The name is Bennett," he would say, "With two *t*'s."

I got a call from Captain Ed Dahill, S-1, Personnel, at 3AD.

"Harry, you have a guy with you now named John Bennett. Watch out for him."

"Why?"

"I think he is some kind of spy. The 100th has had so many losses that they are checking up on you."

"It's about time."

"This guy Bennett is from San Antonio, a member of one of the richest families in Texas. They own the biggest bank in the state and the second biggest ranch. His sisters and cousins are married to half of the big shot generals in the Air Force. When cadets went through Randolph and Kelly, the girls knew which ones to grab."

Bennett unnerved us all. It became good form at the Officers' Club to imitate him: "Sergeant, repeat after me, in the future we will not, repeat not, urinate on the flowers."

"I want to get experience under every circumstance," he said. He flew in the right seat for high and low squadron lead. He flew on the wing, in left and right seat, pilot and copilot. I think he even flew one mission as a tail gunner.

On one mission, when he was filling in as a pilot of a wing plane, his plane got hit over the Rally Point and the electrical system cut out.

That night his copilot had much to say.

"That bastard isn't human. He's a machine. There we were, dropping seven hundred feet a minute, and I wanted to hit the bell. Then I realized with our power out, the bell wouldn't ring.

"All the while that son of a bitch was sitting there fiddling with the standby electrical system, showing about as much excitement as if he was cleaning his fingernails.

"Then the dials flip into position, and we've got power. We're dropping about five hundred feet per, but one by one he pops the engines, and we've got a bird again.

"He slacks back and says to me, smiling like, 'Now, let's get back in the formation, Lieutenant,' he says."

In the 418th, Ev Blakely was trying to shape up the squadron. Most of the crews were still imbued with the idea that raunch was the way to go. Blake's pilots were not eager to tuck their wings into the waist window of their element leaders, and gunners were not convinced that their guns should be ready at takeoff time. No one expected to get in at night from the pubs in time for gate closing. Blake went into his job expecting his squadron to like him, but they were finding him too tough to handle. He was always on the prowl. At night he carried a "torch" around with him so he could inspect his squadron area. Instead of batteries, the flashlight had a device which he squeezed to make the light work. Wherever he went, the squadron could hear him coming, squeeze, squeeze, squeeze.

When the 100th flew again to Norway, to bomb the heavy-water plants for the atom bomb, Bennett turned out to be a superb command pilot.

Maybe you didn't like the guy, but you had to respect him.

On February 13, we were alerted for a "Crossbow." At the time the Germans were demolishing English cities and industrial plants with their V-1 buzz bombs and their V-2 rockets which they launched from huge platforms that looked like roller coasters or reverse ski slopes.

"Go get 'em," said General LeMay.

I set myself up to fly with Valesh and his splendid crew. When the phone rang, it was 0200 hours instead of 0300.

"You and Valesh's crew are going to fly with the 385th."

In a rush we hurried to Hang the Expense V and took off, flying at about eight hundred feet to Great Ashfield. When we got there, a young, slim, full colonel came up in a jeep and climbed through the nose hatch into the pilots' compartment.

Two hours later, our formation together, we made a dogleg as we crossed the coast.

The colonel came on intercom.

"Crosby, look at your 100th."

I stood up in my compartment and looked out the celestial dome. There, as high group of the wing behind us, were the Square D's. All the other groups were in tight formation, but the 100th was all over the sky.

The command pilot came back on.

"That's why all the other groups like to fly with the 100th. The Luftwaffe go to them instead of to us."

I remember that mission well. Our waist gunner was killed, an unusually messy death. A 20-millimeter shell from a JU-88 hit him, and exploded. I went back to the waist to administer morphine, but I didn't know which part of him to put the needle in.

But almost as bad as that death was what the colonel had shown me. He said the rest of the Air Force liked to fly with the 100th because we got the Luftwaffe attacks.

CHAPTER 14

GOING NATIVE

✈ Being Group Navigator was different from
being on a crew. I was combat, but I was also staff
and expected to fit in with the high rank.

As Group Navigator, I had to decide what uniform
to wear. As long as I had on my leather A-2 flight
jacket and ate in the Flying Mess, I was dutifully acting like a soldier. When I ate in the Officers' Mess, I
wore my Class A blouse with all my ribbons, the blue
combat patch behind my wings, and the diagonal
gold slash on my sleeve to show I had been overseas
six months. When I ate there I noticed that Jack Kidd,
John Bennett, and I were the only staff flying officers
who still had the grommet in our hats.

In the Air Force, a flyer wanted to be "hot." He
wanted to be able to handle his liquor and his
women. When he got his picture taken, he wanted to
look like a "rock," short for "hot rock." When a rock

went into the air and put on his radio headset, the stiff top of his hat kept his headset from fitting close to his ears. So out came the stiff wire circular grommet.

It never went back in, and the hat with the "hundred mission crush" was born. The more disreputable the hat, the better for the rock.

In the Officers' Club, I felt something was wrong.

You don't dress up to fight a war.

Besides the dining room, the Officers' Club had the lounges, bar, poker tables, bridge games, and magazines. Because of my still-retained prudishness, I did not like the drinking and gambling at the Officers' Club. I did not feel comfortable with the braggadocio of the flyers who had ten or fifteen missions. At the Officers' Club bar, double double in hand, they latched onto the new crews and tried to flak them up with yarns about how rough the bogeys were. I would look around and there would be clusters around a rock. The rock would have his hands out, flat and in formation. Then his right hand would change from a B-17 wingman to an ME-109. His face would contort into a tat-tat-tat, and his hand would batter the air as it sprayed out imaginary 20-millimeter shells.

I got enough of that from the real enemy.

I felt strange about having a good time in England. Okay, we were flying combat. Okay, the Eighth Air Force combat losses were higher than those of any other military service. Our one air force, the Eighth, was losing more men than the entire U.S. Navy.

When I was flying on a crew, my whole life was flying, and recovering from it. I lived with combat crews. I ate with them in the Flying Mess, with the fresh eggs, Canadian bacon, and fresh orange juice.

When I joined Eager Beaver Blakely's crew, I spent most of my time in training, and I was exhausted. As my missions stretched out and I flew less often, I missed my friends who went down. When I went on pass, I usually checked in at a Red Cross club and I spent most of my time sleeping, trying to recover from the exhaustion of altitude, responsibility—and loss.

It didn't seem right that after a mission I could go down to London and see a stage show. The G.I.s on Guam or at Kiska spent the night in their foxholes.

It got to me.

Now that I was Group Navigator I might lead a task force to Germany and then not fly a mission for a month. During that month, my friends went down or home. When I thought of my friends, Sergeant Lyle Nord, Hambone, Brady, Charlie Via, Ernie Warsaw, Jim Scott, or Sumner Reeder, I had to sort them out, KIA, MIA, POW, stateside hospital, interned in Switzerland, or rotated.

It got to me.

I found myself rather numb to it all. I did my job, but I don't remember much of it.

I was on a train compartment on the way to London. Sitting across from me was a tall, raw-boned Englishman, his hands calloused. He was not well shaved. Maybe he had been drinking. He kept looking at me.

"Yah-ink," he said. "You are different from the rest of them."

I thought I knew what he meant. In fact, I had often wondered what the staid British thought of Air Corps sloppiness. It was wrong for me. I was not raunch, or undisciplined, or sloppy; I was Class A, disciplined, G.I.

"Thank you," I said.

"What do you mean, thah-ink you? I like the others better. Yah-inks are not like us. They are Yah-inks."

I was boiling. What a rude guy! Wishing to avoid an international incident, I elected not to respond to him. Instead I buried my face in *Stars and Stripes*, the service newspaper. But his remark stung.

I remembered what my father said: "Only fight the fights you can win." What was I trying to prove?

When I got to London I checked in at Grosvenor House and slept from twenty-hundred hours till oh-eight-hundred. Then I located an American PX—and bought an Air Corps hat. Instead of felt it was a kind of twill or canvas. I removed the grommet before I even tried it on. I noticed that the chunky, well-formed little Irish clerk smiled at me when I took it out.

"You're a flyer, Yank," she said.

I put the hat on, and cast it at a rakish angle.

The Irish girl smiled. "This is the best job in London to meet aviators, but the best ones are married." She had seen my wedding ring.

"Does that matter?"

"It matters with me."

Back at the hotel I went into the bathroom. Buck naked, I stood before the mirror. I put the hat on. I tried it at several angles, over one eye and then the other. I pushed it back, with just the appropriate carelessness.

"Crosby," I told myself, "you are a rock."

I remembered reading about the British who went to the colonies in India and Africa. They wore their sun helmets and their whites. They shaved.

Time passed.

They grew a beard and left it untrimmed. They turned to gin and native girls. They went barefoot.

They went native.

Had I gone native?

Men at war were different from men at home. Whatever they were stateside, they were more of in England. Whatever was good in them became very good; what was bad became very bad.

Whatever feeling men—or the men-boys I was associating with—normally had for women, it was intensified in England. We needed women, and we missed them. As I came to know them, I observed that married men seemed to need women even more than the bachelors did.

Those were good years for us to enjoy women.

Glamour was in. At movies we saw Betty Grable, Rita Hayworth, Lana Turner, Jane Russell, Greer Garson, Bette Davis, and Ann Sheridan, all of whom had "oomph." On the radio we heard Ginnie Simms, Helen Forrest, Dinah Shore, and Helen O'Connell, and we heard the Andrews Sisters' plea that we not "sit under the apple tree with anyone else but me."

Cheesecake was much more important than Spam. When Betty Grable posed for the pinup picture in that white bathing suit while seductively looking back over her shoulder at the camera, when Hayworth, looking boldly at us, posed in a bed with that filmy negligee, when Jane Russell posed in the haymow with her blouse tantalizingly off the shoulder, they did more good for the troops than if they sank a German battleship.

When I think back over those days and my thoughts roam to English girls and women I feel a deep sense of gratitude. They served, in their way.

They served, as American women and girls did, in the ways that would make feminists proud. They ferried our planes across the Atlantic. They talked us in through the overcast. If you want to know how gratitude can feel, think of being in a B-17, or any aircraft, with two engines out, with a hole in your starboard wing and two of your crew dying of shell fire. Then think of being lost. You are in white, fleecy clouds, and you can hardly see the tips of your wings. Then think of a woman's voice, coming in to your headset: "It's all right, Yah-ink, I'll get you in." Then her British voice from Flying Control nestles you down, "Eye-zy, mite, you're just starboard of the glide path. Heading two-fy-uv-nigh-yun."

The mind boggles, the heart flutters, the eyes mist.

That role, and the myriad other official services performed by women during World War II should make the most dedicated feminist very proud. I hope they also understand and take pride in how much we men appreciated the other role that women played. When women were what we thought of then as womanly, or female, they were wonderful.

American women were marvelous during World War II. They truly served—in both ways. They served as Rosie the Riveter, and in the Women's Auxiliary Corps, the WAC. But still they were women. When I show my young friends in the 1990s pictures of girls in the 1940s, the women of today say about the women of that yesterday, "Girls wore nicer clothes then," or, "Such pretty hair styles." The goal was glamour, and men appreciated it. The music that floated around them was part of it. Big bands and swing music and songs like "That Old Black Magic" and "There, I've Said It Again" were made for romance.

But American girls were in America.

English girls were in England.

And so were we.

Maybe never in history was there so perfect a fit between the women that men needed and the men that women needed.

If a forty-year-old fat captain ordnance officer wanted to cycle down the road and spend the evening with a pleasant, robust woman his age, he could find her, or she found him. She might sit there knitting, and he might be writing a letter home to his wife, but that was what he wanted. She enjoyed his company and the chocolate cake he brought from the mess hall.

I think we were surprised at how well we got along with English girls.

Reserved? As the expression went, "We never had it so good." Every man who came back from pass had a story to tell.

Many of the young soldiers were overwhelmed by the hundreds of prostitutes walking along Piccadilly. Many were pretty. They were all anxious to please. The price was two pounds, about eight dollars. There was a girl for every taste.

Every fly-boy had a different version of his conversation with the French girls. With their dark-rimmed eyes, long lashes, rouged cheeks, slim skirts, strapped bodices, they spoke of a different kind of love for sale: "Lieutenant, I will take you to zee clouds, higher zan you have ever been before. Zen I will bring you down, happier zan you have ever been."

The French girls had staked Duke Street out as their own special province. If any competitor encroached on their territory, they were warned off by the fierce growling of a Dalmatian dog that was standard equipment for the ladies from Paris. We heard the French accented threats: "Buzz off! Do you want my dog, or my knife?" Click!

If a twenty-year-old Nebraska farm boy wanted to indulge his wildest sexual fantasy there was a Piccadilly Commando on Duke Street in London.

And there was everything else.

Many of the prostitutes were bright, witty, well-dressed. One of them, Maria, plied her trade near the Officers' Mess at the Grosvenor, where I ate. Although I never sampled her wares, she recognized me each time I was there. When I was promoted, she noticed. "Hello, Yah-ink, no longer a leftenant? A captain navigator?" At another time, she asked, "Any rough missions, Yah-ink? Want to tell me about them in my room??

Loose lips sink ships. No thanks. Good-bye, Maria.

There was a blonde buxom young woman, probably from a farm but now serving in the Land Army. Standing on a Piccadilly street corner, she said, "I am not a whore but I need two quid and I know what you need. We could spend the evening together at the pictures and end up in your hotel. Do you want to have a go at it?"

Business was brisk for the professionals, but there was really no need for them. There were plenty of other English girls who were friendly to the Americans. Many of them were decent, attractive young women who surprised the Americans by being compliant. Americans believed that nice girls didn't; in England, many nice girls did.

There were nice English girls at the Red Cross clubs who only wanted to dance and learn to jitterbug. There were mature women at the English Speaking Union who liked to take Americans on a tour of the Parliament. For some, sex was not an issue; for some it very much was.

We were a temptation for them. When I was in the 418th our first sergeant told me he was dating a girl in London. The girl told her mother, who said, "Your Yank makes more in a day than your father makes in a month. You will be able to go places I have never gone. Of course, you should do your part to keep the Americans happy. I would."

Another story along the same line. I talked to a farmer on the base. "I never thought I would let her do it. But one of your master sergeants, even without flying pie, gets more in a fortnit than I mike in a year. If I went to the Dorchester Hotel in London, they would look at my jib and keep me out. When my girlie goes to London with her Yah-ink, they sty at the Dorchester." He stopped and thought, "Her laddie is in Eyefrica with Monty's desert rats." With a little translation I got his point.

Besides Jean's wonderful letters, I think that what kept me reasonably true to her was my own exhaustion. When I became Group Navigator and could schedule my three-day passes in advance, I learned that I could rent a room in one of the finest hotels in the world, the Grosvenor House, for about twelve dollars. The price included a hefty breakfast of kippers, powdered eggs, tomatoes, and black tea, which in those days was wonderfully tasty. I often slept twelve hours without waking up. Then I soaked and scalded in a huge tub, drying myself with a thick towel kept warm by a combination radiator and hanging rack. Then I had dinner at the

Officers' Mess in the hotel and saw, on occasion, Jimmy Doolittle, Omar Bradley, and Dwight Eisenhower. I happened to sit with a WAC full colonel and figured out that she was Oveta Culp Hobby. Then, rested, I went back to the base, ready to face the enemy, or—what was worse—wait for days to face the enemy.

Jean's letters. The same stationery. Dainty. Feminine. Brown on tan. Distinctive, always the same, always to Lieutenant and then Captain and then Major Harry H. Crosby, always from Mrs. Harry H. Crosby.

It wasn't till the end of the war that I learned why there was always "another one today." Jean soon learned that many days went when the whole base got no mail. Maybe a U-boat got the transport that day. Maybe our bag of mail was off-loaded for a Pratt & Whitney engine. Whatever.

Addressing her letter to "Postal Officer, 100th Bomb Group, Station 139, APO 559, ETO," she wrote, "On some days, maybe every two weeks to keep the dates right, I will write several letters to my husband who is the Group Navigator on your station. I hope you will instruct your mail orderlies never to give Captain Crosby more than one letter per day. In this way they will accumulate. When there is no letter for him that day, it would be good of you to provide him one from the reservoir. I am sorry to be imposing upon you in this way but, as you may know, his tour has been protracted, and I hope that this little conspiracy will help make his life more endurable."

I should have suspected. The dates told me nothing because our mail often got mixed up. One shipload went faster, or more direct, than another. Even so I should have wondered how it could have been I would get a letter when no one else would.

Her letters were works of art, routinized, but dear, a paragraph about how the war was going in other theaters, a paragraph about how she, Ham's wife, and Blake's wife were doing. She told me how she and Ev's wife tried to console Ham's wife. He'll be okay, they promised. Perhaps her letter had a paragraph with news from our mutual friends at the University of Iowa; always there was a paragraph about her job. She worked for radio station WLS, first as an assistant to the news director and then with her homemaker's program, then with a discussion of plays, books, and movies. Then a caring, loving message about our feelings for each other. I read each letter no less than ten times.

I was in my quarters, writing to Jean.

My phone rang. It was Ellis Scripture.

Scrip was now the Third Air Division Navigator, working on the staff of General LeMay.

"Croz, Dot is in England."

Dot, the girl who was special to me before I married Jean.

"What? Is she ferrying planes?"

"No, she's in the Red Cross."

I asked where she is.

"At the Red Cross club in Cambridge."

I thought about it for a while, several days.

Then I phoned her. I had trouble getting her. When the operator said, "Trunks heah," I didn't know what she meant.

"Then press button B for further instruction."

I finally got Dot.

"Yes, Harry, I would like to see you."

Way behind in passes, I had no trouble scheduling myself for a three-day.

I was with Dot three times.

At Cambridge we "did" the town, the university, the museums, the theater, the wonderful, wonderful pubs. We walked along the Cam. She stayed at her quarters and I stayed in a private home recommended by the USO.

We went to London twice together.

In London, I had it all. The rank, the medals, the wings—and an attractive American Red Cross girl. There were places in London that British girls could not go, like the Officers' Mess at the Grosvenor Hotel. Dot could use the London PX and buy clothing unavailable to an English girl. We could use USO and Red Cross tickets to the theaters on Piccadilly Circus. I was conscious of eyes on us, a lovely American Red Cross girl with her Air Force captain, a rock, with all those ribbons.

I had an idyll going. Plenty of flying pay. Letters every day from a wife I loved very much. Respect on the base. Good seats at the movie. My own jeep. A shower which I shared with only three officers. Lots of interesting friends on the base. A batman to pick up my laundry and cart it back and forth to the laundry lady just outside the base. I could at times forget the missing crews.

So far I had come back on all the missions.

And I had Dot.

Was this too much?

There was Jean at home caring about me. When her picture appeared, all legs and smiles in the

Chicago Tribune with Gerry Hamilton and Margaret Ann Blakely, she got a series of calls from men who wanted to take her out—and she refused. And here I was with Dot. Dot and I were ridiculously moral. We stayed in different hotel rooms.

Through the years I have come to believe that it rarely works out for a married man to have any kind of affair—even as innocent as mine was with Dot—with a woman who is not his wife. But it is worse for him to confess, and expect his wife to forgive him. When he keeps silent, he at least carries on his own shoulders the burden of guilt. When he confesses to his wife, he shifts the burden to her—and expects her to be "understanding." It is his choice, and he should suffer the consequences, not dump them on his wife.

I confessed to Jean. I wrote her a letter telling her that Dot was in England, that I had seen her in Cambridge and London.

I remember her response.

"I married you, Binger, because I love you and I look forward to whatever life we will have together. Now we are separate and living by rules different in war than in peace. All I can say is that you should do what is right for you, and I will try to understand."

That was more than I could handle.

I did not end the matter well with Dot.

I wrote her and told her that I could not betray Jean, which was unfair to Dot because I don't think she would have permitted that anyway. I told her we had to cancel our next meeting in London and I could not see her again.

She did not answer. I heard later that she had married the drummer in an Air Force band. I never saw her again, but even now I think occasionally of her. I realize that having her in my life before I married Jean contributed in some way to what I was, at least to my confidence. I think she helped.

I shall always be grateful to her.

CHAPTER
15

LEARNING ABOUT AMERICANS FROM THE BRITISH

In October, when we got shot up over Bremen, our crew was scheduled to go to the flak shack. Our gunners went, but when Blake became Squadron Commander of the 418th and Doug and I moved up to headquarters, we were too busy with our new jobs to leave the base.

When I got my feet more or less under me, I applied again for R&R. Instead, the Group Adjutant, Major Karl Standish, came into my office.

"The Allied Command has scheduled a high-level conference to see what can be done about the problems we are having with fraternization on the one hand and squabbling among the Allies on the other. I think you might find it interesting. It's at Oxford University."

For two weeks beginning February 21, 1944, I "studied" and "conferred" at Oxford University, one of the high points, intellectually, of my life.

It was all very official. In the usual cryptic fashion, my orders read, "The foll named personnel will proceed on TD for app fourteen (14) days o/a 21 Feb 44 fr Sta 139 to Balliol College, Oxford University to carry out instructions of the Commanding General, Eighth Air Force, and upon completion of this temp dy, return to proper station." Then, on one line, my name, rank, and serial number. The next two paragraphs described the finances: While on "TD," I was to get four dollars a day for "qrs" and $1.25 for "rats," an elegant way of abbreviating "quarters" and "rations." I was provided an additional two dollars a day for "subsistence."

I became a member of Balliol College and had a place to stay in the "court." Billeting was mixed. Americans were not quartered with each other, but with other nationalities. When I arrived I learned that my flat mate, Subaltern A. M. Wingate, would arrive two days later. I didn't even know whether a "sub-all-turn" was a private or a general.

The conferees were from all the Allied countries, British, Canadian, French, Dutch, Polish, the Low Countries, the other occupied nations, the U.S., the works. They were all ranks, from private to general and admiral, more high rank than lower. I was honored to be among them.

I had never seen as erudite a group of men as the Oxford faculty who worked with us. A. D. Lindsay, Master of Balliol. When I heard him lay out our schedule, I knew I wasn't in for R&R. I knew there would be precious little "rest." A. L. Goodhart, of University College. When he contrasted American character to British personality, I felt he helped me understand my strict Calvinist background and, because of it, my near obsession with responsibility and the work ethic. John Lowe, Dean of Christ Church. In a serious but funny way he told us what Oxford stood for. "Let us now praise famous men," he said, and I was humbled to learn who had studied in the very seats where we sat. F. A. Burchardt. He had something to do with statistics, which he used to make sense of international trade and cooperation. Deane Jones, from Merton College. He was really telling us about the "Making of the British State," but in contrast I got new insights into American history and the United States Constitution. A British major general, L. A. Hawes, explained their colonial system by tracing England's relationship to India. I suspect that he deliberately chose India because whenever we Americans got too close with questions about Englishmen and "the white man's burden," he would subtly bring up how we treated our own "Indians," the native Americans. For Deane Jones, history didn't just mean wars; it included sociology, economics, and literature.

At the sherry hour, 4:00 P.M., we were invited to a "musical evening" as guests of Miss Margaret Deneke and Dr. Ernest Walker. "It will be," we were told, "laid on at Gunfield." Gunfield was "next to Lady Margaret Hall," wherever that was.

On the second day, Giles Allison, the Balliol don who was in charge of the whole project, got us going again with his analysis of what causes progress. "The inventors, the poets, the missionaries, the soldiers, the politicians, they all make contributions, but the heroes unsung for their contribution to progress are the trimmers."

"What's a trimmer?"

"On a small boat, the trimmer is the fellow who moves to the side of the boat that is highest. His weight puts the boat back on the straight and level.

"The same thing works in history and politics. Progress may come when the Have-not fights against the Have, or the Liberal against the Conservative, or the Progressive against the Reactionary, but more often it comes from the man in the dominant party who sees what is wrong with his own group. Since he is respected in his own party, he can help it improve. Since he is part of the system, and understands it, he knows what needs to be done. Since he has succeeded in the system, his opinion is respected."

His point was somewhat less than subtle. We were selected because of our position in the system. We were expected to be trimmers.

The classes were demanding. During the first two days, in a crash course which was to be the foundation for later discussion and problem solving, Professor Giles Allison and several other dons took us through two thousand years of European and American history.

With only a short break, we worked from 9:00 A.M. till 4:00 P.M.—and I relished working again on the civilian clock, not oh-nine-hundred hours till sixteen hundred. I wrote so fast in my notebook that my fingers ached. We stopped at eleven for "cho-coh-lot," but I used the time to organize my thoughts.

The professors—or "dons"—actually wore their robes to class. As much as they had to say, the dons still managed to get us to participate in the discussion. Uncomfortably I realized how little I knew about England and continental Europe. I knew nothing about what Giles Allison called "the history of ideas." Zeitgeist? The Greek view of life? Classicism? Feudalism? Romanticism? Gothicism? Victorianism?

Lord David Cecil, who lectured on the plays of Shakespeare, gave me an opportunity to observe British nobility up close. Interesting sort of duck, he was. Tall, aquiline face, self-effacing, quick to make fun of himself and his own pretensions.

Till my roommate arrived, I enjoyed being alone in the "flat." It had two bedrooms, a bathroom, a large sitting room with a wicker sofa, two wicker chairs, a fireplace. Each morning a batman came in, stirred up the fire, and served me steaming, bitter tea.

A major problem we studied was excessive intimacy between the sexes. Americans liked British women and girls, who in turn liked Americans.

That was the rub.

From Africa, the British "Desert Rats" who were fighting across the Sahara with General Montgomery learned that their wives back home were "shacking up" with American soldiers. They learned that their daughters were pregnant from American G.I.s. Members of other Allied armies complained that we received unfair advantages.

The Allied High Command tried to do something about it. We were encouraged to raise our savings allotments of war bonds to keep our money at home instead of spending it in Piccadilly. Some towns were placed off limits for Americans. We were given lectures by the chaplain.

The Allied Conference at Oxford University was another attempt to face the problem.

At the end of the second day, a break. "We've got some lighter moments laid on for you," said Dr.

Lindsay. A walking tour of Oxford. While we were on the streets, aged men, left over from earlier wars, stared at our rank and tossed stiff salutes. An "informal party at Rhodes House, with dancing," given by the "warden" of Rhodes House, C. K. Allen, and Mrs. Allen. A "warden"? Sounded like a prison. As guests of the British Council, whatever that was, we would see Noel Coward's *Design for Living* at the playhouse. Be sure to bring your gas masks, the invitation said. "Since townspeople are getting slack at carrying their masks, the Lord High Mayor has decreed that they will not be admitted into a public place unless they are carrying their masks."

The play was a happy choice because the first act took place in "Otto's studio in Paris," the second act in "Leo's flat in London," and the third in "Ernest's apartment in New York."

The play had been brought up to date. In the third act we could hear a record player, with Harry James and "I'm beginning to see the light" playing softly in the background. In the English flat, the background music was Vera Lynn singing "When the lights go on again, all over the world." In Paris, it was Marlene Dietrich singing "Lili Marlene."

I was more at ease at sherry time than I was during the classes. In the classes I could barely keep up. At sixteen-hundred hours, it was quite a different story.

Most of my "classmates" were much older and higher ranked than I was. If a British officer had a hat with a red band, he was a brigadier or above, and there were many red bands. Only the U.S. had sent enlisted men. The only branches who had sent lower-ranked younger officers were the USAF and the women's groups.

As a navigator who felt he had been promoted more slowly than the pilots, I sympathized with the women officers who were with us. Although they were, judging by their competence and brightness, the pick of WRENs, WAAF, WAC, the Army Territorial Service, the Women's Land Army, NAAFI, and Red Cross, not one of them had the equivalent rank of anything higher than major.

Maybe at first there was a spot of tension. We heard, once again, the "overpaid, oversexed, and over here" lament. To our credit, I heard no American give the pat response, "Yeah, and the British are underpaid, undersexed, and under Eisenhower."

I heard an RAF group captain—the equivalent of our full colonel—say, "We fly at night and you Yah-inks fly during the day, but you are the ones who have I.L.S., the Instrument Landing Service. When we come back after a long one, and our station is fogged in, we have to land at your airfields and see the food you get."

At the sherry hour, besides their faculty and the students, Giles Allison invited several Oxford townspeople. At first I was put off by them. They were a horsy lot, long in the nose, tweedy, the women big hipped, in olive drab cotton stockings, the men in loose jackets with patches on their elbows. When one of them laughed, it was with a pinched, elevated nose, pursed, rounded lips, and a two-syllable "Huh-kwuh."

I soon realized they were informed, witty, and extremely interested in the young American flyers. They were interested in me. That made a difference.

When I noticed that most of the civilian Englishmen wore bow ties I commented that I had always wanted to learn to tie one of them.

"What do you wear at full dress parties?"

"Oh, I have a bow tie, but I bought it already tied."

The Englishman looked at me for a moment; then he said slowly, "I don't think we would consider that sporting."

I met one elderly lady, tall, sturdy, veddy British. She was introduced as Lady Tweedsmuir.

"Oh, Captain Harry Crosby? My word, you have your initials at more places than Winnie does."

I didn't get it.

Initials? Winnie?

Bang! I caught it.

Oh, yes, although I had never thought about it before, there was an H and a C on the water faucets in every British bathroom. Hot and Cold. But Winnie?

Oh, yes, Winnie, Winston Churchill, W.C.

In England the toilets are called water closets, and they are identified by "W.C." on the door. Yes, I guess that H.C. on the hot and cold water taps did appear in more places than W.C. on the water closets. Clever, this old gal.

Lady Tweedsmuir invited all the young Americans to her home for sherry the next day to meet "another American," her friend, "Tom Eliot."

I begged off. I had just been informed that my delayed flat mate would arrive then and I thought I should go back to my quarters and be sure it was in decent shape to welcome Sub-all-turn Wingate.

I learned, but I learned later, that Lady Tweedsmuir was Mrs. John Buchan. Her husband was the author of *The Thirty-nine Steps*, *Greenmantle*, *Mr. Steadfast*, *The Four Hostages*, and many other novels. I had seen the movie of *The Thirty-nine Steps*. Mrs. Buchan had just come back from Canada. Her guest, whom Lady Tweedsmuir called "Tom," was T. S. Eliot, the American turned British poet.

When I got back to what the dons called my "digs," I saw that the batman had the place in good order, even to a cheery blaze going in the fireplace. By twenty-one-hundred hours, when I returned from the talk in the common room, Sub-all-turn Wingate was still missing.

I decided to take a turn around the court and look at the stars. It would be great to see them and not worry whether the sky would be clear to get a bomber formation together in the morning.

When I returned, I opened the door and—startled—said, "Oh, excuse me."

A woman, a pretty woman, looked at me and smiled. "Come in. You must be Captain Crosby."

"I am." I caught on quick. "And I see that the subaltern turns out to be in the ATS, the Army Territorial Service, instead of the British army."

She smiled again. "You expected a man?"

The smile remained. "And we pronounce it 'subble-trun' instead of 'sub-all-turn.'"

We talked for a while. She had signed her name "A. M. Wingate," because, she said, "We are encouraged by the ATS to conceal our feminine names." That's why the bursar put her with an American officer.

"I suspect we can maintain a decent existence. Your wife has nothing to fear from me. We can take turns with the W.C. and bath. We have our separate bedrooms."

Her first name was Alexandra, which she had shortened to Landra. She was a Scot, a graduate of

Lady Margaret's at the University of Edinburgh. She was attractive in a clear-eyed, straight-on sort of way, average height, brown short hair, nice figure, pretty legs even in the cotton stockings.

When she started attending our sessions at Balliol the eyes of all the men turned to her. The young officers swarmed around her.

Intellectually she soon became a force in the discussions. When a pompous Indian army brigadier made a rather extravagant statement, she said, "Sir, I feel I must challenge you on that." She did, and demolished his assertion, all in a very nice way. When I complimented her on her logic, she said, "I was good at games at university."

"It is natural," she told me the next evening, "that since I am a Scot, I drink Scotch." When I went to get her a drink, I asked, "Have you acquired the American habit of taking ice?"

Firmly: "In Scotland we believe that Scotch should never be diluted."

I asked Landra what her job was and got a noncommittal answer. For security reasons it was at the time considered bad form to press a person about his or her duties, and I did not ask more questions.

As I came to know her, I was amazed at her command of languages. "Let's see," I said. "You seem to speak several languages."

She smiled. "Yes, the only language here that gives me trouble is American."

All during the conference, no matter what the announced subject for discussion, we always kept returning to two knotty problems, disharmony among the Allies and too much harmony between the genders.

"It isn't a matter only of forward American men taking advantage of willing English girls," the statistician said. "If it goes on the way it has started, we estimate that 60,000 English girls, after they have married their American boyfriends from the Eighth Air Force, will have to adjust to American life."

The purpose of the conference was not to come up with some kind of plans for solutions, but to encourage an increased understanding among ourselves. Because we were in key positions in our commands, it was hoped that we might eventually contribute to making improvements.

Because I operated on the very lowest military level, I had no idea of the jockeying going on in the ETO among the brass. I did not know of the rivalry between Montgomery and Eisenhower. I did not know that until the U.S. Army Air Corps became the U.S. Air Force it suffered in disputes with the Royal Air Force about daylight versus night bombing, bomber escort versus attack bombing, and so on. Until Hap Arnold, my top boss, got those extra stars, he was outranked—and ignored.

All the other services were frank about their problems with the Americans. I learned that as an American captain on flight pay I got a bigger salary than the highest British admiral at the program. "Captain Crosby," an admiral said, "your blouse and trousers are twill. Mine are barathea because that's all I can afford."

A Polish officer added, "My uniform is left over from World War I."

The English language came in for some knocks. "How can you defend a language which has *pi*, *pin*, *pint*, and *pinto* in it?" a Polish officer asked. "Every time you add a consonant you change the sound of the vowel."

One member of the RAF, an Australian, often came in for a ribbing about his language. When he told us how much he liked "American khaki color," we puzzled until we realized that was how he pronounced "Coca-Cola." He didn't like English chocolate because it tasted "sipey," with the first syllable rhyming with "pipe." What he meant was "soapy."

Trying to keep calm, we each told what we found both admirable and objectionable about people from the other countries. All the Allies were grateful that the Americans had come across the Atlantic to help, but a Frenchwoman was bitter. "The English didn't come across the Channel until it was too late."

We Americans admired our Allies for their brave fight against the Germans and Italians. We objected to the British smoking in the "cinemas." To us, their cigarettes smelled repulsive, and the odor permeated the theaters, particularly in the balconies.

My new friends objected to American spitting. I had never noticed it before and I began to think about it. Yes, American soldiers, as they walked along the green in Diss, or St. James's Park in London, everywhere, felt free to hawk up and spit out a glob.

The flyers thought the infantry had the toughest war, and the infantry thought the airmen had it worst. "When we get hit," one corpsman said, "we don't have so far to fall."

What rankled the men from the other countries most was the American way with women.

"You Americans are, I judge, a bit more zesty about sex than we of the U.K. are," tutted one British army brigadier.

"Yes," said the RAF Group Captain, "most of your planes have pictures of nude women on them." A pretty little WREN told us about her reactions. "I work in Flying Control. When a Yah-ink crew lands at our base, I sometimes am shocked at what's pinted on the back of their flight jackets." The word she pronounced "pint," like half a quart, was really our word "painted." She was amazed at what we "pint-ed" on our jackets.

We Americans smiled, and she smiled.

"One crew had the picture of a nude girl, and the inscription "Grin and Bare It." She told us how it was spelled.

"What I think it is," said an American chaplain, a lieutenant colonel, "is that our boys are away from home, and they are really living it up."

"The Desert Rats are putting on their show away from home too," said an English commodore, "but all they have are those brown buggers."

The staunchest defendants of the Americans were the women members of the British forces.

"Americans are nice to us," stoutly insisted a petite WREN. "At a dance hall they actually thank us for a dance." Another comment: "They always let us go through a door first."

"An American asks us where we would like to go. An Englishman never asks what film we want to see. It's nice to have a choice," said another WREN.

"The Yah-inks want to go to a different place every time," said a browned, sturdy member of the Land Army, women who worked in factories and on farms but were in military service and wore uniforms.

One florid British general was frank. "Let's face it. You Yah-inks have more spunk with the ligh-dies than we do. When we were young, we turned to chambermaids and barmaids for our early excitement. My daughter will be a duchess but she sighs that her American swine invites her to bed before they even have dinner."

Surprise. Swine? Then we laughed when we realized he meant "swain."

A don came in: "That's what Casanova said to do: treat duchesses like barmides, and barmides like duchesses."

"Maybe that's the explanation," said the American chaplain. "When are your young girls taught to say no?"

The British men looked blank and the British women laughed.

The first WREN spoke carefully. "In England the chambermaids and the barmaids are not supposed to say no to their employers. We don't have to learn to say no to our equals because with us they are supposed to be gentlemen. They don't ask."

"Or insist," said the second WREN. "Americans insist," and, again, everyone laughed.

There was one American WAC, a first lieutenant. She had not said a word during the conversation, but now she spoke very carefully.

"I think I can summarize what it is like in America. With a pickup, like at a public dance hall or at a bar, anything goes. But in a hometown, or on a college campus, it is like a ritual. The boy brings you home from a party, and he kisses you once, maybe just a peck. Same on the second date. If you have a third date, you are supposed to go someplace in a car and neck. You know, lots of heavy kissing but nothing more. On the fifth date, the boy starts fumbling with your blouse buttons or you feel his hand on your knee. He is starting the moves for what we call petting."

The WRENs got into the conversation. "Yes, yes."

"At that point," continued the WAC, "the American girl either stops him or not. Even if she stops him, she is glad he made the pass. She knows she interests the boy. The boy has to make the gesture. He wants her to know he is a man and not something else. It is his duty to make the pass."

The blustery brigadier, interrupting, "I get it. British girls are not trained to say no because we Brits make no advances to girls who are in our social class. In contrast, you Americans make a pass at every girl—and the English girls have no training on how and when to say no."

He paused, proud of his perception. "Small wonder you all sigh you have never 'ad it so good."

The RAF group captain, a handsome fellow, turned to me: "Captain, I see that I am just jealous. May I borrow your uniform some night?"

Everyone laughed.

Giles Allison had a different way of looking at what the Americans were experiencing.

"We Englishers," he said, "are mostly Victorian. We still think we have the empire. Little brown brothers, the white man's burden, the stiff upper lip, and muddling through."

The blimps nodded and smiled. One of them, ruddy face, rotund, said, "Pip pip, and all that. You Yah-inks must think we're awf'ly stuffy."

No American denied it.

"In contrast," Giles Allison went on, "you Americans are mostly Romantics. Your problem is that you are caught up in a neo-Classic job." In summary he said, "you Americans are experiencing an evolution from nineteenth-century Romanticism to preparadigmatic twentieth-century neo-Classicism."

"In translation," said Subbletrun Wingate when we all were quiet, "your American fly-boy individualists are having to learn to cooperate in a war, which is particularly an act of an organized society—and you are finding it strange territory."

The WACs, WRENs, ATSs, and the NAAFIs nodded. The American women looked at each other and raised their eyebrows.

The don went on. "When I call you Romantics, with a capital R, I don't have in mind whether you are amorous or not. I suggest that you are the kind of person whose ideas were described by our poets, painters, and novelists of the 19th century here in England. Shelley. Keats. Wordsworth. That is," he paused, "until our good Queen Victoria changed us all."

Deep silence. The Americans weren't convinced. Most of us had not read the poets.

In came a Canadian. "You know, I think he is right. I think we from the Dominion are Victorians too. When I see some American in us, it is the Romantic type. You all want to be rugged individualists. You hate discipline. I have visited a number of your bases, and none of you can march."

He stopped. "And why do so many of you wear high-heeled boots? Are you all cowboys?"

The two American fighter pilots, both of them wearing boots, laughed. One of them said, "You hit us. Maybe that's why we all wanted to be fighter pilots instead of getting stuck flying formation in the big ones."

A brigadier: "You all wear more or less the same uniform, but you want to be different. Gad, what you do to your hats!"

The U.S. chaplain came in. "Maybe we are all Romantics. But what's this about our being caught in neo-Classicism?"

"Romanticism in the early nineteenth century was a revolt against the eighteenth century. In the eighteenth century, everyone wanted to move from the country to the city. Plays were not about simple people, but about the people in the courts and palaces. They wore powdered wigs, white stockings, brocaded pantaloons, and lace cuffs. That was their uniform, and they liked it. People were supposed to act with decorum, instead of spontaneity. Discipline. When officials gave speeches, they were elaborately reasoned according to form. Regulations. Instead of being condemned, society and government were respected. The military. People preferred to work together rather than separately. That's why you are finding your war so burdensome."

Each night, with Landra coolly amused at the elaborate notes I took, she and I went over what we had discussed.

"The don really put his finger on it," I said. I told her about the leadership of the 100th. I told her how raunch was cultivated. "I guess Giles Allison would call that Romanticism."

Bucky Cleven and Bucky Egan, the two squadron leaders who went down over Bremen and Münster, were the very soul of Romanticism. They hated discipline. I told Landra that discipline was called "chicken shit." Like the two Buckys, our pilots all wanted to be dashing individualists.

"I can see that the pilots here are different from you," said Landra softly.

"In the Eighth, we are supposed to be working together. Discipline should be important. Formations should be good. Cooperation between the navigator and the pilot and between the pilot and the bombardier, and among the groups, wings, and air divisions, they are how we will win this war."

"Do you feel out of place?

"Of course. Before I came here, the way I saw it was that I am a navigator in a pilot's air force. The way Giles Allison puts it, I am a neo-Classicist surrounded by Romantics."

She said nothing.

"What I can't really handle is that when Cleven and Egan were still around, the men were happier. With them gone, the heart of the 100th has stopped beating."

Landra changed the subject.

She said, "When you come to London, we won't talk about it."

16

JOHN BENNETT AS GROUP COMMANDER

Air Marshal Goering had long boasted that American bombers would never fly over Berlin. We in the Eighth considered this a challenge. In November 1943, we were briefed for a mission to Berlin, but it was scrubbed. Weather. On March 3, while I was at Oxford, the Eighth tried again. They got as far as the Schleswig-Holstein coast but had to turn back when they encountered thick clouds billowing up over 30,000 feet. Even so, the 100th lost three crews. One of them tried to make it to Sweden and internment, but landed by mistake—a navigator's error—at a German airport in occupied Denmark. Now the Germans had one of our planes, intact, with the big Square D on the tail—and they used it against us.

On March 4, the target was again Berlin, and almost immediately there was trouble. On that day, instead of putting up one complete group formation, the 100th put two squadrons with the 390th and one with the 95th. This was a slap for the 100th, to be placed under the two other groups in the wing, but only one of several indications that General Huglin of the 13th Wing and General LeMay at Third Air Division HQ were down on us.

Suddenly, all over England, huge clouds built up past 25,000 feet. To the west, where the clouds were worst, the commander of the First Air Division could not get his force assembled, and scrubbed the mission. To the east, near the coast, the 3AD air leader had managed to get most of his task force together and headed out over the North Sea. When he heard the 1AD leader abort, he ordered his task force to do likewise. Most of the groups in the 3AD heard the order and returned to their bases, but one group did not.

That was the bastard, mixed outfit with which the 100th was flying.

Either because he did not hear the abort message or because—although he did hear it—he decided, with typical Air Force macho, to ignore it, the air leader of the 95th, with the 100th squadron tacked on it, went on alone, heading for the most heavily defended target on the Continent. Besides the planes and guns defending Berlin that day, the tiny task force had to put up with an irregular sky alternately clear and filled with huge, billowing cumulus clouds. In and out of and around the clouds went this tiny armada.

Fourteen minutes before they got to Berlin, they were hit by a typhoon of German aircraft. One 100th gunner got an ME-109, the first E.A. destroyed over Berlin by an American, but the rest of the attack was a calamity. The 95th leader led the formation down and down as he tried to get out of the clouds. Every time the 17's peeked out of the clouds, they were hit by the Luftwaffe.

The Americans put thirty-one planes over Berlin, thirteen of them from the 100th, the first time Berlin was bombed by the Eighth. Although the 100th lost no planes, the crews were exhausted from so much time on oxygen, our planes were riddled with a network of holes, and many engines were overstrained.

On March 5, the Eighth tried again, but the mission was scrubbed. Weather again.

On March 6, the Eighth put up an M.E., maximum effort, 730 bombers, and an escort of 800 fighters. Thirty-six of the bombers were from the 100th. Because of takeoff trouble, six of the 100th returned before assembly, and thirty of the 100th went on, flying with the 95th in the middle of the long formation.

When the formation got to Dummer Lake, the Luftwaffe hit the leaders, in the First Air Division. Either because of a mistake in the fighter rendezvous or because the fighters went up to defend the front, the German ground control realized that the middle formations of the bomber stream were unprotected. Dispatching two small waves of interceptors to the front and tail ends of the formation, the Germans sent a huge force at the unshielded middle, the Thirteenth Wing.

The unprotected two groups were the 95th and the 100th, who had bombed Berlin two days before.

Catastrophe. A head-on attack. Lead bombardier and navigator are killed in the first sweep. Exploding planes, all ten men KIA. The whole tail assembly shot off one plane. Crews bailing out with their clothing on fire. Chutes on fire. In another plane two engines knocked out, and the bomb bay on fire. Its load explodes.

With the lead plane gone, flights separate from the main formation and are immediately attacked. Planes spin down, the centrifugal force pinning crewmen to the plane. Wings come off and the fuselage twirls down by itself. Control cables sever, planes mush around with no control, smashing into other planes. Some planes head for Sweden, with FW's after them.

Not a plane in the formation escapes being hit.

Soon it is not a formation, just a straggle of crippled planes. Parachutes are dropping through formations.

The attack lasts an hour and thirteen minutes, sometimes hitting the 100th in flights of three, at other times coming in waves of over forty E.A.

Back at the base, the 100th is hearing that our formation is in trouble. At return time, duty stops and all workers look upward.

The sound. It is wrong. Engines missing, engines racing too fast. Pilots are having to work their remaining engines too hard.

Then the formation. One, two, three. The plane that has taken over the lead is missing the whole trailing edge of its starboard wing. Four. Two engines missing.

Red-red flares, injured aboard. Five, six, seven. Two engines out, one of them ripped completely off the wing. How on earth do those Forts still stay in the air? Eight.

Nine. Ten. That poor bastard of a pilot with his whole left elevator missing is still trying to keep in formation. Ragged.

Eleven. Twelve. Is that all?

No. Here come three more. Or rather, parts of three more. One of them has a hole clear through the fuselage.

Red-red flares from every plane.

Fifteen planes.

No more. Missing: half of what went out.

One of the worst days of the Eighth. All told, sixty-nine bombers were missing, fifteen of them from the 100th. Again, we had the worst loss in the whole Air Force. In the Eighth, 349 planes were damaged so bad they couldn't fly the next day, six of them so bad they had to be salvaged. Every plane in the 100th was hit, bad.

This was the end for Colonel Harding. For weeks he had been in and out of the infirmary, his face gray with pain from some stomach ailment. The docs told him he should go back to the States, but he steadfastly refused.

"The 100th never goes off ops, and I don't either."

Finally the S.M.O., station medical officer, told him he had no choice. Back stateside to have an operation for gallstones.

I had mixed feelings about his departure. He was a decent human being, and he had treated me well.

John Bennett, who had gone from replacement pilot, to Squadron Ops, to Squadron Commander, to Air Exec in a matter of weeks, was in charge.

A lieutenant colonel, he was now the acting Group Commander.

We shivered.

On the seventh the 100th was given a milk run and managed to put fifteen planes and crews in the air. In the customary gesture of new commanders, Bennett flew as command pilot. One crew did not return.

On the eighth, with John Bennett again scheduled for the right seat of the front plane, the crews assembled at briefing.

Berlin again.

The Forty-fifth Wing was scheduled to lead, with the Thirteenth next. The 100th, putting up fifteen crews, was leading our wing. This would be Bennett's first wing lead. Jack Swartout, whose crew competed with us for the lead of the Regensburg mission, was the lead pilot, with Leonard Bull as the navigator.

At Dummer Lake, where the 100th had been hit so disastrously two days before, John Bennett felt comfortable as he saw what he thought was a cover of Mustangs off to the right.

It was a ruse. On that day the Germans imitated American fighters by seeming to fly escort.

Suddenly the "escort" peeled off and hit the Forty-fifth Wing head-on. More than 150 E.A. in one wave.

The Forty-fifth Wing lead went down. The deputy lead went down. More planes went down.

Attack after attack, and soon little was left of the Forty-fifth. Its planes fell back and fitted onto the 100th, leading the second wing.

Now, with John Bennett in command, the 100th was leading the whole formation to Berlin.

On the two previous trips to Berlin there had been full or partial cloud cover.

Now, in the clear, American bombers were flying over Berlin, and the Germans below could see them. On that day, 539 bombers floated over the city. The attacking bombers a few days before were obscured by clouds. Today, the first bomber the Berliners could actually see had a Square D on its tail.

For the next few days, the losses were heavy.

In retaliation, perhaps, for our attacks on Berlin, the Luftwaffe started attacking American air bases. Almost every night, the sirens wailed. Red Alert. Into the bomb shelter. The smell of men packed together, scared.

Strange sounding engines, neither British nor American. A roar. A bomb on the runway. The earth shook.

Almost every night.

Usually when an officer took over a command temporarily, as John Bennett was doing, he conducted a holding operation.

Not so with this guy.

When the replacement crews came in he gave them "the tough talk" and put them into the air to practice formation and do takeoffs with a full load. He walked from plane to plane inspecting them before takeoff. If a gunner didn't have his machine gun clean and in its mounting, Bennett peeled his skin off.

A strange man. Older than most of us. That funny talk, part Texas, part Princeton. He kept saying, when he issued an order, "Now repeat after me . . ." He treated privates and majors alike, and all of us like children.

When the group took off on a mission, even if he wasn't flying, he took off too. He bird-dogged them even after they joined the rest of the division. That voice, Texas, Andover, Princeton, all rolled into one, grating out, "Leadbelly Charlie, your port wing belongs in the starboard waist window of Leadbelly

Able. If you want to come back from the mission, put it there."

Ev commented about Bennett. "I'm glad he's here. Before he got here, I was the son-of-a-bitch."

On the seventeenth of March, the 100th heard that we had a new Group Commander, a full colonel, new from the States, name of Robert Kelly.

He didn't show.

When we learned that he had gotten sick on the way over and ended up in the infirmary, the wags had a comment: "He has heard about us, and he's dogging it."

When he did arrive, he lasted one week.

Although he had never flown a mission before, on the first mission after he arrived, he put himself in the lead ship, right seat, with Bubbles Payne as his navigator. Air Force macho. I began to wonder whether West Point taught its cadets the difference between bravery and bravado. Between courage and brashness.

I thought of the lectures at Oxford. With Kelly we had another rugged individualist, a Romantic when we needed a neo-Classicist.

Although the mission was supposed to be a milk run to the French coast, all targets had flak. When the group got to the target, Colonel Kelly started yelling to the bombardier and the pilot. When they got to the target they were so far off that the bombardier elected to hold his bombs. The 100th floated over the target with their bomb bay doors open. No bombs dropped.

With uncommendable brashness and derring-do, the inexperienced colonel decided to go around again and make another pass at the target, same altitude, same speed, same direction, same wind deflection. Down below, ack-ack corrected their settings—and blew the 100th out of the air.

The lead plane went down, taking with it a splendid crew. When Bubbles Payne and Bob Peel were deposed from Group Navigator and Group Bombardier, they asked to be placed on the same crew. Possibly to show that they should not have been demoted, they became a superb team with many successful missions.

Both of them went down with Colonel Kelly.

My good friend Bubbles, the one who had been so nice to Jean.

When Colonel Kelly was shot down, there was John Bennett, all ready to take over again.

And take over he did.

He set up an extra office in Group Ops and watched everything we did. He had me show him how I made out a flight plan for a mission. He had Doug show him how bombsight settings were computed. He even sat behind the cryptography clerk and silently watched him accept a field order.

He decreed that we would fly every day, if not in combat then on practice missions. Sack time was out. Leaves were canceled.

In the air I heard his voice over intercom. "You are flying formation like Lancasters and Halifaxes." This was a horrible insult. The RAF flew missions at night, about a football field apart. "Tighten up. Put your wing in your flight leader's waist window."

That voice!

I was taking a shower in my quarters. It was about seven o'clock, 1900 hours, too early for the field order.

The Bennett voice. "Captain Crosby will report to Group Ops."

What's going on? I had a phone in my room. Why didn't the son-of-a-bitch use it? Why the hell blast my name all over the base? He was calling to me on the Tannoy, the public address system with the British name, which had a huge loudspeaker in every section on the base.

Quickly, because I tried to be a good officer, I turned off the water, toweled myself, and started dressing.

The damned Tannoy again. The voice. Texas and Princeton. "I repeat. Captain Crosby is wanted immediately at Group Ops."

Hair still wet, no tie, jacket in hand, I tore out to my jeep and fired it up. Just as I screeched my wheels at the end of the WAAF site, I heard it again.

"Captain Crosby will run, not walk, to Group Ops."

I was furious. I covered the distance to Ops in nothing flat. I jumped over the sideboard of the jeep and into Ops. Two squadron commanders, Group Ops, some other officers, and Bennett were huddled in some kind of talk.

"Colonel Bennett," I said, boiling, "I got here as soon as any man could."

I had more to say and I wanted to say it, but he held up his hand, like a traffic cop, stopping me.

"Captain, come into my office."

Into his office we went, he all prim and straight, me steaming, all the other officers and the enlisted men white and silent, hurting for me.

They watched us go into the office and they watched through the huge front glass, Lieutenant

Colonel John Bennett, sitting at his desk, talking, stern. Captain Harry Crosby, angry, standing at attention, braced, before the desk.

"Captain," he said, his face fixed, firm. "How's your wife?"

Surprise on my face. "What?"

"Your wife, Captain, your wife? I hear you have a nice wife back in the States who gets letters through to you every day."

What in the devil was this guy up to?

"I wonder if the good work you do here on the base and in the air is helped by the support you get from home?"

I started to relax a little. I looked around for a chair.

The ice and the steel came back. "Captain," he grated, "you will remain at a-ten-HUT!"

Snap. Back in the brace.

And so, for the next ten minutes, the onlookers sweated for me. Old Croz was really getting it.

I finally did get it. This SOB was making an example out of me. And who better? If he demanded this much of Straight Arrow Crosby, the rest had better shape up. That guy Bennett even chewed out one of the originals. We better pop to.

His expression never changed. What I suspect was on my face was pure wonderment and awe. We talked about Jean, the University of Iowa, and, finally, just a little, about his dreams for the 100th. He told me what I had been feeling.

"The leaders of the 100th think they are making a movie, not fighting a war. We have to get serious."

He finished the conversation. We went back to the other men.

"Captain Crosby," Bennett said, "has been ordered not to divulge the contents of our conversation."

The other officers looked at each other and shivered in their seats.

Within the next few days the word was out. Heads were about to roll. There was going to be a meeting in the S-2 War Room and only the New Leadership would attend.

How did the story get out? A careful leak? I didn't know. I got my invitation early and I passed the word. There is some sense of relief. Remembering the Tannoy incident my friends said, "At least the bastard doesn't hold a grudge."

I noticed that at the club two officers were particularly nice to me. One was the Ground Exec, the other the head of S-2, both retreads from WWI.

"Harry," said the Ground Exec, "Don't you think I have been doing a good job?" He had never called me by my first name before.

Secretly I thought he was doing a terrible job, but I didn't say so. I said something kind and cowardly.

His head's off, I thought.

The afternoon of the War Room meeting came. I looked around.

What a swath! Two new squadron commanders, a new ground exec, a new air exec. New S-2. A new adjutant. Same engineering officers, Rovegno, Blazer, Herlihy, Carleton, and Clift, all top-quality officers.

Blake, Doug, and I survived.

I was dazzled. He got rid of the deadbeats, the Hollywood fly-boys. He promoted the good guys. We now had the men to fight a war.

In the next two months I saw more good leadership in action than I had seen in all the rest of my time with the 100th. Jack Kidd was just as good a leader, but he was hampered by the two men above him. He gets credit for most of the good that the early 100th accomplished.

This guy Bennett wanted to make us into a good group, and he wanted it yesterday. We cleaned up our quarters, we policed the areas where we lived. We washed our jeeps. We had parades, with the light colonels out on the drill field like the buck privates. We checked our equipment. We had machine gun practice, even I who believed I should never take my attention from navigation and fire a gun. We washed our jeeps again.

Over Tannoy, for all the base to hear. "This is Bennett. Until further notice, there will be no beer, wine, or hard drinks sold on the base. I repeat, all bars will be closed."

We flew and flew and flew. Crews were moved around and changed. If a good crew had a poor navigator, he was put on a poor crew, and with a new navigator the good crew came into lead crew training.

Always that voice, that damned voice. Over Tannoy. "This is Bennett. Tomorrow at oh-eight-hundred hours there will be full company drill for all who are not on the mission. I repeat, full company drill, at oh-eight-hundred hours on the tarmac."

In two months our wonderful mob became a war machine. From the front plane I would look out my astrodome, back at the high squadron. All six planes were right in their diamond, perfect.

The Voice, from the command pilot's seat. "Well, Fireball, that is something like what it should be." Even on practice missions, we had code names.

Today Fireball was us, and Fireball was one sweet-looking formation.

Over Tannoy, for all to hear. "This is Bennett. Bar restrictions have been removed. I repeat, bar restrictions have been removed."

That's all. No explanation. No praise. No thank you. Maybe a little less ice and fire in his voice, but that's all. Even so, we all felt we had been promoted to lords and given a share of the British Isles.

He wasn't all iceberg. When a new crew arrived and its first three missions went to Berlin three times, he wrote them a citation for their survival.

The pilot, Red Harper, still had the letter forty-five years later. "Getting praise from that bastard was like getting a popsicle from Satan himself."

The 100th stopped losing more planes than other groups. Our bombing got better. Our gunners reported more kills. We felt better about ourselves.

I doubt that any one of us ever thanked John Bennett enough for what he did.

For our successes.

For the lives he saved.

17

TOM JEFFREY BECOMES GROUP COMMANDER

✈ John Bennett lasted only two months as Group Commander.

As great a job as he was clearly doing, the Air Force Higher-Ups could not give him a permanent command. He was not career. He was not Regular Army. He was not West Point. He taught himself to fly and passed a flight test for the Air National Guard. His pilot rating was recognized by the Air Corps a year before Pearl Harbor.

So onto the base, on May 7, 1944, came a slight young blond lieutenant colonel. He was our new Group Commander. He was not from West Point, but he was from VMI. Virginia Military Institute. That was where General George Catlett Marshall graduated.

The new guy, Thomas Jeffrey, was not new to air combat. He had flown missions as Air Exec of the 390th. He could fly a B-17 with the same competence we knew in Bucky Cleven, Bucky Egan, and Jack Kidd.

He was soft-spoken, self-effacing. "Anyone can fly this bird," he said. "The B-17 is a forgiving aircraft."

When he had distinguished himself with the 390th he was offered the command of either the 95th or the 100th. With the 95th, which had the reputation of being a good, steady, dependable outfit, he would only conduct a holding reputation. In the 100th, with its losses, and its notoriety, he saw a challenge.

Since the Higher-Ups questioned the old 100th leadership, he was given some fifteen captains and majors from other groups, a pool for new appointments. Although neither he nor we knew it, some of them were excellent; some of them had been shucked off by groups happy to get rid of them.

John Bennett and Tom Jeffrey on the same base? Franklin D. Roosevelt and George Washington in the White House at the same time?

Instead of putting him back in his old position as Air Exec as Colonel Kelly had done, Colonel Jeffrey got rid of John Bennett in the usual way: he kicked him upstairs.

Out went Bennett, up to some kind of position at 3AD. In came Lieutenant Colonel Fred Price. Colonel Jeff was really his own Air Exec, the way some presidents are really their own Secretary of State. All Fred Price had to do was listen to Jeff think and stay out of the way. He did the job well. He was also a good command pilot.

Even Colonel Kidd went home.

That was as it should be. For the entire war so far, Jack Kidd had been carrying the 100th. He was the best air leader, and he flew all the tough missions when the 100th was out in front of task force. Until Bennett came, he was the Air Exec and Group Ops. To the degree that Harding and Kelly let him, he was the Group Commander. He was the Group.

At twenty-three when he looked eighteen, he was one of the handsomest men I had ever seen. Now, after months of war, he looked fifteen years older. He was gaunt. His regulation hat, not the hundred-mission crush type, was too big for him. His uniform hung on him. Al Dahn, the Group Dental Officer, told me that Jack's gums were withdrawing from his teeth. He was exhausted.

Since he flew only when we were task force lead, he had not completed a tour. When Tom Jeffrey came on the base, he knew how great Kidd had been, but he knew that a man can only take so much.

"Jack, you have had enough. You are going home."

"Thanks, Jeff."

I did not know it at the time but I had witnessed the beginning of four great military careers. Bill Veal, Jack Kidd, John Bennett, and Tom Jeffrey all became major generals, and there could never be a better testimony to the awareness of the Air Force as to who their leaders should be.

Planets apart in temperament and method, each in his own way was superb.

Under John Bennett and Tom Jeffrey and continued by Fred Sutterlin, when Jeff finished his tour, the 100th became a great group. We bombed well. We lost fewer planes. Before Bennett and Jeff arrived, one of our squadrons had the highest combat failure record in the 8AF. For whatever reason, more of that squadron refused to fly than any other. After Bennett and Jeff, we got awards for our engineering record. We got cited for our good formation and excellent bombing results. Maybe in the early days, it was more dramatic. We were a bunch of wild characters, with wild leaders, and we liked that. But Bennett and Jeff made us into a different outfit.

And I almost missed being part of that story.

When Tom Jeffrey came over from the 390th to the 100th he had been told that our leadership was, as he put it, a "bunch of fuck-ups." To a degree he was right. We had some great flyers, and some great leaders, especially Cowboy Roane, Sammy Barr, Olin Turner, Ev Blakely, Bob Rosenthal, and Jack Swartout, and Colonel Jeff soon came to appreciate them.

For Group Bombardier he had Don Ventriss.

Jim Douglass put up no opposition. In contrast to my chances to fly as command navigator, there was no place for the Group Bombardier to get in his own missions. Doug trained the lead bombardiers well. They knew of his triumphs, and they respected him. But he rarely flew a mission. The end was nowhere in sight. For him, Don Ventriss was an opportunity for him to go home.

And he did.

In my case, there was a question.

On the day Jeff arrived, I flew my twenty-fourth mission, the next to the last.

We put thirty-two planes into the air heading for Berlin. Due, no doubt, to the heavy strain on both crews and planes from our recent demanding missions, ten of the planes aborted, and we went on with a straggling group formation and a half.

When we got to Berlin, we had a complete overcast. Since we couldn't see Berlin, we bombed on

Pathfinder and watched our gaggles of bombs disappear into the clouds.

What a way to fight a war, I thought. We couldn't see them, and they couldn't see us. We destroyed a whole section of the city and never saw it.

One more.

Wrong.

Until then, 8AF losses were about four percent per mission. Theoretically, by the time we had flown twenty-five missions, we were KIA or POW, and we had to be replaced. If we bucked the odds, we got to go home. Since the Eighth couldn't plan on our being there we might as well not be taking up bunks and rations.

Now, losses declined a little, down to about three percent, and our human logistics changed. We had to fly thirty missions. For the twenty-four I had flown, I got credit for twenty-seven. I had three more to fly.

As I saw it after my study at Oxford, Bennett and Jeffrey had changed the 100th from its original hot fly-boy individuals to twentieth-century work-together warfare. From Romanticism to neo-Classicism. History in the making.

I was tired of being part of history. I wanted to go home. Let the new guy take over.

The replacement on tap for me was a captain named Leafy Hill. That is really not his name because I have resolved never to reveal the true names of officers and enlisted men whom I did not admire. War does bad things even to good people. Many of the misfits, the incompetent, the exploitive, and the cowardly whom I met at Thorpe Abbotts have gone on to put together good lives, have had good jobs and good families. I choose not to reopen old wounds.

Leafy thought he was the Group Navigator from the day he walked onto the base. He immediately scheduled himself as the command navigator on the next mission. I hit the sky and stormed into Jeff's office.

"Even command pilots fly high squadron lead on their first missions. I want to know what Leafy Hill can do before I put him up in front."

This was my first encounter with Jeff. He smiled, and talked with me the same way Charlie Via did, Virginia talk.

"Okay, don't pull the hoose down. The 100th is flying low in the wing. In the nose with a good lead crew navigator, he can't foul up too much."

When the planes came back, the crew with whom Leafy had flown were wild.

"The guy is off his rocker. He yelled over intercom all during the mission. From takeoff to landing."

The crew navigator was shaken.

"That screwball actually wanted us to abort when we were on the bomb run. I think he wanted to make the run alone so he could get some kind of medal. I won't fly with him again."

I checked Leafy's log. His ETA's and routes were a tangle of misinformation. He claimed to have seen fighters and flak not reported by any other navigators.

I read the lead crew pilot's official report: "A five-hour trip. Major Rosenthal was command pilot and Captain Hill went along as second navigator. The mission was good as far as the leading went, but Captain Hill screwed up our bomb run. Our navigator gave me a 68-degree heading from the Initial Point to the target which would have been swell, but

Leafy said the target was at one o'clock and the bombardier swung over as he ordered. Then he saw the target back at ten o'clock. By the time he got his course correction killed his rate was over and we messed up the run. So that's what one man can do to mess up the works."

In no time every navigator at Thorpe Abbotts was sure that Captain Leafy Hill was nuts.

But I could go home if he became the Group Navigator.

I did not have to solve the problem myself.

I was long overdue for a pass, and I decided that a London trip to see Landra Wingate might clear my head.

When I returned to the base, I heard quite a story.

One of the really great command navigators, Stewart Gillison, decided after he finished his tour that he wanted to stay in England. I welcomed him into Group Headquarters as my chief assistant. I could trust him with briefings.

Stew was not your normal guy. Under the circumstances of war, none of us were exactly level on course, but Stew was really something. At night, when he went to bed, instead of turning out the light, he shot it out with his .45 revolver. The ceiling of his room looked like a sieve, and the batman had to put in a new bulb every day.

When I got back from London, Leafy Hill was gone.

Stew had assigned Leafy Hill to fly as fill-in navigator with a crew Stew himself had flown with before he became lead. The crew flew out on the mission and came back.

Except that Leafy Hill was not with them.

When I asked Stew Gillison what happened to Leafy Hill, he said with deference unusual for him, "Major Crosby, I suggest that you don't ask."

I did ask. The pilot wouldn't tell me. The bombardier wouldn't tell me. But the copilot did.

Stew, their former navigator, instructed the crew what to do.

After the target when the group was at the R.P., a gunner called out, "We've been hit!"

That part of it was true, but that was standard. To some degree, we were almost always hit by flak over the target. Sometimes it hit the crew, and we died or we got Purple Hearts, but usually the flak only jarred the plane.

"We really weren't hit at all. The pilot only waggled the wings." The copilot continued the story.

This is what he said happened.

"Okay, pilot to crew, prepare to bail out. See you in Stalag."

"Roger, pilot." This was a chorus from the entire crew.

The pilot rang the alarm bell.

Whoosh! Out went, not all ten of the crew, but just Leafy Hill. He wasn't in on the joke.

When I heard the story I thought it was funny.

Leafy spent the rest of the Air War in Europe in a prison camp, wondering what happened to the rest of the crew.

And I spent the rest of the Air War in Europe as Group Navigator of the Bloody 100th.

18

HARD LIFE AT
THORPE ABBOTTS

✈ John Bennett should get some of the credit, because he was the one who started to turn us around, but with the arrival of Lieutenant Colonel Tom Jeffrey, everything seemed to go better with the 100th—and me. We still lost plenty of planes and crews, but as time passed, we no longer felt that the whole German Luftwaffe and all the antiaircraft gunners in the Third Reich were aiming solely at us.

Things were different. The two Buckys were gone. It wasn't the same old 100th. Some of the old swagger was gone. Perhaps because of the excellent leadership of John Bennett and Tom Jeffrey our losses went down and successes went up, but it was still a tough war.

So much routine. Up in the air, destroy a city, and come home. Write a letter to Jean.

On one day we were sent up for two short missions, one of them to bomb airfields on the Pas de Calais coast. We liked that. We got just as much credit as when we went to Berlin, and it was a lot shorter.

Most important, we felt as though we were getting ready for the invasion.

The mission should have been a milk run but over the target an inexperienced crew tried to dodge flak and during the evasive action dropped a bomb on one of the planes below it in its own formation. The bomb hit a plane from the 100th, did not explode. It lodged on top of the plane's tail, pinning the gunner underneath.

The plane and crew got back to the base and made a landing. The problem was how to get the tail gunner out of the plane without setting off the fused bomb.

An ordnance corporal climbed into the tail and, working around the unconscious tail gunner, put a defusing wire through the detonating mechanism. Our Group Surgeon, Clifton Kinder, then dragged the gunner out from under the still dangerous bomb. Later, with the help of an RAF bomb disposal squad, our ground crews got the bomb off the plane.

Defusing that bomb and saving that tail gunner's life took more courage than that demonstrated by any of the combat flyers that day. We now knew that, given the opportunity, our ground enlisted men and officers could be just as heroic as we were.

An important day for the 100th.

Since I was not flying on missions, life at Thorpe Abbotts should have been easier for me.

It wasn't.

As I look back I think the losses were beginning to get to me. Brady and Ham, with whom I had gone through phase training, were in a Krieg camp some-where—as were most of the original 100th—if they weren't dead.

We went to England on May 31, 1943, with thir-ty-five crews. None of the complete crews finished. One crew got nine members through, with one being killed while flying with another crew. Of the thirty-five navigators in with the originals, only five got through. The rest were either KIA, MIA, POW, or wounded so badly they were sent back to the States.

Fourteen percent got through. Eighty-six percent loss.

I don't think I worried so much about getting shot down myself. Instead of my leather A-2 jacket, I wore my Eisenhower jacket on missions, with my medals. If I got shot down, I wanted to be well dressed, with all my ribbons on display. When I went into the air, I felt the weight of the whole world on me. What if I screwed up and missed a rendezvous and left the 100th unprotected? What if I had been the lead navigator at Münster, or on the bad Berlin raid? All those losses attributable to me?

If I got shot down I wouldn't have to worry about the war anymore.

I was, perhaps, inclined to overdramatize what was happening. I saw myself as involved in too many major conflicts. Us against the Germans. Navigators against the pilots. After the lecture I heard at Oxford, I saw myself as part of the conflict between the indi-vidualist fly-boy Romantics and the work-together neo-Classicists, Them against Me. Now that the head fly-boys were gone and we had the Bennett-Jeffrey leadership, the neo-Classicists were in the command pilot's seat.

THE 100TH'S
AWFUL EIGHT MISSIONS

August 17, 1943	Regensburg	9 crews lost
October 8, 1943	Bremen	7 crews lost
October 10, 1943	Münster	12 crews lost
March 6, 1944	Berlin	15 crews lost
May 24, 1944	Berlin	9 crews lost
July 31, 1944	Merseberg	8 crews lost
September 11, 1944	Ruhland	12 crews lost
December 31, 1944	Hamburg	12 crews lost

Did we deserve to be called the "Bloody 100th"? Other outfits lost more planes and crews than we did. What marked us was that when we lost, we lost big. These eight missions gave us our notoriety. Then too, we lost with panache. One Group Commander lasted only eight days. One crew did not even get unpacked.

On the Münster mission, we only sent out thirteen planes. That was all we had after the losses and battle damage over Bremen. Since twelve went down, among them almost all of the last of the originals, only one crew, *Rosie's Riveters*, came back. That is the stuff of which legends are made.

I should have felt better.

But I didn't.

Everyone else seemed to have a life that had limits. They either flew their missions and went home, or got shot down. Kaput.

With me it went on and on.

Sammy Barr, who had been an original lead crew pilot, was now the C.O. of the 349th. The former 418th Ops officer, Bucky Elton, had the 350th. Ev Blakely had the 418th. We rarely saw each other.

The missions were bad enough. Send out twenty-one crews, and count them when they come back.

Work stopped about a half hour before they were expected back. I went out to Flying Control. Up the stairs. Outside. We looked east. We looked at our watches. We didn't talk much. Jeff. The new Air Exec. The squadron commanders. The weather officer. Me. The top brass of the outfit.

The roar. Dim at first.

Stragglers.

We heard the radio downstairs. The command pilot talking to the formation.

"Come on, Redpath Able, Baker, and Charlie, let's pull it together."

Always the attempt to fly tight over the field.

Red-red flares. Four planes with injured. They peeled off on the first pass over the field. SOP. Standard operating procedure.

Around again. Pilots with dead engines and feathered props revved the good engines up. An awful, discordant din. Wounded engines hurt like wounded men.

"Four missing. Looks like the 350th got it."

As the wounded planes came in, all the pilots at the tower called out help which could be heard only by us.

"Up, up, dammit! You're too low!"

"Stall it, stall it! You're still flying the thing. Get out of the air!"

Life on the base was not easy.

At Thorpe Abbotts, we didn't lose men only on missions. We lost them on bicycles, as Americans tried to cycle home at night from the pubs. Dark. No lights. Into a culvert. A broken shoulder bone.

We lost crews when we shouldn't have lost them.

A pilot going up to slow-time an engine after it was overhauled was busy looking at his instruments at the head of the runway. He began to roll just as three other planes came in from a practice mission.

Crash. All four planes piled into each other. Only two men killed.

On one mission, with an experimentally heavier bomb load, three planes could not lift off and smashed into the revetment at the end of the runway. All crews lost. Thirty human beings.

On another occasion, seven planes piled into each other as they all tried to land at once. Five men killed and seven planes salvaged and cannibalized. Carnage.

This was getting to me.

CHAPTER
19

D-DAY

✈ During the month of May, Jeff's first month with the 100th, we all sensed that the opening of the western front was coming. In Russia, Joseph Stalin was harshly critical. He felt that the fighting in Africa and Italy was a diversion. The real support he expected from his allies had to be an attack across the Channel from England.

At Thorpe Abbotts, we felt the pace go up. In 1943, our strength was around thirty-five crews. Usually each squadron would have two crews stood down, perhaps because they were on pass or at the flak house. Perhaps they had been shot up so badly they were training a new pilot, or a new tail gunner. That meant three squadrons could put up two flights, totaling six, and a spare for supernumerary, or alternate. The fourth squadron would be recuperating.

Then we started getting extra crews. In the weeks before D-Day, we put up two whole groups, the 100th A and the 100th B, forty-two planes plus twelve supernumeraries. On May 1, early in the morning, we bombed a secret target in France and Belgium.

The briefing was terse: "We can't tell you what it is. Just bomb the hell out of it." We dropped every kind of bomb we had, from thousand-pound demos to sticks of incendiaries. When the crews were debriefed, we knew what was happening. We were softening up the whole coast from Holland south to Spain. We were going everywhere. We were part of the deception.

In the afternoon, the 100th went out again, briefed to bomb railroad marshaling yards in Sarreguemines. When the target was obscured, our squadrons split up and dropped G.P.s, general purpose bombs, on every railroad track and car they saw on the way home.

One crew got lacerated by flak, and prepared to go into the water. When they came in low to ditch in the English Channel, a German E-boat came out after them and started firing 20-millimeter cannons up at them. The crew threw out all their guns and everything else that was loose. They skimmed their lightened plane over the water till they were able to dump it in the first airport they saw. Just like our return from Bremen.

The stood-down crews were sent up for "pre-invasion practice." They went up to 12,000 feet and simulated runs on the English coast, practically abreast. A very dangerous kind of formation.

When we had rotten weather and no mission, all crews were assembled for aircraft recognition and target identification.

The Invasion felt very near.

The program General Eisenhower set up to make us "informed personnel" was going full time. The enlisted men went at any time for a briefing in their Aero Club.

On May 4, we were supposed to go to Berlin. The load was "twelve fives," twelve 500-pound incendiaries in our racks, and "three thousand-pounders," huge general-purpose demolition bombs. The load was so great that in the Flying Control tower we strained to get each plane in the air.

"Not yet, Lacey, not yet. Keep it down, get your speed," I heard Jeff call out.

The planes hardly cleared the fence at the end of the runway. They flew between the trees. We were glad we had cut down the Queen's trees beyond the runway for a thousand yards or so.

When the task force got out over the Channel, the muck came in and the planes were recalled. They had to turn around and fly back in the soup—and land with their heavy loads.

Several of them blew out their tires at touchdown and skidded crazily down the runway.

On the fifth of May, briefing again for Berlin, but the mission was scrubbed. Soup up to 18,000. Planes trundled back to their hard standing. Bad weather for us. What about the Invasion?

On the seventh, we went to Berlin. I flew in the lead plane as what we now called "command navigator." If anything had gone wrong I would have interceded. All I did was keep my mouth shut and let the crew DR navigator and the Mickey operator do their machine-like precision job. We bombed through the clouds. I was so fascinated by the smooth operation of the lead crew that I hardly noticed the flak and fighters.

But opposition we had. In a crew behind us a navigator was killed and the plane knocked out of formation. On the way home, they got lost and a Little Friend, a P-47, guided them home. Another plane lost two engines, dropped to the deck and came home with another Little Friend as escort. A German plane hit another Fort in the pilots' compartment. The cannon shell ignited all the flares and the whole plane became an inferno. The crew beat at the flames with their jackets and sprayed them with fire extinguishers. They crashed in a woods near us, killing five. Years later, the farmers and village people who saw the plane crash built a memorial to the dead in their local chapel.

On May 8, the 100th bombed more military and railroad targets.

What a drama! Novels, nonfiction, television, movies have tried to tell the story of the Invasion. Its mammoth expanse, its complication, its grandeur, its heroism, its screw-ups still boggle the mind.

I missed it all.

Having flown on the longest mission to the north and south, Trondheim and the Africa Shuttle, having flown to most of the tough targets including Bremen, Berlin, and Frankfurt, now being one of the four original 100th flyers still on Ops, I expected to fly on D-Day. The mission was so immense that I would play a small part as a navigator, but at least I would participate in history's greatest pageant.

We were to fly not one mission on D-Day minus two, D-Day minus one, D-Day, and the next D-Day plusses as long as we could endure, but five to ten missions a day. Our planes were to be briefed, take off, cover the sky in huge waves of bombers, drop their bombs, land, be debriefed and briefed, and take off again.

Each air force, each division, each wing, each group, each squadron had a patch in the sky over Normandy which it was to patrol. We had promised the G.I.s headed for Omaha Beach and all those other cauldrons that every plane they saw would be ours. On the maps the sky was marked in colors, and we had a part in the spectrum.

During the week before D-Day I worked twenty-four hours a day. I had to superintend the preparation of maps and flight plans. I had to set up the formations for over a hundred different missions and variations. I had to brief all our navigators as a group and each lead navigator as an individual.

I was a minute part in the whole operation but I worked for seventy-five hours without even seeing my bed. I didn't shave. My orderly brought me a change of uniforms. I don't remember eating. I remember gallons of coffee, each cup so hot and strong it shocked me into wakefulness.

The night before D-Day I was a zombie.

"Croz, go to your quarters and get some sleep."

"Sir, there is too much to do."

"I know that your department is in good shape. The job is done, but so are you. Go to bed. That's an order."

"Yes, sir."

On the way to my quarters I almost ran my jeep into a tree, I was so nearly out. I fell onto my bed without even loosening my tie or removing my shoes.

Twenty-four hours later I awakened, and it was all over.

On my radio I heard BBC announcing that "Allied armies have landed in France in the Havre-Cherbourg area." Axis Sally also was on the air: "The center of gravity of the attack is Caen."

"That's one of the places we bombed," I thought out loud. "We fooled her."

General Eisenhower came in, "We can now assure you all that France will soon again be under the command of the French." Then, more soberly, from President Roosevelt, "Yes, we have made the first move on the new front. But victory still lies some distance ahead. It will be tough, and it will be costly."

Group Ops and the Assistant Group Navigator had decided they didn't need me. The missions went off perfectly. My lead and command navigators performed like the heroic professionals they were.

And I missed it all.

THE TACTICAL AND
STRATEGIC WAR

✈ Because of General Eisenhower's edict that all troops should be fully informed about what was going on, the 100th current events room was a masterpiece. Two officers from S-2, our Intelligence section, and two enlisted men devoted almost full time to keeping it up.

There was news from home. Both political parties were getting ready for the next election. Against President Roosevelt, the Republicans planned to run two governors, New York's Tom Dewey and California's Earl Warren. They were trying to get the candidate of four years before, Wendell Willkie, to cooperate. Baseball's New York Giants and the Brooklyn Dodgers played a special game to raise money in the fifth war bond drive.

Every week we got a batch of newspapers from different parts of the country. They were usually about ten days old, but they gave us a chance to see what was going on in our own parts of the country. From the *Des Moines Register and Tribune* I learned that the University of Iowa had become a Navy pre-flight training school and the cadets were having a ball dating Iowa coeds. My former girlfriends. I envied them. They were a million miles away.

From flimsies made from messages that came in over the code wires in our cryptography section, we got up-to-date reports on the positions of our troops in all theaters. On one wall map a ribbon stretched along a series of pins represented the slowly progressing front in France. On two other wall maps, we could see the CBI, China-Burma-India, and the Pacific theaters.

In the *New York Times* I read that Omar Bradley and his American troops had captured Cherbourg and 30,000 prisoners. In just three weeks after their original landing in Normandy, Allied land forces had "liberated more than 1,000 square miles of France, captured more than 50,000 prisoners, and had destroyed four German divisions."

That was why we pounded the French coast so much.

Apparently our attempts to be deceptive, all those bomb runs on different parts of the coasts of Holland and France, were to some degree effective. I read that a British naval intelligence officer said that the Germans had been so skillfully outmaneuvered that they massed their defenses at Calais and Boulogne, leaving Normandy without protection.

Axis Sally had been wrong. We fooled the Germans.

Thanks to the reading room, for the first time I began to appreciate the Fifteenth Air Force, which was operating out of Italy. On a day we in the Eighth were stood down because of clouds piled 25,000 feet over England, "the 15th went out in full force and bombed Vienna. About 700 war planes were in the air." The Fifteenth was getting as big as the Eighth.

Fascinated in the reading room by the moving lines of pins and red string, we watched the Fifth Army fight its way up the Italian boot. Way out in the Pacific, in Saipan, our boys were fighting for every inch. Marines had "scaled Mount Tapotchau and dug in at the summit." Navy planes were bombing Guam. Allied forces had captured Mogung in Burma and gained on all fronts from the Indian border to China. The Japanese were attacked in Hunan Province.

For the global war out there, we were spectators. In England, part of our war was the same. A few months before, we could see our targets, the cities, the planes on the runways, the antiaircraft blinking up at us. Now, with blind bombing, not only did we not see the cities, we didn't see the bombs explode. They just disappeared into the clouds.

We had two missions, strategic and tactical. The first, bombing Germany, knocking out factories and communication, through the clouds, was called Operation Clarion. It was unreal. During the tactical part, when we were a tiny segment of Operation Overlord, we flew in low to destroy bridges, railroads, and airports. On those missions, we could often see the troops we were supporting.

On June 17, we went through a briefing, got ready to bomb a French airfield at Melun, and waited at the takeoff strip.

Mission scrubbed. Weather.

On the eighteenth, we were briefed to bomb an oil refinery in Ostermoor, Germany. Since the 100th was to lead the whole task force, I would fly. The lead pilot was Frank Valesh, with Al Franklin as navigator and Jack Johnson the Mickey operator. This crew had once been called "the worst fuck-ups in the Eighth," but now they were one of the most disciplined and highly skilled. I looked forward to flying with them.

The crew was so good that for almost the whole mission all I did was just sit there. No way for me to screw up.

I went into action just once. After the navigator got the wing together he headed for the division rendezvous, climbing on the way. As we climbed, the tail wind increased and Al and I could see we would be six minutes early.

"Radius of action to the right, Croz?" Al asked.

I nodded.

We were supposed to fly about three minutes off 45 degrees to the right—which was upwind—and then make a 90-degree to the left for about two and a half minutes—downwind—and back on course with a 45 to the right.

As we went out to the right I sensed that something was wrong. I couldn't see anything but clouds but I had the radio compass tuned to Splasher Six and the pointer was changing too slowly.

I went on intercom.

"Command navigator to pilot, you better rack it around ninety degrees to port."

Valesh was not happy about my interference.

"Al, what's going on?"

"Goddamned if I know. But you better do what he says. He's been here more times than we have."

The command pilot came on.

"Croz, you better be right."

I didn't feel very sure, and I began to sweat.

When it felt right—and I didn't have any better evidence than that, I came back on the phone.

"Now 45 to starboard, on original heading."

I quickly flipped our radio to the buncher at Great Yarmouth where we were to meet the other wings. Thirty seconds for the ETA.

Not at twenty-eight seconds, nor at thirty-two seconds, but at thirty seconds, the needle went around. The pilots saw it. Back in the radio compartment the Mickey operator saw us cross over Great Yarmouth on his radar. He came on intercom.

"Goddamn, Captain Crosby, how did you do that?"

How? I had no idea. Aerial navigation was no exact science, and I always felt I was less exact than anyone else. Skills? Experience? Luck? I had no idea. Was this the navigator who, just a year ago, missed England by a hundred and fifty miles?

The mission with Valesh when we saw almost no opposition made me realize dramatically that the Eighth was doing its part in winning the war. We had knocked the Luftwaffe out of the sky.

That we were winning the war was demonstrated by another development. On all bulletin boards a notice appeared: "From this day forward, officers will no longer be required to wear side arms." Nothing more, but we knew what it meant. We no longer expected the Germans to launch an invasion of England. I was glad to get rid of the heavy, dangerous .45 revolver. From then on, I carried it only on missions.

I always felt strange about carrying a gun. Most of the time I could help to destroy a whole city and sleep that night. But I never liked carrying that revolver. I might get shot down and have to shoot someone.

As June was becoming July, it was deep and shallow, shallow and deep. Germany and France, France and Germany. If the weather was bad, we went in deep. If it was clear, we went to France.

On the long runs, our crews took off, hit the soup at 200 feet and broke out at 22,000. With no sight of land, but with the guidance of the Mickey operator, they coasted along over those billowing pillows for three hours. The command pilot called for the pilots to tighten up. The formation made a hard left turn, dropped its bombs onto something, and came home.

On the whole mission, the only evidence of the enemy was the flak over the target. There were black bursts of flak as the groups made the hard left turn at the I.P.

In the pictures which the photo officer brought home, those explosions out there, as the planes floated along, looked like black blossoms in a white, billowy, and lovely world.

CHAPTER
21

THE RUSSIA SHUTTLE

✈ One bit of information we got as we went each day to the reading room was that the Russians were not very happy with us. Before Operation Overlord, Joseph Stalin complained that the western front was long overdue. After D-Day, he complained that there was not enough cooperation with the Russians.

We could see why the Russians were dissatisfied. They were taking terrific losses. When they conquered Vitebsk and Zhlobrin near the Polish border, Stalin complained that his troops, with heavy losses, had captured the "anchors of the Fatherland Line" and captured 45,000 Germans, while the Invasion was moving too slowly.

The 100th flew every day the weather permitted. On the fourteenth they went out, supposedly to bomb an airport in France, Le Culot, but the clouds were so bad the lead crew never did find the target. The task

force wandered all over Belgium and brought their
bombs back. On that day our new chief S-2 officer,
Marvin Bowman, and Colonel Jeffrey went to 3AD
HQ where they were told we would go to Russia on
the next day.

We became part of the American answer to Stalin's
complaint. We became part of "Operation Frantic."

On June 19 the Eighth bombed airfields all over
France. Our target was Cormes. A good lead crew
did a good job. Everyone felt good about helping the
troops down on the ground.

On the evening of June 20, while I was in my
quarters writing a letter to Jean, my phone rang. It
was the duty officer.

"You're due at Ops, Captain."

"What's going on? The light's green."

"I know, Captain. It will soon change to red. It's
Operation Frantic. The colonel wants to see you right
away."

I went to Ops where I found most of the group
brass already assembled.

Colonel Jeff filled us in on what was up.

"The mission is a shuttle. The task force will
bomb Berlin but our wing will hit an easier target.
We don't want to lose planes over the target. The
main task force will come back to England but our
wing will go on to Russia and give them a show.
Roosevelt wants Stalin to know that we are in this
war together."

He turned to me.

"Croz, who is your best command navigator? Part
of the mission will be low level."

I didn't think long.

"Big Pete."

"Okay, get 'im here. I bet he's at the club. Tell him we got a long one."

Big Pete was the group clown. Late at night, just before the bar closed, the hangers-on began to applaud and eyes focused on Big Pete.

He began his act. He was the German commander of a U-boat, imitating how he acted with his periscope.

"Up der U-boat. Ach, vee haf surfaced. Up, periscope. Ach, I zee der Blooty Hundret. Ach, they will miss der target and bomb der brussel sprouts. I don't like der brussel sprouts. Let dem pass. Down periscope. Down, U-boat." And many other lines.

Big Pete saw me coming.

"Ach, der duty calls."

At Ops he and I worked with S-2 in the map room to see what kind of supplies navigators would need. As he and I worked out the mission I thought about my own role. Then I went to Colonel Jeff.

"I have been on the farthest mission to the north, to Trondheim. I have been on the farthest to the south, to Africa after Regensburg. This is the farthest to the east. I want to go on this one to fill out my record."

"You are grounded, Croz. Nothing doing."

"But if I fly to Berlin, that's one mission and I will have credit for twenty-six of the twenty-eight I am supposed to fly for my tour. If we fly one on the way back, that will make twenty-seven. I still will have one more. I still won't go home."

He thought for a while.

"Okay, you can go."

I felt funny putting Big Pete in the lead ship and myself in the high squadron which was deputy leader but statistically safer. I reminded myself that Big Pete was better at low level than I was.

All night long, crewmen gathered equipment "to last a week." Ordnance. Engineering. Armament. Operations. All busily preparing for an M.E.

What a scramble! Toothbrush, bug repellent, field rations, an extra blanket, changes of underwear and socks, hurried conversation: Where is my escape kit? How much money shall I take? Should it be English, or American, or Russian? How much is a ruble? How cold is Russia? Did you hear that Major Rovegno, the Engineering Officer, and Captain Bowman, the Intelligence Officer, are going? I wonder how those ground officers will feel with their feet in the air? How can I get all this junk into one bag? Be sure to have our dogtags. If we get past Germany we still may have to prove ourselves to the Russians. I hope we don't have to crash-land behind the Russian lines. I've heard the Russians are in a hurry to shoot people they think might be spies.

On the twenty-first, the 0130 briefing was orderly, swift, a strange note of festivity.

Our target was Ruhland, no milk run, but a lot safer than Berlin.

Besides the usual view of the target, briefings about the group, wing, and division rendezvous, and reports of enemy resistance, there was instruction about which Russian ranks to be saluted. On the blackboard was a space for the estimated time for return. The briefing officer jokingly inserted "July 4" in that space, little realizing how prophetic he was.

Each ship had some particular item to take care of for the whole group. Some planes carried the engineering kits, some the field rations, others the luggage of the P-51 Mustang pilots who were going to escort us all the way. The plane whose safe arrival was the most desired was the one which carried our entire supply of toilet paper. Another one we were interested in was the one which carried the medical supplies. One box contained a liberal supply of contraceptives.

When Doc Kinder listed the box of condoms, he was asked, "Do you think Russian girls are available?"

"I don't know whether Russian girls are available," he responded, "but I know the clap is."

We groaned when we learned that each plane would have thirteen men in it. Each of us had to carry supernumeraries, to perform needed jobs in Russia.

While the planes were taxiing out from their hard standings to the takeoff strip, two of them banged into each other, which dashed the hopes of two crews for this jaunt. The only officer who spoke Russian was supernumerary in one of the planes. The formation took off with no interpreter.

We flew the northern route to Germany, climbing northeast to a point above the Frisian Islands, then heading due east as though we were heading for southern Denmark. We penetrated the German coast between Flensburg and Bremen, my old nemesis. We were miles from Bremen, but their gunners still aimed at us with flak and sent up a smoke screen over the city. The air was black for miles around.

In the high squadron lead I was flying with Captain Richard Helmick, a quiet, nice-looking Glendale, California, boy. No hot pilot or rugged individualist he, he wanted to finish up, go home, and get married. The bombardier, Captain Paul Gregory, was one of four squadron bombardiers. Flying in the right seat was a captain, a new squadron commander, Joe Louis Zeller. He had been in the military a long time and could tell stories well, and more or less accurately. One of our supernumeraries was Sergeant Joe Picard, the ground crew chief who was our extra load, his job to work on the planes when we landed them in Russia.

From the German coast on, all intercom talk stopped. Our gunners scanned the skies for fighters. If they were friendly we relaxed. By now we were on oxygen and we had connected our heated clothing. With all those wires, if I turned around twice in the same direction I would feel as though an octopus had me. I never got accustomed to all those wires around me, interphone cords, oxygen tubes, electric heating lines, and the parachute harness, all tangled with my chair, and my desk, and the machine gun.

Every fifteen minutes I sang out a position report. We were on a guided tour of northwest Germany.

Up ahead the copilot of the lead plane, sitting in the tail gunner's seat and acting as Formation Control Officer, blinked his lights. I.P. Prepare for bomb run.

Bomb bay doors open. Hard, rocky flying as the two pilots jockeyed the plane into the tightest possible formation. The talk on interphone: "More manifold pressure . . . Watch number three. It's running high. Damn! Our left wingman almost collided with us . . . Bogeys, two o'clock high . . . You idiot. That's a Little Friend . . . Bombs away!"

Gregory hit the toggle. We jerked upwards, our load gone. We were six thousand pounds lighter. A sudden turn to the left. As SOP, standard operating procedure, our formation lost altitude to confuse the flak. We went down so fast our eardrums popped. Bomb bay doors ground shut. The flak was black. Out there, so far about a hundred feet away, the spitting explosions. Small black clouds. The plane shook as the chunks hit us. We listened to see if we had been hit in a vital part.

The ball came on. "Sir, Three is smoking."

"Command here. No sweat. It's been doing that, but we are okay. Picard, you've got a job when we get on the ground."

We went on. No hits in the tanks or engines or control surface. Bless the old 17.

But we wished the Old Bird had a better heating system. God, it was cold!

From the target on, it was easier. We lost a few more thousand feet which improved living conditions. Warming up, we loosened our clothing. Then eastward across Germany and into Poland. The 51's were out there. Even they were in neat formation, in flights of two stacked together.

I heard the fighters calling to each other. They were actually complaining that the Berlin guys got all the action. They were spoiling for a fight.

Near Warsaw they got it. The weather changed. Off to port huge cumulus clouds built up and the lead group changed course to the south. From behind the clouds a flight of planes careened out towards us.

Bogeys. 109's.

After seven and a half hours of flying, our pilots had relaxed.

Snap! Back into formation.

Yelling with delight, our Little Mustang Friends

went into action. They dropped their extra gas tanks, called out signals, and dove at the 109's.

It was no fight. Our boys were eight to one to the Germans. In no time, seven bogeys went down and the rest of them went home.

"Good show, gang," I heard the fighter leader call out.

"Piece of cake."

As we crossed the Dnieper River, the sky cleared again, and we saw what the Germans had done to Russia. The scorched earth. From Poland to central Russia, every acre of land had a trench or a bomb crater. The whole land, scarred and pitted, had been a battlefield.

We were supposed to fly this leg at eight thousand feet, but instead of stopping there as briefed, we kept on descending.

Down to about eight hundred feet. Not a very safe way to fly all these big planes. Down below, people. Waving their hats. Waving flags. Their faces looking up at us.

At this low altitude the plane was rocky, and I began to get sick. I flipped out a grocery sack and began to stink up the compartment.

Staring at me in disbelief, the bombardier left and went up to the pilots' compartment.

Our field. Tight formation. The peel-off. Bumpy landing strip, made out of some kind of heavy metal fencing. The Rooskies made a landing field for us just by laying down a metal carpet.

"Picard here. What this stuff will do to our tires!"

Instead of being guided to a mooring position, we rolled straight on and were flagged to a stop. An American master sergeant and a Russian soldier came on board. For all we knew, he was a general, so we saluted him, and he saluted us.

The crews were gathered up in trucks; the pilots and navigators in command cars. A Russian woman in a uniform was our driver. She had about the biggest bust I ever saw. There was hardly room for the steering wheel.

"Comrade," she said.

"Comrade," Zeller, Helmick, and I said. Zeller rolled his eyes to the high heavens. "Mother Russia," he said.

We came to a huge tent. We stopped, went in. Colonel Witten, who had moved up from 390th C.O. to OIC, Thirteenth Wing, was in charge of interrogation and indoctrination. Two Russian officers talked to us, and we pretended that we understood his English.

Soon we were caravanned into the town and deposited before a battered schoolhouse, where we were to be quartered. Instead of beds, there were long benches about three feet off the ground, and sloping down from the wall. They were covered with hay. We opened our bags, ate some K rations, cheese, canned meat, crackers, and dried fruit. I gave my cigarettes to someone.

With our clothes still on, we climbed onto the benches with our heads near the wall, our bodies sloping downward, our feet pointing toward the center of the room.

"Goddamned sardines," someone said, but I went to sleep at once.

On the next morning, groggy, no place to shave. We went to the windows. Red banners and pictures of Stalin everywhere.

A truck came for us. We drove somewhere. All along the road, Russians waved at us. The women threw flowers at us.

At the mess hall, Russian women waited on us. They were all top-heavy.

"I'm in heaven," one enlisted man said. "Does every woman in Russia wear a size-D cup?"

"Can't you tell, man? They don't wear any cups."

Hot coffee. Cold cereal, Kellogg's Corn Flakes, just like home. Huge pitcher of milk.

The first guy tasted it, made an awful face.

"My God. Sour."

No one ate any cereal, but there were oranges and apples. Very good.

That afternoon a problem developed. German reconnaissance planes droned over the field, looking at us. The Russians had no antiaircraft. Russian pilots in America Airacobras went up, and the Germans, apparently Stukas, went away.

Colonel Jeff was uncomfortable.

"We're naked in front of those guys."

He talked to Colonel Witten. Shortly before dark, we took off and flew, low enough to escape the German radar screens, to another airport, at Kharkov, distant enough to be safe. I was glad I wasn't navigating in the plane. Low-level navigation. I used four paper bags.

When we landed at Kharkov it was dark, and we could see little of the city as we were trucked to our barracks. We did notice that about every mile the road was blocked by a gate and a sentry. As we drove up to a gate, a sentry barked out, "*Stoy*," and pointed a rifle. The driver "*stoyed*."

Then the driver's copilot would say, "*Ed-dee*,"

which we gathered meant "Un-*stoy*," and off we would go.

When we finally arrived at our barracks, a damaged building like before, with "beds" like before, we started to climb in even though there were several Russian soldiers in the room talking to each other.

Just then another Russian soldier stalked into our boudoir and started jabbering. We paid no attention to him until someone said, "Hey! He's talking English!"

Sure enough. It wasn't good English, but it was English.

We learned that he had been studying American history and language at Stalingrad and had boasted in a conversation with his mates around a vodka bottle that he could speak English. When they volunteered him to be an interpreter, he felt bound to deliver but shaky about the outcome. A pleased expression came over his face as we zeroed in on him and finally began to understand what he was trying to say.

In the morning, with our new interpreter taking us in tow, we trooped out onto the streets lined with pictures of Stalin. We rode a block or so to what was to be our mess hall. We had spaghetti and Spam in sour milk, beets with sour milk, coffee with sour cream and rock-size sugar, dessert with sour cream.

One enlisted man said, "I used to have borscht in the Catskills, but I didn't know they put sour milk on everything."

By now we were too hungry to be choosey. We scraped off the sour milk and cream where we could and did manage to eat a little.

After the "meal" we sat around and talked about how strange it was for us from Iowa, California, Pennsylvania, and all over the States to be gathered around sour milk in Russia. A fellow from New York said he hadn't had such good borscht since he used to visit his Jewish grandmother. A fellow next to him hit him and sent him sprawling.

Another topic was the apparent healthiness of Russian women. The girls who were waiting on us were built like our driver the night before, with tremendous top shelves. "I think they would all take G cups," said someone.

Our waitresses seemed to think that our remaining at the table meant we wanted something more so they brought us in a pot of some kind of fruit tea. We guessed it was made by pouring tepid water on dried apple slices, a fresh berry or two, a pear peeling, and some tiny seeds. The result tasted like warm water with a slight fruit flavor.

They kept bringing it to us.

The routine went something like this. The first cup we drank. The second cup we struggled over and finally downed. The third cup we poured into the empty cups of the fellows who had left. That illustrates how hard we were trying to cultivate Russo-American friendship.

On the next morning we started looking for a place to shave and clean up, and learned that out in the courtyard a huge basin, much like a horse trough, had been filled with water for us. This community project worked satisfactorily if we didn't mind shaving in ice water.

Another example of Russian hospitality. Girl soldiers stood by the trough and, cupping their hands, poured water over our hands as we washed. The girl soldiers were everywhere, doing what they thought would please us.

"What a healthy bunch they are" was the standard, amazed expression. All G cups. An articulate G.I. compared Russian women to American architecture: "Every one of them is built like a brick shithouse."

Colonel Witten had established his headquarters at one end of the building, and nearby was a bulletin board which announced that we were free till 1500 hours, at which time there would be a meeting for all personnel.

Outside our quarters was a great open yard. Into this yard went the Americans to see the Russians, who were already there to see the Americans. About fifty Russian soldiers were stationed nearby to aid us. Some were truck drivers, cooks, and orderlies, and some were guards. Many of the guards were boys, and at least half of them were women and girls. All well developed.

By now, several of our enlisted men whose parents had "come over from the Old Country" were beginning to remember the Russian, Yiddish, and Ukrainian their parents had spoken around the house, and—with our volunteer Russian interpreter—we could communicate a little.

We heard tragic and fierce stories of what total war meant to Russia. All the civilians had come through the forty-five-day siege of Kharkov. This part of the country had been through two wars, the scorched earth policy of the Russians when they retreated before the Germans, and then, eighteen months later, the vicious battles that drove the Germans from Russia. When we noticed that many of the men and women wore a square red medal, we asked what it meant. All who wore the medal, soldiers or civilians, had been in the Battle of Stalingrad.

We met one rather plain-looking girl, very thin, almost boyish, no front. We noticed that the Russians treated her with respect. Since she was intensely solicitous about helping us, when she disappeared, we asked about her.

Early in the war, she had fought heroically as a foot soldier and was frequently decorated. She became an officer. She was sent to flying school, became a fighter pilot, and shot down sixteen German planes. She had parachuted five times from stricken planes. On her last drop, something snapped in her leg. Because of sloppy surgery, she was through flying. Back to the infantry she went, now with two full sets of medals. She was given a commission and placed in command of a company defending Stalingrad. The Russian command decided this was too passive an assignment for her, and she was sent behind German lines to fight as a guerrilla. Finally she was given a rest leave, back to her home in Kharkov and her two children. Her husband was off somewhere on the German front.

How did she spend her R&R? By doing hard manual labor, swinging a sledgehammer with the men who had laid down the metal landing strip at our landing field. When the Americans arrived, she poured water on our hands.

Even the boy soldiers had killed Germans, stopped tanks, and been wounded by German grenades. They had medals to prove it. One of the middle-aged women who cleaned the dining room had killed a German soldier molesting her daughter. The women who worked in our mess hall were front-line nurses home on leave.

Russia was the only place yet that I found to be like Hollywood's version of it. It was just like *Song of Russia*, but without Robert Taylor. In Russia, people actually gathered on the street corners to sing. On duty, when they marched, platoons sang. Instead of "Forward, MARCH!" apparently the leader said, "Singing, start!" and off they went. It wasn't just singing amateurishly in unison, and off key, it was grand opera, high, soaring tenors and deep, profundo basses, full, strong harmony, and lots of vigorous rhythm. Off duty, they met on street corners at night, and sang. Men did a whirling, knee-bending, foot-kicking, jumping kind of dance that brought out yelps and "ki-yi" from the spectators.

As we sat in the courtyard the Russians put on a show for us. Everyone could do something, some form of entertainment. They did solos, duets, trios, quartets. They got up in pairs and apparently put on little playlets, with dialogue that brought out brays of laughter from the audience.

Then the Russians stopped and sat down.

They looked at us. They had done their thing. Now it was our turn.

Who of us could sing? Or dance a solo? Or put on a play?

We had too much of our lives listened to radio and watched others perform. We sat in embarrassed silence.

Finally a Russian soldier began to play American music, dance music, and the Russians got up and danced, with strange couples, man and man, woman and woman, and man and woman. They looked at us beseechingly.

Two Americans got up and tagged a Russian girl couple. The girls smiled, and fell right into step with the Americans.

That did it. All of the Americans stood up and tapped girls. When I selected a partner, I had to bend backward because of the double protrusion. What an armful!

Suddenly the music stopped and our interpreter told us, "We want to learn to jitterbug."

A G.I. went to the accordion player and asked for his instrument. He fiddled with it for a while, made a few squeaks, smiled, and began the song: "Mairzy-Doats."

Several of the Americans began singing, "Mairzy doats and dozey doats and little lambsy divy." Six G.I.'s tapped six girls and away they went. Jitterbug. The girls struggled at first, and then got it. The earth moved, and so did the girls' tops.

From then on, it was a party. An American picked up a tin can and became a drummer. Another man borrowed a fiddle from a Russian. We had an orchestra. Everyone danced, sang, and laughed. "String of Pearls." "Dipsy Doodle." "That Old Black Magic." "In the Mood." Russo-American relations. We hoped that Stalin heard about it.

Time for our meeting. A bugle call. The dancing stopped.

Comments like, "Most of the gals were so top-heavy that I was off balance most of the time."

"Yeah, but those women could really follow."

"Every man's dream!"

At the meeting Colonel Witten told us that the Thirteenth was all that was left of the task force that flew to Russia.

Our trip flying low on the deck had saved us.

While we were sleeping in Kharkov, Stukas dropped flares over the field at Mirgorod that we had deserted and the occupied field at Poltava where the other wing's planes were moored. Without a shot being fired at them, the Germans bombed under their chandelier of flares. They dropped bombs for an hour and fifty minutes.

They destroyed seventy-two American planes on the ground. When the Germans left after their repeated bombing runs only three planes were intact. The Luftwaffe had destroyed a combat wing. It was our own little Pearl Harbor.

It was bad enough that the planes were destroyed. There were so many bomb craters on the landing strips that there were no fields with runways long enough for us to take off with a bomb load.

While our leaders decided what to do by conferring with the American Air Force through phone lines that went through Moscow, we kept pretty much to our own quarters. For one thing, we were restricted to very limited parts of Kharkov. We couldn't see the heavily bombed parts. We couldn't see Russian military quarters. We couldn't trade with the Russian people. We were not permitted to have conversations one-on-one with the Russians. When an old fellow came up to me and tried to show me something about "my Mosca" in a newspaper, two Russian soldiers came up and roughly pushed him away.

We could only talk in groups. We did learn that several of the Russians were pilots flying P-39's which we had Lend-Leased to them. The Russians had modified them a lot, but they would not tell us what changes they made. Parked near our planes were two American C-47's, with machine guns added. When we went out to look at them, two soldier boys, maybe thirteen or fourteen, came out with their rifles leveled at us.

"*Stoy!*"

We *stoyed*.

In front of our quarters we were permitted to exchange souvenirs. Our boys wanted rubles for their Short Snorters and the Rooskies wanted cigarettes. One package of Yank smokes for one ruble. We learned later that the Russians would have given two rubles for one cigarette. Souvenir insignia traded about even.

In the late afternoon, Colonel Witten walked into the yard with his new find, a satisfactory interpreter. This one was a double threat: besides knowing English she was a cute young woman, slender everywhere but on top.

Junior Lieutenant Maja Krootz, pronounced "Maya," was so good that she rather dismayed us. When Colonel Witten introduced her to me I was so accustomed to talking about Russians in front of them that I said, "She is one neat number, Colonel," and she responded, "Thanks, Captain. From your accent, you must be from the Middle West."

When she talked with any one of us, she talked the way we talked, our exact accents. When she joked with Bucky Mason, from Texas, she sounded like a cowgirl. Southern "you-all," Midwest twang, she had them all.

Maja was a gem. She could work telephones. She blasted our way through Russian and American liaison. She was tireless, efficient, and bustling. Bustling?

We learned that she was just nineteen. She was a split personality, one moment an efficient soldier and the next moment very aware that she was surrounded by attractive, eager American males. In one minute she would show briskly how to field strip a pistol, and in the next she would demurely wait for one of us to pull out a chair for her. She was a born flirt. She had learned that the word "Brooklyn" in any context was funny to an American.

Question: "Where did you learn English?"
Maja: "Brooklyn." (Laughter)
Question: "What do you hope to do after the war?"
Maja: "Marry an American from Brooklyn."
(More laughter)

She was delighted by American slang and regionalisms. When Butch Rovegno trotted out his deepest Alabama, "Well hush mah mouth and stuff it with yams," she made him say it over and over till she could imitate him exactly.

She told us she hoped to go to Washington, D.C., to the American embassy—"That's near Brooklyn, isn't it?"—and she took all our addresses and promised to look us up.

Thanks to Maja, Jeff and Colonel Witten were able to give us progress reports relayed through Moscow.

Our main takeoff strips were being repaired. More landing netting had been trucked in.

Bombs and fuel, blown up by the German Stukas, had been replaced.

We would fly a mission on the next day.

We were to leave Kharkov, fly on the deck to Mirgorod, and land. That night our planes would be fueled and loaded with bombs.

Kharkov gave us a grand farewell. The women apparently had stored their more gaily colored dresses but they got them out and wore them to say good-bye to us. Some of them dug up rouge and lipstick. They all hurled roses at our trucks. Little girls gave us bouquets. Everywhere we went the Russians said, "*Do svedanye.*" They formed quickly into groups and sang, in parts and in English, the words over and over, "Farewell till we meet again." Then they stopped singing and said something in Russian that sounded like, "*Poka du solve stra.*"

For me the short flight back to Mirgorod was torture. Although I had by then nearly a thousand hours in the air I still got violently airsick, especially at low altitude where flying was particularly turbulent. For the millionth time since I had joined the Air Corps I regretted not having joined the infantry.

The flight took forty minutes. It was hot and the fumes from the engines were almost visible. I used up twelve of my precious paper sacks and almost turned myself inside out three times. I stunk up the plane so badly that everyone else got sick. Gregory left the nose and went back to the radio compartment and threw up. That made all the gunners sick and they threw up. Then the pilots got sick and took turns throwing up. None of them was prepared, and they used compass covers, ammunition boxes, lunch sacks, and their hats. The pilot, from his remote control, opened the bomb bays and the whole crew stood in the catwalk and let go.

"I have never been airsick before," said Joe Zeller, "and I hope I will never get airsick again."

On the way we flew over Poltava and surveyed the damage done to the other combat wing.

It was tragic. Fifteen acres of junk. It looked like a city dump, with smashed old cars. Three once-proud flying groups were now trash. We looked away and didn't look back. Those poor old battered Big Gas Birds.

At Mirgorod the runways were repaired, but the rest of the field looked pitted like a kitchen colander. Crews were walking up and down with flak vests and exploding delayed-action and dud bombs.

We landed and were asked to remain at the planes till they were refueled and our bomb bays loaded.

A fuel truck came up and with a hose pumped 2,780 gallons of gas into the tanks, making sure that our regular and wing tanks were topped off.

Then a truck came up with a driver about twelve years old. He was so small he had to pull himself up with the steering wheel and look over. He made a sweeping circle and stopped by the plane. He got out, went around to the back, climbed up and lifted off the end gate. He threw it aside, jumped to the ground, and returned to the front. He drove forward slowly and carefully, then shifted into reverse and gunned the engine. When he was backing up fast, he jammed on his brakes, and his entire load, six 500-pound demolition bombs, tumbled off.

"Hit the dirt!" Every American voice.

Down we went.

Nothing happened.

Under the direction of Joe Picard, we rolled the bombs under the plane, snapped on the plane's hydraulic lifting gear, and slowly pulled the bombs into place. Our bombardier said he would arm them just before takeoff.

Then we sat down. Those of us who smoked, smoked. The rest of us just sat there, quietly, and sweated. Flying missions was safer than this.

A truck came by with coffee. We got out our store of C rations and began to eat.

It got dark soon and someone turned on a battery-powered lamp. The radio operator tuned in Berlin, and we heard American music. "Lili Marlene." "That Old Black Magic." "Mood Indigo." We sat in a circle, still quiet. When it got cold, we moved into the waist of the plane to eat the rest of our meal. The lamp battery wore out and someone turned on a flashlight and laid it down on the catwalk. We spread out our C rations in the cone of light.

We could smell each other's flying clothes. One fellow said, "Sling me one of those biscuits." A hand went into the cone of light, picked up a biscuit, and withdrew.

"Hand me the Spam."

Another hand in the light.

"Thanks for the caviar."

We could hear each other breathing and that was all.

Outside was Russia. Tomorrow we would, we hoped, be in Italy. The States were so very far away. We were young, we had seen too much, destroyed too much. It was June 25.

Somebody came by and briefed us. We would sleep in our planes, take off very early. I got a packet of maps and a set of coordinates. I saw where the target was. It was Drohobycz, in Poland. Mission twenty-six of my twenty-eight.

The last word of briefing: "Get your fans started when you hear some rifle shots and see yellow-yellow flares. Turn your radio on." He gave us a frequency.

"If your fans don't start, just stay in your planes. Some ATC types will come by and pick you up. You will be taken to Moscow. From there you will go to Teheran, and then to Cairo and Morocco, and then back to England. You will be TDY, rations and quarters allowance. It will take about a month."

Wow! Did that sound good. TDY meant "temporary duty," which meant we got six dollars a day for food, another six for quarters, and some allowances for other expenses. At that time that was a rich man's salary. No one would shoot at us and we would have a sight-seeing tour. A dream.

In the next morning, after a restless night where we tried to sleep on the ground outside or in the plane with jackets and parachutes for mattresses, we stiffly went to our takeoff positions—and hoped for a trip to the fleshpots of Africa.

"Start One."

Number one started. Damn!

"Start Two."

It started. Damn again!

"Start Three."

The fan went around, almost caught, and the engine died. Great! North Africa. Here we come.

"Engage Three again." Against all our silent wishes, it caught.

"Start Four." It didn't. Not one of us made a sound, but we all cheered.

"Joe, go out and see what you can see."

So out went Joe Picard. Somehow he managed to climb up on a wing and open the cowling. Just then a truck came up, and Picard motioned the driver—it was the kid who dumped the bombs—into position by the engine.

Picard went to the waist, got his tools and some boxes. In no time at all he changed a whole bank of spark plugs. The driver pulled away. Joe went back to work.

Soon he waved to the copilot.

"Copilot to pilot, engage Number Four."

It started.

When Picard climbed into the plane, he looked all proud of himself, but the crew in the waist glared at him. Every one of us had an imaginary gun in our hand, aimed at him. We pulled the trigger.

No TDY to Algiers.

The mission was uneventful. We hit our target.

Credit for twenty-six for me. Two more to go.

We lost no bombers. One plane lost an engine, which the whole formation thoroughly enjoyed because it was the one that one of the engineering officers was riding in. The pilot was Bucky Mason, who called out in the clear, "Put the engineering officer on intercom."

When we heard Major Rovegno's Deep South come on, Bucky said, "Hey, you old coot, you better have your hammer and nails ready in Italy. This duck I'm riding in is about to fall apart."

That is what German eavesdroppers with their ground radios heard as we flew by.

Of course we had to show off. When we got to Italy, Jeff and Witten called us into tight formations. To show the Twelfth and the Fifteenth how the Eighth flew, our pilots almost made their wing tips touch the waist of the flight leaders. It is a wonder we didn't lose more planes than we did at Poltava.

We landed at the base of the 99th Group, which formed just before us and trained before us. Half of my navigation class went to them. They were all gone now, but the ground people remembered them and told me what happened. There had been almost no casualties. They all went home.

The 99th whistled when I told what had happened to my classmates. More than eighty percent of them KIA, MIA, or POW.

"I guess what we've heard was right," one of them said, "that the Eighth had it rough."

We stayed there for a week. We swam in the Adriatic. We visited the coastal fishing villages and saw the damage done during the landings. We took off, flew over Rome. I gave the crew a guided tour— "That's the Vatican," and "There's the Coliseum, where the Christians fought the lions." We flew around Vesuvius.

We took a bus trip to Naples. We saw small boys hawking their sisters. "Hey, Yank, you wanta fock my seester? Two dollas or two packsa cigs." The "seester" might be twelve or fourteen. We saw adult men hand over the cigarettes, walk to an alley, and then get the job done, the child with her skirt up and the man with his pants down. All the while the boy would be lining up customers.

We drank Italian wine with Italian girls, big eyes, dark skin, low-cut dresses. What a way to fight a war.

Expecting to have three more days, we went to an underground wine cellar, watched a show of dancing and music, and flopped into bed at 0200.

An hour later, an Italian voice: "Okay, Yank. Up and attum. You're going on a mission." This was July 3.

Someone got the idea that we should demonstrate solidarity by flying a mission with the Twelfth. Our target was Arad. I didn't even know what country it was in.

This was really the way to fight a war. We flew in a loose, strung-out formation, at 12,000 feet. We didn't wear our oxygen masks most of the time. We put on our flak vests but didn't see a burst of flak or a single E.A.

Milk run.

I didn't get airsick on the whole mission. I sang most of the way. Colonel Jeff hadn't expected this extra mission. I now had twenty-seven of my twenty-eight. With the mission we were scheduled to fly on the way home, I would have the twenty-eight I was supposed to fly.

United States, here I come.

On the next day we finished the triangle. Another milk run. We bombed an airfield and a marshaling yard in Béziers, in France. We did a good job. Little flak and no fighters.

I sang all the way home. Twenty-eight missions. A full tour. Jean, here I come.

I thanked my lucky stars that I still had a few more weeks as a captain. At that time the Higher-Ups had decided that field grade, majors and up, were professional and had too much knowledge to waste. When they finished their missions, they either had to fly another tour or take a ground or training job somewhere in the ETO. If I were a major, I would have to stay in the ETO; as a captain, I could go home.

When we left the French border and saw the English coast, I heard the pilot talking on radio for landing instructions at Thorpe Abbotts. The voice from the control tower was that of the new Air Exec, Fred Price.

I broke into the conversation. "Hello, Colonel Price, this is Captain Crosby, with twenty-eight missions."

"I read you, Croz." There was a note of triumph in his voice. "I read you loud and clear. But it is now Major Crosby." He puts emphasis on my rank—my new rank.

The rest of the crew came on intercom. "Congratulations, Major."

"Thanks a lot."

No rotation home for me.

WITH LANDRA
IN LONDON

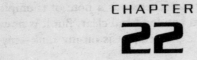 As I went up the ranks I became a different person with each promotion. As a second lieutenant on Brady's crew, I was eager, unsure of myself, navigating by keeping my eyes on the plane up ahead. As a first lieutenanant on Blakely's crew I was still eager and unsure of myself, but I was in the plane up ahead. To do my job, I almost tore myself in two. Missions drained everything out of me that was in me. As a captain Group Navigator, I was still eager and unsure—no planes were in front of me, and the missions still took everything out of me. When I got out of a plane after a mission I was so exhausted I could hardly walk. I smelled so much of sweat I left my flying clothes outside my barracks to air.

As a major, established by luck, experience, and rank as a prominent figure in the 100th, I was different. Everything I once did by myself I now had someone else do. For every formation I had three highly skilled navigators for the lead plane: the Mickey operator, the lead crew DR navigator, and the command navigator. If the lead was group or wing, I sent one of the squadron navigators in the command navigator function. For the division and task force leads, I sent Captain Ed King, my current Assistant Group Navigator for Ops.

I also had the Assistant Group Navigator for Training. He took care of getting new navigators ready for their missions.

For myself I reserved the job of training lead crews.

Big deal.

The rest of my life was routine. Every morning I received a letter from Jean, sensitive, informing, and caring. Every night I wrote to her. The miles between us began to stretch. I looked at her picture, as I wrote, trying to remember who she was. I wondered what it would be like when I was with her again.

Routine.

I wasn't flying missions, but my friends were.

Some of the missions were successful. Some were not.

On July 6, we sent the group to Fleury-Crepeuil to destroy a mystery target, which was identified as "No-Ball." When the crews returned, they told us what they had seen. The targets were launching racks for V-1's and V's, rockets aimed at London—and our bases. The lead bombardier saw the target too late, and missed. Navigators and bombardiers—and I— smarted under the resulting criticism.

We were sending out so many formations that we were even shorter than usual of good command pilots. Back in the States, Hap Arnold had decreed that every flyer in the Training Command and the Air Transport Command had to fly a tour of combat. This order shook a lot of high-ranking pilots out of their cushy jobs.

In the 100th we got more than our share of them. Some of them were able and willing, some of them were so frightened they turned in their wings rather than fly combat. All of them were inexperienced— and all of them had the rank to become squadron commanders, and to fly in the right seat of the lead plane on a mission. They did not get the training we gave lead crews, and they did not know enough to keep their hands off the wheel during a bomb run.

On July 7 we were supposed to send the group into Germany, to Bohlen and Merseburg. Since Merseburg with its oil refineries was one of the most heavily defended targets in the hinterland, this was bad enough, but the weather was foul and wings went in alone, no fighter escort. Our inexperienced command pilot had the group climb too slowly. His wing men slogged along and nearly stalled out. The lead crew could not locate the target in the clouds and it didn't show on radar. The 100th dropped its bombs on an air depot in Toggingen, with poor results.

The report from 3AD said, simply, "The 100th missed."

Hard on me.

On July 8, with Frank Valesh and *Hang The Expense VI* in front, the 100th was assigned to bomb a railroad bridge at Clamecy-Joigny. When the weather turned bad, Dick Johnson tuned up his radar, found a railroad bridge at Bourth and a railroad junction at Le Lente, and smashed both of them. Valesh's plane was damaged so badly it was salvaged.

From 3AD: "Excellent results."

Good for me.

During this week the 100th suffered an indignity which should have embarrassed us. It didn't.

Most of Curtis LeMay's Third Air Division flew B-17's. Five groups, however, flew B-24's. We were accustomed to seeing Liberators with the huge white circle on the tail, the sign of the Second Air Division. When we saw them with the white square of the Third, we felt it was wrong. Apparently someone else did too because the 3AD Liberator groups were given Forts, and taught how to fly them.

One of these groups was the 486th, which had a huge O in the square on the tail. When its commander, a colonel named Overing, suddenly realized that his Forts would be flying with a Square O, he feared his unit's new markings would look very much like the 100th's Square D.

This would never do. Like every other member of the Eighth Air Force, he was certain that the German Luftwaffe had a vendetta against the 100th because of the wheels-down story. Colonel Overing therefore insisted that his group get a new insignia, a huge W in a black square. He did not want his group to be confused with the Bloody 100th.

We should have been angry, or hurt.

Instead, with the typical perversity of the 100th, we were either amused, or proud. It made a great story to tell the new crews. "That will flak 'em up good," said one of the veteran copilots.

On the tenth, the weather over the Continent was

good and the crews could have earned a mission credit by bombing Berlin. Instead, they were briefed for a low-level job at Mery-sur-Oise, north of Paris, but after we briefed them, the weather did not clear and the mission was scrubbed. A waste of time. Much grumbling.

And so the month went. Down on the ground in France the troops were trying to capture St. Lô. Our planes went out in support of them, sometimes helping, sometimes hindering.

On the nineteenth, Frank Valesh's crew flew their last mission. As usual, they drew a tough one, to Schweinfurt. As usual, they did a good job. On the way home, Dick Johnson, the Mickey operator, walked into the bomb bay to make sure the racks were clear. There he saw Valesh busily dumping cans of an easily identified fluid out into the air. Frank had gone around to all stations, picked up their relief bottles, and dumped them out. As Dick watched Frank drop each container, he saw Valesh mouthing the words, "Piss on Hitler."

As usual, their plane, on this mission, *Hang the Expense VII* got hit hard. Frank skidded the plane in for a landing with the whole rudder slashed off and most of the vertical fin missing. Salvage.

Then the crew went home.

And another batch of my friends were gone.

On the Russia Shuttle I had come to know Bucky Mason, the pilot from Texas who flirted with Maja Krootz, our vivacious interpreter. As a command pilot he was highly respected by my navigators. He went out on what was to be his last mission—and did not come back. The whole low squadron got blown out of the air, and none of them were in the forma-

tion that flew, after the mission, over the control
tower. As I stood there waiting for them, two planes
ran into each other on the runway. They blew up,
killing nineteen men right in front of me.

It wasn't only that my friends were gone. The spirit was gone. The laughter. Ham, Brady, Warsaw,
Crankshaft, Solomon, Murph—always good for a
laugh—were gone. Under Darr Alkire and Chick
Harding as Group Commanders, anything went with
the 100th and it did. When Bucky Cleven and Bucky
Egan were setting the tone of the 100th, there was
dash. There was derring-do. Flying the war was an
adventure.

Now, under Bennett and Jeffrey, we were doing
what we should have done. We hit targets and we
lost fewer planes.

On missions almost no one wore a white scarf.
The flamboyance made the war endurable. Now it
was gone. The 100th was a quieter place.

On the twentieth, we sent the group to Merseburg,
and they got smacked by the worst flak barrage until
that time. As we waited for them at the control
tower, we counted. Eight missing.

Hard on me.

The best moment of my day was when my orderly
brought me the beige envelope with the writing in
brown ink: from Mrs. Harry H. Crosby, to Major
Harry H. Crosby.

But she was four thousand miles away.

I started going on pass to London regularly. Three
days off every two weeks.

Off base, my new rank made a lot of difference.
On Air Force bases there were many majors. Airmen
came to England. Since so many were shot down,

there were openings above them. If they survived, had lots of courage and even modest ability, they fitted into responsible positions, got promoted, finished their tours, and rotated back to the States. A major or lieutenant colonel at twenty-three or twenty-four was not unusual. As slow as my promotions were, in part because I was a navigator instead of a pilot, I had gone from second lieutenant to major in eleven months, a phenomenon rare if not impossible for the infantry, navy, or the British.

In London, officers had advantages over enlisted men. The USO and Red Cross, as democratic and equalitarian as they admirably tried to be, had to hand out invitations to English parties, some of which were open only to officers. Company grade, that is, second lieutenant, first lieutenant, and captain, got invitations to nicer parties and more interesting events than enlisted men. Now that I was "field grade," I got even more interesting invitations.

And I had Landra to take with me.

In London there were clubs for British, American, and other Allied field grade officers. I received an invitation to join something called the Churchill Club, on Dean's Court, as I remember. I went to parties where most of the men were ten years older than I was and their medals were from the last war. In contrast to them I was slim, I had hair on my head, I had five Air Medals, two Distinguished Flying Crosses, and a Presidential Citation. I had the French Croix de Guerre. I had two hash marks on my sleeve to show I had been overseas for a year.

Just being in the Bloody 100th made me a celebrity. Edward R. Murrow, Homer Bigart, Andy Rooney, Tom Considine, Walter Cronkite, Larry

Winship, the editor of the *Boston Globe*, and other radio and newspaper celebrities either came to our base or interviewed us in London. I was interviewed by BBC and the recording played in Iowa City, Rockford, and Chillicothe, making me a hero for my college friends, family, and in-laws.

In the language of the time, I was hot stuff.

In London, this all paid out in attention. For the first time in my life, I got advances from unescorted women. When they learned that I was a survivor in the notorious Bloody Hundredth, they thought it was their duty to be especially nice to me. Never before in my life had I been a target for good-looking women.

I had Jean at home and Landra in England.

I started seeing Landra every time I could.

I never really knew what she did. I never saw another unit patch like the one she wore on her shoulders. She told me her office was on Sloane Square, but once when I went there to surprise her, I found no military office at the address. When, on trunks, which was what the British called their long-distance phone lines, I tried to phone her at the number she gave me, I felt my call was forwarded through three and four exchanges. At each exchange I got a guarded voice—"May I ask who's calling, please?" or, "May I ask the purpose of your call, please?" The voice might say, "Subbletrun Wingate is not available, sir."

"Is she out for lunch, or will she be gone a long time?"

"I am not at liberty to say, sir."

Most women in the British services were promoted slowly. I think Landra skipped a rank, because she soon became a captain.

"I will request that Captain Wingate answer your call, but it may be a while."

"Can I reach her at another number?"

No answer. Just dead silence.

When we were together she was interested in what I thought, careful about what she thought.

Like me, she felt the need to put a lot into our three days. Since it was available at the 100th PX, I often took a fifth of Scotch to her and marveled at the way it disappeared. She didn't use a shot glass, she put the whisky in a tumbler and drank the whole glass. No grimace, no eyes closed, no shudder like an American doing chug-a-lug. No reaction at all. It was like water.

I never once saw her affected in any way by the whisky she consumed.

In wartime, London was battened down. Much of what usually appeared in museums was stored in basements somewhere.

And Landra knew where to find it all.

Landra knew flowers, and we visited all the great London gardens. I remember Kew Gardens most of all. She knew historical documents, and we read the Magna Carta and saw the Rosetta stone. She knew books and we saw first editions. She knew gravestones, and we read the inscriptions of Shakespeare, Chaucer, Henry VIII, all of them.

We sat behind the back bench of Parliament.

She knew all the high rank.

"That's Lord So-and-so. He's from Norwich," she said. "He has the P.M.'s ear."

Landra failed where I should have helped her succeed. Even with its wartime strictures, England was still the center of much intellectual excitement. There were lectures and meetings which should have interested me. Landra knew about them and would have liked to attend, but what I wanted from my leaves and passes was escape. I didn't want to know about any more problems or how to look at them. I was still muddling over what I had heard at Oxford. I missed what should have been invigorating contacts. I did not get to know all the cultural greats who were then doing all they could to entertain the troops—Dylan Thomas, Stephen Spender, Louis MacNeice, Dame Edith Sitwell, George Orwell, Evelyn Waugh, Laurence Olivier, John Gielgud.

That was my fault, not Landra's.

She knew, better than I did, what was happening on the Continent. From her I first came to realize the extent of the Holocaust.

"Jews in France are being systematically removed from Paris and Nice. They have disappeared from the villages."

Was she a spy? Was she dropped into France? The Low Countries? Certainly her strange disappearances suggested that. Was she in Intelligence? Certainly her knowledge of languages and strategy, concealed though it was, made that possible.

I never knew. I never asked. She never told me.

All I knew was that she was making my life much more endurable.

I did not tell Jean about Landra.

R&R WITH JEAN

 The flyers who came over with the 100th in May 1943 were now few and far between. Ollie Turner was still C.O., of the 351st; Sumner Reeder had the 349th, with Sammy Barr as his Ops. Bucky Elton had the 350th, and Blakely had the 418th. During their stay they had all moved up from lieutenant to major or lieutenant colonel.

With them, Colonel Jeff—whom I had come more and more to respect—knew he had a batch of burntout cases. He managed to rotate Reeder and Turner back to the States. Bucky Elton finished his missions. Three of my friends gone. A good job, well done. Sumner Reeder was assigned to fly C-54's and crashed somewhere over the Carib. Dead.

Jeff arranged thirty-day R&R for Sammy Barr. He went home and came back, refreshed, and became C.O. of the 349th.

Blake and I were still there.

By this time I was an automaton. I got up, did my job almost without knowing what I was doing, and fell into bed, often without removing my clothes.

Blake and I were in the latrine at Ops with Colonel Jeff, and he saw us both in the mirror. Two skeletons. Our hats were too big. Our ears stuck out. Our A-2 jackets hung on us. Neither one of us bothered to have our pants pressed. Our shoes weren't shined. Our shirts were ringed with sweat. Around our eyes were dark circles.

Colonel Jeff knew cruel and unusual punishment when he saw it. "You two need a rest."

Blake went home first.

For a few days, before Sammy Barr and Ev Blakely came back, I was the only original 100th flyer on the base. I had outlasted them all.

On the twenty-fourth of July, 1944, the Fifth and Nineteenth U.S. Army Corps of the First Army were face to face with the Germans. To help them, we sent the Eighth up to blast a corridor 4,000 yards wide in the German lines southeast of Caen.

We sent up another formation to repeat the job. Absolutely pinpoint bombing was required. Colonel Jeff was command pilot. The mission was scrubbed.

On the next day, they went up again. This time we sent up three complete group formations of twenty-one planes each, the most we had ever put into the air. From just our base, we sent up sixty-three planes, what the whole Eighth Air Force had put up for the Trondheim mission. When the three groups got to where the infantry was fighting, the smoke and haze were so bad they had to go down to 12,000 feet. Easy range for anything to shoot at them.

Visibility was zero. The lead bombardier held his bombs, thinking that they were short of their target. The B and C groups dropped into the smoke. As they dropped their bombs, they heard voices on the ground radio liaison frequency. "Hold your bombs. You're dropping short."

On the way home, the air was full of recriminations. Why were heavies being used for this kind of work? Had the bombs gone short? They were 100-pound frags. What a mess they would have made of our men.

At briefing: "You killed the head of the infantry in that sector, General McNair."

Who did it? Photos completely exonerated the 100th, but it was a mistake made by a navigator in another group.

I was devastated.

Without permission I left Thorpe Abbotts, went to London and was rude and irritable with Landra Wingate.

I came back to the base ashamed of myself.

Although Jean still got a letter to me every single day, I began to skip writing to her. I complained that she was not banking our savings properly. This was the first time I ever wrote harshly to her, and she was deeply hurt. Penitent, I wrote to her that I shouldn't care about the money, and she should go out and buy herself a fur coat. When I insisted, she bought the coat, and sent me back a picture of her in July, in a beautiful gray squirrel coat.

My phone rang. Colonel Jeff himself. Usually an orderly or his adjutant placed his calls.

"Croz, we can't stand to have you around. We want you back, but we want you to go home for a while. You will have thirty days in the States. Tell Jean I would like to meet her."

Going home.

The procedure to get me back to the States. R&R personnel had a very low priority for seats. I was sent to an embarkation center with a pool of enlisted men and officers who were going home. The injured got first priority. Permanent transfers, the ones who were going home for good, were next. The R&R group, who would be back, were last.

I spent hours in the Officers' Club waiting for a seat on a plane or a berth on a ship. Nothing.

Time for self-examination.

What was I like? What would Jean be like? What would she think of me?

What would I think of her? Protected in the States as she was, how would she compare to Landra? Now that I had grown so much, had such experiences, how would Jean and I fit together?

An orderly came into the club, got our attention.

"A war-weary B-24 is being sent back to the States as part of a bond tour. The navigator got appendicitis. Is there a navigator here who can get a Lib across the Atlantic?

I did not volunteer. No one did.

More self-examination. Why did I reject the opportunity? Was I afraid I couldn't navigate across the ocean? Did I have a prejudice against a B-24? Was I afraid of seeing Jean?

I went to Ops. The offer was still open.

I spent six hours refreshing what I knew about celestial navigation. We took off and I fretted about sitting backward as I navigated. Dumb way to put an aircraft together.

To my surprise, I found Iceland, Greenland, Newfoundland, and the United States without any trouble. I rushed into New York City, where every G.I. and gob on the street almost broke his arm in an eager salute to me. The rank, the medals, the hash marks. I stopped at the first restaurant I saw and ordered a steak and fresh milk, six glasses of it. The waitresses all stood around me and cheered as I chug-a-lugged each glass. I then stopped a cab and asked to be taken to the Waldorf-Astoria.

"It's full up. You won't find a room."

The receptionist at the Waldorf, ogling my medals and rank, could not refuse me.

"Excuse me. I will get the manager."

The manager looked at me.

"Isn't that a Croix de Guerre?"

"Yes, sir."

"You have been overseas more than a year?"

He looked where I had signed my name.

"You are Major Crosby. Harry Crosby! That's Bing Crosby's name too, the way he signs it on the register. He is here now. Maybe we can get you two together for some publicity pictures."

"You have a room for me?"

"No, but we have a suite, and we will let you have it at the same price."

"Hello, Croz."

I turned around. Behind me was Colonel Chick Harding.

"Dodo, this is Major Crosby. I have told you about him. Harry, this is my wife."

That night, the Colonel and his Lady—no, I was to call them Chick and Dodo—had dinner in the Starlight Roof Garden, with Guy Lombardo in the background. The headwaiter gave us the best table, right up in front. Three waiters seemed to be giving us their complete attention.

"Major, may I dance with you?"

I looked up to see a svelte young woman, floor-length skirt split up to reveal long slender legs, shimmering pageboy bob, dark hair, luminous eyes. She was one of the singers in the band.

I looked at the Hardings, saw their approval, excused myself, and danced.

She was so good that she made me dance very well. I took long steps, easy, not too much the show-off. The singer nestled into me and sang into my ear. It was Jean's and my song, "At Last."

She ended up with the last line, "And here again, home again, at last with you."

The music ended and people applauded, apparently at us. A girl came up, short skirt, a camera in her hand.

"We would like some pictures."

Two days later, I was reunited with Jean, the moment I had yearned for—and dreaded.

It was at Camp Kilmer, in New Jersey. I met her when she got off the train.

I recognized her immediately.

But she was taller than I remembered.

She was slimmer.

Her hair was longer.

Her eyes glowed.

She was the most beautiful woman I had ever seen or imagined.

Four weeks. Four long and wonderful weeks.

The train trip back to the Midwest. Meeting our parents. Nights in hotels. Days with friends, and days alone.

Okay, so I had grown a lot when we were apart. But she could pack a suitcase better than I could. She was positively inspired when she ordered at a restaurant. She could read a train schedule. In an instant she could neaten up a hotel room. She smiled with dignity when an enlisted man in Chicago insisted on carrying her bag. There was always something to talk about.

I had grown one year, she had grown three.

After about a week, at breakfast, I started laughing.

She looked mystified.

"I'm laughing at myself. I was so smug. I feared that with all my experiences overseas, I might find you lacking in sophistication."

"And you don't?"

"I guess not! You are way ahead of me."

She smiled.

"That's a relief. I had the same fear. I worried that I might disappoint you."

An idyll.

The whole month went very well, and very fast.

Jean was more than I remembered. The photographs she had sent me had done her little justice. The months had treated her very well. When I went overseas, I left a girl. I returned to a woman, a lovely one.

In contrast to the days when I had courted her so strenuously, I had the comfort of knowing the race was over. She was my wife. I could just relax and be nice to her, and she with me.

One memory: One morning, while we were at Jean's parents, my first batch of mail came. I sat in the living room and opened it, Jean at my side, her father and mother with us. To them I read a report from Ed King, a note from Ev Blakely, to keep me posted on life at Station 139. Two letters from friends from the University of Iowa. They were 4-F, wanting to wish me well and express their envy—and their frank relief that they had escaped what I had endured. I read those letter to Jean and her parents. I opened a large envelope from the Waldorf-Astoria Hotel, pulled out an eight-by-ten black and white glossy. There I was dancing at the Starlight Roof, my profile to the camera, in my arms a tall, svelte girl, eyes closed, her face nestled against me. Whispering? Singing to me? Her dress, being backless, seemed to leave her practically nude.

Jean, her mother, her father, and I looked at the picture, saying nothing. I explained how I happened to be dancing with the singer.

Dances. Visits. Long mornings with breakfast in bed. Walks along the main street of any town. A burly old policeman in Chicago saluting me, shaking his head and saying, "My God, they are letting kids run the army these days."

There was a war on. In Guam, Wake Island, on the Rhine, flying the Hump, hundreds of young men were getting killed, but I was home, with my wife.

We talked about our future. We would go back to Iowa City, and I would continue my master's degree. Teaching still seemed what I wanted to do. Because we believed I would not fly any more missions, the future looked reasonably secure.

We made an important decision. During one of those happy nights our first child was conceived.

CHAPTER
24

ROSIE

 When I returned to Thorpe Abbotts, I found, that the 100th had a new hero.

Robert Rosenthal seemed to have a charmed life. He flew his first mission on October 8, 1943, and watched the two leads, Bucky Cleven and us, get shot out of formation. He saw eight planes go down. Two days later he saw the whole group go down. His was the only plane that returned from Münster.

He finished his tour, during his first twenty-five missions moving his way from the wing up to flight leader, and then to low squadron lead. At the end of the tour, most of his crew went home, but he stayed on, first as squadron operations officer.

He started his second tour. He volunteered especially for the tough ones. He went to Berlin several times, Frankfurt, Bremen again. He became Squadron Commander of the 418th.

What made him fly? The story was that his family was part of Hitler's Holocaust. His grandparents killed on Crystal Night. I never knew for sure, and I didn't ask. All I knew was that I liked him very much. We laughed a lot together. When I went up with him once to check out a new crew, he told the pilot that no good B-17 pilot ever did a buzz job, but he could buzz clouds.

So for the next half hour we flew in and out of the clouds, up and down, like Tinkerbell, but in a man-made monster of an aircraft. I got violently airsick but the rest of the crew had a joyous time.

With Rosie, life was fun.

Then he got shot down. On a mission to Nuremberg, he got hit over the target, limped as far as Belgium, and crash-landed in France. Jack Wallace took over as 418th Commanding Officer.

Three weeks passed. Rosie came back to Thorpe Abbotts. With the help of the Underground, he made it out in record time, his broken arm in a sling.

This time he became 350th Squadron Commander.

Later, he got shot down again and managed to land where some French Resistance picked him up and shipped him to the American troops.

The 100th had a heart and a spirit again.

Rosie made a difference.

He wasn't much of a soldier. Instead of returning a salute, he smiled and waved. The story was that he had played football with the writer Irwin Shaw at Brooklyn College, but he certainly didn't look like an athlete. He walked with his toes turned in. He never really fit a uniform. No 100-mission crush hat for him; he usually went bareheaded. He and Butch

Rovegno, the Group Engineering Officer, argued a lot about who was the ugliest man on the base.

Jack Kidd, John Bennett, and Tom Jeffrey showed us how to win a war. Bucky Cleven and Bucky Egan gave the 100th its personality. Bob Rosenthal helped us want to win the war.

When Rosie started on his third tour, many flyers volunteered for their second. They wanted to be like Rosie.

Life for me, when I returned from stateside, was very different. I had longer letters to write to Jean since we had so many more new experiences in common. Her letters were filled with reports on her pregnancy. We deliberated on what we would name our child. We got it down to three names, two for a boy and one for a girl. Stephen Patrick or Jeffrey Allen. I leaned toward naming a boy after Colonel Jeff. For a girl we came up with Evalyn, in honor of her two grandmothers, Eva Crosby and Evelyn Boehner.

On the orders of Colonel Jeff, Rosie and I intensified lead crew training. While Ed King did most of my work as Group Navigator, I spent hours in the air with lead crew and command navigators helping them learn how to make rendezvous, how to compute ground speeds and winds—and communicate the data back to the rest of the navigators. Rosie and I helped the DR navigator, the command navigator, the Mickey operator, and the rest of the crew cooperate with Command Pilots, who now took part in air leadership training.

I was amazed at how good they got.

Ed King, John D. Carpenter, William Dishion, Jack Wild, Big Pete, Kelsey Wilcox, Bob Kirby, Charlie Gunter, Walt Klinikowski, Lee Raden, Carl

Roesel, Seymour Passan, Ray Miller, Julius Krepisman, Leo Kimball, and several others were in my Hall of Fame. They became truly great, either as lead crew DR navigators or as command navigators. Two Mickey operators, Dick Johnson and Storm Rhode, became so good at their job that they really were command navigators. Any one of them could lead the task force as well as I had. In fact, we had so many great lead crews that we could afford to fly them as deputy lead. When the group lead went down, we had a skilled crew as deputy, leading the high squadron, so that we no longer had the catastrophes we had over Bremen and Münster.

My consolation as I compared myself to them was that I had led the whole task force on more M.E.s (maximum efforts) than any of them. They started leading the Air Force when they had about twenty missions, but I did it on my third mission, to Trondheim. They did it not only with two navigators in the nose of the plane, but also with a Mickey operator. In the early months, Leonard Bull, Bubbles Payne, Tony Gospodor, Howard Bassett, and I did it all alone.

Partly because the Third Air Division Staff Navigator, Ellis Scripture, knew me and gave me credit whether I deserved it or not, and partly because those lead navigators did so well, Group Navigators from other commands came to study what I was doing. They just could not believe that I looked at navigators' logs after every mission and graded them for thoroughness and accuracy. For flying combat missions, I gave grown men marks from F to A. The visitors shook their heads in disbelief.

They all lamented how slowly navigators got promoted and how rarely they got medals. When he learned that I had got myself put on the awards and decorations board and made sure that navigators, bombardiers, and gunners got as big a chunk of the medals as the pilots did, one of the visitors said, "You are not a Group Navigator, you are a politician."

I worked with the Personnel Officer to make room for more captain navigators. According to the Table of Organization, our group was entitled to one major navigator—me. We could have four captain navigators, the ones holding the position of Squadron Navigator.

At first, when we had only thirty-two crews in the group, the Higher-Ups held us to this T.O., but when we grew to seventy-five crews and flew several missions a day, they slacked off. Although I could not promote my assistant, I could transfer captains from one position to another. When a lead navigator made captain as Squadron Navigator, I immediately transferred him on paper to Group Ops as my assistant. Then we would put another lead navigator in the squadron into the opening for the captaincy.

I got so slick at this that at one time I had four captain assistants and four captain Squadron Navigators, twice the number we were authorized. When one of my captains went to London, he met one of his navigation school classmates, who was still a second lieutenant. "Oh," the lieutenant said, "You must be in the 100th with that Major Crosby."

When my captain came back to the base he said, "Sir, you are a legend."

Once a mission got screwed up. The command pilot of the wing lead charged that the 100th arrived late at the rendezvous. The wing got to the air division rendezvous all mixed up and there was much swearing over the air as the maelstrom of planes and groups churned around trying to get into position.

All the lead crews and command pilots were summoned to Wing HQ for a critique. By now Kelsey Wilcox, one of our former leads, was the staff navigator at Thirteenth Wing HQ.

"Major Crosby," he said, "the 100th navigator is in trouble."

At the debriefing, a lieutenant colonel from the 390th stood up. "We were on time for the rendezvous but the 100th never showed up."

The command navigator from the 390th, a major, backed him up.

How could they be so sure? They had climbed up through 15,000 feet of clouds. They could not see the ground for a visual checkpoint. For some reason, no Pathfinders, the planes with Mickey blind bombing equipment, were used that day. There was no radio beacon.

The 100th lead navigator was a child. He looked old enough to be a Boy Scout, but not old enough to be senior patrol leader. His name was Norman Graham, but we called him The Kid. I thought he was one of the best lead crew navigators we ever had.

He looked at me, and shook his head. "I thought we made the rendezvous exactly on time."

A second lieutenant navigator against a major navigator and a lieutenant colonel command pilot? No visual or radio checks to confirm either claim? It looked as though one of Major Crosby's navigators had fucked up. The room was very quiet and everyone looked at me.

"Major," I said to the 390th navigator, "when

was the last time you saw the ground or went over a
beacon?"

"At H-minus 1:32. I saw Lowestoft. A clear visual
check confirmed by my deputy lead navigator."

"Kid, I mean Lieutenant, when was your last visual check."

He gave me a time and a place.

"Major, what was your wind?"

He told me.

"Lieutenant Graham, what was yours?"

The Kid told me. Apparently he thought the wind
was much stronger than the major did.

While everyone in the room watched me I plotted
the two positions on a chart on the wall. With a pair
of dividers, I measured the distance the two groups
had flown, and wrote it and the time on the blackboard. I put the major's arithmetic and The Kid's in
two separate problems. When I picked up my E6B
computer, Kelsey Wilcox and The Kid began to
smile. Kelsey told me once I could make an E6B talk.

"Lieutenant, according to my computations, if you
arrived on course when you said you did, your
ground speed against the wind was 162 knots.
Kelsey, what does his log show?"

"164."

"Major," I said to the 390th command navigator,
"If you started out where you said you did, your
ground speed upwind to get to the rendezvous had to
be 640 knots."

Much buzzing in the audience. I turned to the
Wing Commanding Officer and then back to the
390th navigator. I admit that I was guilty of phony
dramatics. I said, "Major, has a B-17 ever flown that
close to Mach One?"

The 390th major and the lieutenant colonel looked at The Kid. Then they looked at me. The major said, "Crosby, you son-of-a-bitch."

The 100th cheered.

On the next morning, orders went in for The Kid to become a first lieutenant.

As my navigators got better and better and turned in great missions, I got the credit, and I was awarded a Bronze Star. Lots of other Group Navigators in the seventy-five commands who now made up the Eighth Air Force had the Distinguished Flying Cross, but, to my knowledge, I was the only one who got the Bronze Star. That meant a lot to me.

As the missions passed and my kid captain navigators went out and flew flawless missions, I began, slowly, to realize that I was treated like a has-been. New crews saluted me, and called me "Major Crosby," and smiled at me, but they considered me a relic of another kind of warfare. When I worked with lead navigators in the air on practice missions, they saw that I knew my stuff but there was something missing.

Then, too, I had never flown a mission with Colonel Jeff. All the other leaders in the group were his appointments, but I was part of the Old Guard. I felt he treated me like an outsider. I respected him so much for what he was doing with the 100th that I wanted to be sure he knew what I could do.

So I decided to fly with him.

The next time the 100th was to lead the task force, Jeff put himself in the lead plane, and so did I.

"Now I will see you do your stuff," he said.

"Likewise."

The target was a deep penetration, to Frankfurt, with heavy flak. We could expect heavy fighter attack but our escort was going with us, all the way.

Briefing, normal. Bomb load, normal. Crew assembled at the hard stands, talking quietly, cleaning their guns. Normal. The lead crew navigator and I conferred carefully, making sure we had an effective division of labor.

"Major Crosby, will you make the task force rendezvous? I have put the group together and the wing and the division, but I have never worked with the Libs and the First. I have heard you were"—he corrected himself—"are the best at it."

I agreed, pleased with the opportunity.

At the appointed time Colonel Jeff's jeep drives up, the Air Exec with him. He passes out Hershey bars to the crew. They like that. He is a good guy. He asks, "Do you have any special rules that I should know about intercom procedure?"

The pilot shakes his head. "No dumb jokes. No shouting. Keep the messages short. No one but the navigator, bombardier, and pilot on intercom during the bomb run. Pilots are hands-off on the bomb run."

Jeff smiles. "Wilco. I get the message."

Engines start. I hear Colonel Jeff dutifully doing the copilot's role for start-up procedure. We have number one and number four roaring. Chocks are removed. We start to roll. We taxi with the outboards and pull out into the perimeter strip. As we pass by, other planes roll out behind us. I look back and see a string of air monsters behind us, their outboards whirring.

At the head end of the takeoff strip, the pilot starts number two and number three and runs them up, step by step, with the procedure. I hear that mercury pressure is good, the flaps will work. They run the engines up, the plane straining against the braked wheels.

Engines at idle, the bombardier and navigators standing behind the pilots with the top turret gunner. No one is ever in the nose during takeoff. Behind us all the gunners are sitting down on the floor, their backs to the bulkheads. SOP. Standard operating procedure.

We peer out to the right, watching the control tower.

Green-green flare. The two fiery pom-poms loop out over the takeoff strip. Jeff turns his head to the left, looks at the pilot, who nods.

The pilot firmly pushes the four controls forward and the engines roar. He gets the power up with the brakes on and the plane shudders, straining to move forward.

Brakes off. We roll, the engines thundering, the whole airframe shuddering, faster and faster. We pass the control tower. Everyone on the roof is waving at us.

After we get into the air, the crew navigator and I go down into the nose. I stand up, my head in the astrodome, watching other planes on both sides. The lead navigator is working on his log and E6B. He writes, "T.O. On time, as briefed." He marks down the time. "0515."

We hit the overcast at 4,000 feet, and it is like flying through milk. Now the hardest part of the mission, for me, begins.

Round and round over Splasher Six. It is not as hard or dangerous anymore now that we have the Mickey operator giving position reports to the lead crew navigator. On intercom, we call him "DR." DR plots the positions on his chart, and I see a tiny circle of dots around the base. Wonderful. Now we navigators can do what we are supposed to do.

The top of the clouds is at 16,000.

We break out into blinding sunlight. Normally the high squadron comes out first, but today we took off ahead of them. We are the only plane in the whole wide world, and the whole wide world is spread out all around us. We are over The White Meadow of Heaven. It is blindingly beautiful.

A lovely day to go to fight a war.

The other planes pop out.

"Command to top turret. Fire flare."

"Roger dodger."

"Pilot to top. Can the funny stuff."

"Roger . . . sir."

"That's better."

The group comes together, high in place, low at first strung out, a wingman missing. A supernumerary fills in.

"Command navigator to command pilot, group formation, normal and on time."

Wind direction and speed as briefed.

Wing assembly. Normal and on time. Not merely right as to minute, but right as to second. Getting sixty-three planes in such precise formation is an art. DR probably can't see it through my oxygen mask, but I smile at him. I hope my pleasure is pardonable. I have taught him well.

The 390th is high, on the starboard. The 95th is low, port side.

I hear Colonel Jeff talking to the 390th, whose Air Exec he was. He joshes the 390th.

"Has Scrubbrush Baker forgotten to fly formation since I left? Pack it in."

At the division rendezvous one of the wings is early. They will need to ess. They have to get behind us.

We are on time. Jeff calls the early wing and approves their maneuver to get back in place.

Now to get the three divisions together. For some reason the Libs are lower than we expected.

"Lead navigator to command navigator. It is your show. The wind is a lot stronger than briefed."

It is indeed. In fact it is more than seventy miles an hour.

"Command navigator to pilots. The wind is seventy knots portside."

"Roger, pilot to navigator."

I do not hear an acknowledgment from Colonel Jeff, but I don't think anything about it.

Piece of cake. As planned, we have twelve minutes to play with before we go direct to the meeting with the First and Second.

I twirl my E6B, the lead navigator watching me, making sure his oxygen tube, radio wires, and electrical underwear connection do not get in my way.

I call the pilot. Heading to rendezvous, 84 degrees."

"Roger."

Colonel Jeff comes on. "How we doin', Croz?"

"Command to command. Very well. We have twelve minutes to lose."

"Right. An ess."

"No, a radius of action."

But Jeff is on another radio channel, talking to the First and Second Division leaders.

No problem. In lead crew training, we have practiced the maneuver. The pilot and I will handle it.

We smooth into the heading. 110 degrees. 100 degrees. Ninety. Eighty, then easy back to 84.

"Pilot to command navigator. In two minutes do an R.A., five and three. Port side.

"Roger."

The maneuver is clear. In 120 seconds he will turn 45 degrees to the left, fly the heading for five minutes and then rack the formation rather hard onto a 90-degree turn to the right. In three minutes he will do a 45 to the left, back on course. It is important that we turn into the wind; otherwise the high wind will hit us before we make the turn and blow us far to the starboard. Every navigator knows you never do an ess or a 360 by starting downwind.

I relax, waiting for the stately maneuver.

Two minutes pass. Nothing.

I start to call the pilot. Then, to my horror, we start turning starboard, downwind. The lead navigator looks up, stricken.

What's up?

"Command navigator to pilot."

"Pilot here." His name was Austin Dunlap.

"What are we doing, turning right? The wind is portside."

"Sorry, Navigator. The colonel has the plane."

Colonel Jeff is making the turn? Does he know something we don't? Has the mission been recalled?

I hit the intercom button.

"Command navigator to command pilot."

Nothing.

"Command navigator to command pilot."

A click. "Pilot to Major Crosby."

"Go ahead, Pilot."

"The colonel is on the task force channel."

"Will you punch him for me. I need to talk with him."

"Captains don't punch colonels, sir."

By now we are going full tilt downwind, away from course. We will not get back on course on time.

I stick my head up in the astrodome and signal frantically to Colonel Jeff, making motions at my throat mike.

"Command to command. What's up, Croz?"

"Sir, we had a mixup on the rendezvous procedure. We are now behind for our assembly."

Mild profanity. "What went wrong?"

"Sir, I don't have time to explain. We need to take a direct heading to the Assembly Point, but we will still be six minutes late."

Stronger profanity.

Colonel Jeffrey is on the air, giving the bad news to the other divisions. Up ahead I see the Second on the left and the First on the right. They planned to fall into trail behind us but they are ahead of us. I can imagine their navigators figuring out how to lose those six minutes. Not enough time to do anything very scientific. I watch their strategy.

The Second, those 24's that look so different from our Forts, turns right, toward the course; the First, 17's like us, turns left, also toward course. That should have been all right, since the Libs were briefed to be a thousand feet higher than our division and two thousand higher than the First.

But all hell breaks loose. I switch to command channel.

If the Germans who are monitoring our radio understand the American language, they know something has gone wrong. I hear choice expressions like "fucking bastard," "shit house mouse," and "goddamn asshole," most of them aimed at Scrubbrush Able, us.

Apparently the Second got started late in their climb and they are a thousand feet lower than briefed. They are at 15,000 feet, our altitude. The First were supposed to be at 14,000 feet, but when they got there they were still in the soup, and they kept on climbing. They leveled off at 15,000.

So here we are. Every aircraft and crew that the U.S. Eighth Air Force can get into the air for an M.E. are flying right at each other.

Maelstrom. The three divisions converge. Their command pilots yell at each other and at their formations. Even the atmospherics are against us. All three divisions are laying contrails like highways.

It's a beautiful sight. Hundreds of planes. Mammoth ribbons, as big as superhighways. Dozens of flares, red-green, green-green, yellow-yellow, yellow-red, yellow-yellow, all the possible combinations as the lead planes try to identify themselves and keep their formation together. Fourth of July.

I cover my ears to keep out the sound of the crashes I expect. Planes veer in every direction to avoid smashing into each other.

Suddenly we are in the clear. We have made it through the melee. Colonel Jeff calls the high group.

"Scrubbrush Able to Scrubbrush Baker. Lose anyone?"

"No, by the grace of God."

God seems to have been with us. No losses. A miracle. I even hear some laughter on command channel. From Toothloose Able Leader I hear, "Scrubbrush

Able, the rest of the mission can't be any harder than what we just went through."

Then, Colonel Jeff wants to know what happened. I tell him, and he gets mad, and then I get mad, and we start shouting at each other. A full colonel and a major yelling at each other over intercom. No Tail-End Charlie's wing crew would have permitted that during a mission. Actually we both made a mistake. I should have made sure he Rogered or Wilcoed when I announced the wind change. He, as the command pilot, should have let the lead crew pilot do the ess. We finally get it straightened out and click off the interphone, more or less friends.

From then on, the mission goes very well, and Colonel Jeff does a great job as formation leader.

We cut short on one of the doglegs and make up time. We arrive at the fighter support rendezvous right on time. So do the P-51's. A few HE-110's pop up out of the clouds, but they are outnumbered ten to one, and they dip back into the clouds.

Fifty miles short of the target the skies below open up and we can see all of Germany. Beautiful country. Rolling hills. Lovely villages.

Smooth at the I.P. Bomb bays open. Easy, easy run, the bombardier in charge, no sudden corrections. The heading we gave him exactly right.

Bombs away.

"Ball turret to command pilot."

"Speak, Ball."

"Sir, we creamed the target, tight pattern."

So much for Frankfurt.

We lose no planes. A few Purple Hearts for flak injuries, but nothing serious. We get back to England. Normally, when there is a mission with no losses, the command pilot calls the loosened formation in and we buzz the base.

Not today. We come straight in.

I do not feel I have impressed him.

That night I see him at the Officers' Club. He is pleasant, but distant. I think to myself, "I screwed up."

I have a short conversation with him.

"Crosby, did you hear Axis Sally just now?

"Yes, sir, I did. She said, 'Today the Eighth Air Force was out in force. They bombed Frankfurt. They killed 5,000 people and they left 50,000 homeless.' That was all she said."

He looked at me and said nothing.

"How did it make you feel?" I asked.

He continued to look directly at me. "I felt okay. It was our job. And we did it well."

I took a moment to answer. "I guess I felt okay too."

He smiled slightly, nodded, and walked away.

CHAPTER
25

LONDON JUNKET

✠ When I returned from the United States and my idyll with Jean, I knew I had to do something about Landra.

For a while I solved the problem by doing nothing.

Readjusting to my new life in which I flew almost every day with Rosie and the lead crews took time. Since he was no longer a member of a squadron he moved into the WAAF site, which was for the leaders of Group Headquarters. Since no ground officers rotated home, the only ones who left the 100th were the misfits and incompetents. As openings developed, many of the best and brightest ground officers of the squadrons were promoted to Group HQ jobs—and moved into the WAAF site, where Rosie, Blake, and I lived.

Here, the talk, and the friendship, and the dumb, ribald, practical jokes made life a delight.

Letters every day, back and forth, to Jean.

Finally fate forced me to go to London.

As the 100th flew its missions, we threw huge parties to celebrate the 100th and then the 200th mission. I missed the first one because I was sent to Alconbury to learn how to use some new technical equipment. I heard it was quite a bash. There were still girls in the barracks on Wednesday. The next party to celebrate the 200th mission was to be September 30, 1944, and I didn't want to miss it.

The 100th could really throw parties. For the 200th Mission Party, we signed up a whole carnival with ferris wheels and rides. We invited almost a thousand English girls. In fact, whether she knew it or not, every girl in England was invited.

Wars being what they are, and soldiers being what they are, we began to accumulate all the alcoholic beverages we could acquire. When our PX officer, Al Paul, heard that a huge supply of whisky and vodka had arrived in London, the party committee commandeered a plane, the *Mason-Dixon Line*, to fly to London to pick up crates and crates of supplies. We got Duncan Shand to act as pilot. Since the trip assumed the proportion of a mission, Cowboy Roane volunteered to act as command pilot. I was asked to be the navigator.

I had to go to London. I had to say goodbye to Landra.

She was, of course, highly decent. She had seen it coming.

"When a month passed after you were to return, and you did not phone me," she said, "I suspected that it was over. You found things good with Jean?"

I told her about R&R in the U.S. I told her more

about Jean. I told her about Stephen Patrick, Jeffrey Allen, or Evalyn.

"When I realized you were gone," she said, "I no longer said no to a nice American at my office. I have been with him several times. I like him."

"I'm glad."

"He is not married. He is not so dashing as you, but we have good times together."

Me "dashing"? That was not my self-image.

So much for Landra.

Actually it was not so much for Landra.

Landra was a superb young woman. A brave lady making the most of her duties with the military. She taught me a lot. She was an intelligent, witty woman, a companion when I needed one very much. I shall always be thankful that I knew her.

The trip back to Thorpe Abbotts in a war-weary plane, heavily laden with crates of party preparation, was one of my toughest missions.

We were scheduled to take off at noon, but it took a while for our party to assemble. There was too much for them to do in London. It was getting dark before we were ready to roll.

When we finally got into the plane we had quite a crew, some of them decidedly hung over. Our crew chief was Joe Picard, with whom I had flown to Russia. Somehow or other, our Group Surgeon, Clif Kinder, who was already in London, heard about the flight home, and he was in the radio compartment. We also had an assortment of air and ground officers and enlisted men who, for some reason or other, deserved to be on the junket. As Doc Kinder put it, the crew looked like the basic cadre of a bomb group.

With Duncan Shand in the left seat and the Cowboy in the right, we begin our pre-flight warmups. Since Duncan knows we will be flying at dusk in the face of nervous RAF antiaircraft, he asks Joe Picard to load our flare pistol with the colors of the day.

Trouble right away.

Number Four won't fire. Grind, grind, grind.

"Let's try to make it start on the runway," says Cowboy.

The idea is that Duncan and Cowboy will go so fast down the takeoff strip that the prop will rotate and ignite the engine.

So, several times, we thunder down the runway. When the engine doesn't start, the pilots jam on the brakes and barely get stopped.

"Okay," says the Cowboy, "let's try it on three."

"Are you serious?" says Duncan. "I never heard of a 17 taking off on three engines."

"There's a first time for everything," says Cowboy.

We roar down the runway with max power and three props whirling. We make it. We get into the air.

Joe Picard starts firing the flares. He is so excited that he puts his weight on the pistol just as he pulls the trigger. The flare goes off in the cockpit and hits the box of flares at Joe's feet.

The box ignites and flares blow all over the pilots' compartment. They go into the bomb bay and burn around the fuel transfer valves. This is where pilots moved gas from wing tanks into the engine tanks. There are always fumes. Why we don't explode I'll never know.

The flares flame down into the hatchway and shoot into the nose, where I am fiddling with my paper maps. Red-red, green-green, yellow-red, yellow-yellow, the whole spectrum, the flares arcing all around us. Fourth of July in the aircraft!

And all the while Duncan is trying to get the underpowered plane under control and into the blue. We are skidding around just over London, near St. Paul's, the Tower of London, and Waterloo Bridge. The Cowboy leaves his seat, takes off his fifty-mission crush hat, and tries to bail the incendiaries out over London. Trying to breathe, Duncan opens his window and puts his head out—and almost loses it to the airstream. The Cowboy sees we are about to stall. He grabs the controls and pushes us into a dive that makes us just skim over some high wires. When Duncan and the Cowboy finally get the *Mason-Dixon* bird under control and we get the fires out, I go back to the radio compartment and learn that Doc Kinder and the other passengers have no idea what is going on. They are thoroughly enjoying their low-level view of London Town.

"It was nice of you," Doc Kinder says.

LAST MISSION

 Our next commander, Colonel Fred Sutterlin, was a good man, but he was new to combat. Rosie and I had to show him how to fly as command pilot with lead crews, and I had to show him the importance of the lead navigator.

The chance comes sooner than I expected. I am sitting in the movie with the rest of the rank in our rows. The red light goes on and I hear the buzz of talk as we file out. The base is on alert.

The field order has a surprise.

It is not our turn to lead. We will be buried somewhere in the middle of the huge formation. Since this is what we expected, the squadrons have let their command navigators go off on pass. Usually their leaves are coordinated through me, but in the roughness of the changeover to a new Group Commander, there's been a hitch. Ed King is gone somewhere, and I am doing the whole load.

The new maneuver is that tomorrow the 8AF will split up. The whole force goes in together and then the first wings turn north, and we turn south. Suddenly the 100th will be leading the formation.

I have to fly. There is no one else.

This is not all bad. Since Colonel Sutterlin is scheduled to fly in the command seat, I will have a chance to show him what I can do.

Not so.

Although he has flown several missions in high squadron leads and even a group lead, he does not have the macho that ruined Bob Kelly. Colonel Sutterlin takes himself out of the front seat and puts himself in low squadron lead. At the time we had two great command pilots, Jack Wallace and Harry Cruver, the best leaders we got out of Training Command.

Colonel Sutterlin puts Harry Cruver in the front seat, right, of the formation lead.

Lieutenant Colonel Harry Cruver is a dream of a guy. Tall. Heavyset. Red hair, red face. Always a smile. From the Midwest, like me. Good natured. No flap. Confident but not overimpressed with himself. Quick on the stories. He laughs about halfway through the stories and almost can't get to the punch line. He got his commission with the ROTC at the University of Wisconsin in Ordnance and went through flying school in rank. He spent a lot of time in Training Command. Now he is Squadron Commander of the 351st. He can fly a B-17.

We don't know where we are going, but the field order tells us something. M.E. Maximum bomb load of 500-pounders. No incendiaries. A factory? No sub pens or harbors. It will be deep.

March 31, 1945, my thirty-second mission actually, but, according to converted bookkeeping, it is listed officially as my thirty-seventh, to Bad Burken, which is part of Merseburg. A bad one, very bad, some of the worst flak in all Germany.

I attend pre-briefing, taking it in instead of giving it out. The telex starts chattering and the message gets unscrambled.

A deep target. Harry Cruver laughs, "We might as well have a big one as a little one." His logic escapes me, but I like him being at ease.

I leave Group Ops and get into my jeep for the drive to my quarters. The base is always blacked out, but the moon is so bright I can speed along.

I look up. There is not a cloud in the sky. I can see all the way to Mars and Jupiter. There is Orion, the North Star. On the horizon I see Aldebaran.

I say something, half prayer, half swearing. Why is the sky so clear now when it will be ten-tenths in the morning? Is God telling the British that they are right to bomb at night? Does He, whoever He is, not want us to violate the airspace over the Continent? I come up with no answers.

Since I am on duty about eighteen hours a day I am usually exhausted. Tonight is no different from the rest. I read the lovely, informative letter from Jean again. Stephen Patrick or Jeffrey Allen, or Evalyn is moving around. I write my response. Tell her how much I miss her. Play a record or two. Take a shower. Chew the fat for a while with Rosie and Butch Rovegno. Serious guys doing their jobs, which is what we talk about.

At 0400 hours, the phone.

"Roger, I will be right there."

The jeep ride. Yes, complete overcast. Ceiling at maybe two thousand feet?

Quick breakfast at the Flying Mess.

Group Ops is the usual hubbub and then a sudden silence as the rank walks in. No, we "stride" in. That's the way we try to look confident and competent. That's the way we try to inspire the troops.

S-2 pulls back the curtain. Harry Cruver, at my left, laughs. Sammy Barr, the major at my right, says one word in Louisiana talk: "Shee-yit." He will be high squadron lead. He has flown over fifty missions.

At the hard standing, the crew is quiet. The pilot is Bill Murray and the navigator is Hiram Johnson. I have flown with them during lead crew training, and they are top-notch.

Engines start. The Birds taxi out, pause at the end of the runway, run up their engines. Green-green.

We roar down the runway. By now the soup is on the ground and we are into the white when we hit the air.

Drone, drone, drone as we circle around Splasher Six.

We go onto oxygen at 10,000 feet and the bombardier and DR put on their masks. As usual, I feel I am in a different world. We break out at 12,000 feet.

Squadron assembly: easy.

Group assembly: I hear Harry, the other Harry, pulling the high squadron in. No problem.

Wing assembly: The lead crew navigator is in charge. On time to the second. I pat him on the shoulder as the second hand hits the top of the face of my watch. He may have smiled. I can't tell through his mask.

Wonder of wonders, a few moments ago there were 12,000 feet of clouds. Now they have burned off. I can see all of East Anglia. Farms. Away to the west is Nottingham Forest. Robin Hood. Under us, the Broads. The villages. Horse and carts.

"Navigator to Major Crosby."

"Go ahead, DR."

"Sir, I feel lucky. May I make the division assembly?"

"Roger."

He sits at his desk and calls to Mickey for a series of fixes every two minutes. He plots them furiously, checking each fix with his E6B. If I were doing it I wouldn't be using the computer. With this kind of visibility I can do it visually. The assembly is briefed for Great Yarmouth, but we are going the wrong way.

"DR to pilot."

"Roger."

"Three-hundred-and-sixty-degree turn to the left, into the wind, port side, around to 87 degrees magnetic.

"Roger."

With the sixty-two planes in the wing with us, we can use up from six to ten minutes, depending on how steep a turn he begins.

DR plots out a radius-of-action maneuver, calls for the upwind turn, then the hard right turn, and then back on course. Perfect.

The pilot, Captain Murray, levels out smooth as silk. He knows his job. Behind us the three squadrons follow him smoothly back to the 87 degrees.

"Good show, Pilot."

I am in the astroturret. High and low groups are in place. I go to the front of the compartment, to the side of the bombardier, and watch us sail over Great Yarmouth. The wings ahead of us are in trail formation. Beautiful.

"Formation Control Officer to command pilot." It is the crew copilot sitting way back in the tail gunner's position.

"Speak."

"Sir, all the wings behind us are in position. I can see their flares."

"Roger, Control. Good show, Navigators."

We have three fighter rendezvous. On time. Nothing for them to do. No E.A. at all.

Halfway in, the groups ahead of us turn left. That is good. They were beginning to leave contrails. We angle to the right. We are now in charge. Smooth.

Fifty miles from the I.P. the German defenses start throwing flak up at us.

"Control to command."

"Two planes in the high group just got it."

"Count the chutes."

"None, sir. Both planes blew up. There is debris all over the sky."

"This," says Command Pilot Harry Cruver, "is one hell of a way to make a living."

No response.

At the I.P., the crew bombardier takes over, makes a few minor but rocky corrections.

"Bomb bay doors going open."

I feel the plane tremble.

"Okay, crew, no one on intercom." It is the pilot.

The slowest seconds in all of time are when we are moving from the I.P. to the target. We are going downwind, but we will still be floating over some of the heaviest flak in Germany for about eight minutes.

"Control here. Three more planes, eight chutes. Low group."

"Later."

"Sorry."

The plane jumps suddenly. A rasping, scraping sound.

"Bombs away!"

Silence.

"Ball to command."

"In the pickle barrel, sir."

"How's the pattern."

"Tight. Nothing outside the target area."

"You hit the haystack, Bombardier."

"Thank you, sir."

So much for another German city.

The Rally Point. Control reports that he has seen eight planes go down, none in the 100th. A couple of our planes have lost an engine. Another plane has lost part of its vertical stabilizer.

"Rough," says command. "Let's go home."

As is often the case, I get airsick, now that I feel relief from the responsibility of getting to the target.

I head for the bomb bay, use up a #10 sack, and throw it out the vent. Maybe I have a grim smile on my face. The sack and its contents may hit some ack-ack gunner on the head.

On course, on time, all the way home. Our formation in tight. We roar triumphantly over the base at 200 feet, even the injured planes keeping up. No red-reds to request ambulances for the wounded.

Eighteen planes roll to their hard standings.

Debriefing. Strike photos show ninety percent of our bombs within a hundred feet of where we wanted the MPI, maximum point of impact. Very good.

Harry Cruver stands up before all the crews.

"Men, today we did just about as good a job as it is possible to do. I want to commend you, and I want to thank you."

He pauses, looks at me, and continues. "And I want, also, to thank Major Crosby. He is the navigator supreme."

Great! I like that.

But on the whole mission I didn't do one single thing. All I did was watch Hiram Johnson.

CHAPTER
27

GENERAL SPAATZ
IN PARIS

 By February 1, 1945, Colonel Jeff had left the 100th.

Darr Alkire, Howard Turner, Harold Huglin, Chick Harding, Bob Kelly, John Bennett, and now Tom Jeffrey. Seven of them. I had outlasted them all.

Jeff had flown a whole tour, and a man can only stand so much. General Earle Partridge, who had taken over the Third Air Division, told him it was time to move. Since field grade didn't rotate, he could not go home. He was transferred to ETO Headquarters in Paris.

I was sorry to see Jeff go. We were never close, but I felt we each had respect for the other, limited by my feeling about pilots and his about navigators. From a good pilot all I expected was a good truck driver. I wanted him to shut up, drive the plane, and stay out of things as the navigator and the bombardier took care of the mission. Jeff was a pilot. From a navigator he wanted a good job of bookkeeping.

My respect for him was increased by my gratitude about what he had done for the 100th. During his tenure, we flew good formation, we developed great lead crews, and we did not suffer heavy losses. He appointed good Squadron Commanders, and he helped them do their jobs well. He was all business, but it was good business. He was an excellent Group Commander.

Our new Commanding Officer was Frederick Sutterlin. Once again I had to earn the confidence of a man who had flown no combat and had little experience with navigators.

Apparently Colonel Jeffrey thought more of me than I thought he did.

I was in my quarters, writing to Jean.

The phone rang. I heard lots of zings and clicks, and an operator talking in a language I didn't know.

"Hello, Croz, this is Jeff."

"Where are you?"

"I'm in Paris, and, Croz, this is the life. You better come on over."

"Sounds great. When and how?"

"The USSTAF Navigator is going back to the States, and I think I can get you his job."

The next day Colonel Sutterlin had me on a B-17 flying to Orly Field in Paris.

Since the early Franklin D. Roosevelt days, the federal government was a melting pot of alphabet soup, like NRA, CCC, and AAA. In the military, acronyms became just as common: there were the WACs, the WAAFs, and the WAVEs. The alphabet was stretched as the proliferation of organizations set up many new names. Since then the women's titles changed so frequently I never knew what to call them.

We of the 100th were in what was first ETOUSA, the European Theater of Operation, United States of America, and then was shortened to the ETO. At first we in the Eighth and Ninth Air Forces were in the United States Air Forces, United Kingdom, till Axis Sally started pronouncing the acronym "Youse-a-fuck," from USAFUK. When all four Air Forces, the Eighth and Ninth in England and the Twelfth and Fifteenth in Italy, were joined, we became USSTAF, that is, the United States Strategic and Tactical Air Forces. Under General Carl (Touhey) Spaatz, USSTAF was divided into two missions. The tactical air forces, the Ninth in England and the Twelfth in Italy, supported the ground forces. They flew low, bombing bridges and enemy holdouts before the advancing infantry and tank corps.

The strategical air forces, the "Mighty Eighth" in England, and the Fifteenth in Italy, did the high-altitude bombing. With the support of the P-47's, the Thunderbolts, and the P-51's, the Mustangs, they destroyed factories, shipping, communication, and transportation. One of our missions was to destroy civilian and military morale. If I became USSTAF Navigator, I would be the navigation advisor for the whole of air warfare in Europe and Africa. I would also become a full colonel.

After my B-17 landed at Orly, I was met by a spit-and-polish first lieutenant who steered me quickly through a private door to a command car.

"Sir, I am to be your ADC while you are here," said the lieutenant, obviously an Eager Beaver.

ADC? Aide-de-camp? French expression. I was in Paris.

We drove sedately through the streets of Paris, with me gawking in every direction.

"Sir, part of your program while you are here is for me to give you a guided tour." The Eager Beaver would go far, I thought.

"The air support staff—the navigator, bombardier, metro, communication, who advise on tactics and strategy—all live together, in the Coty Mansion."

I could see I was in a different world.

We drove down a street of huge, ornate houses. Any one of them could have been a palace. We stopped at the biggest, the most ornate.

Immediately a thin, wiry, grizzled man ran out, saluted on the run, and opened the door. I felt uncomfortable. He was too old, too distinguished looking, to run.

Another man appeared from somewhere and took my B-4 bag; I wrestled with him over my briefcase, with my military secrets in it, and won. He looked hurt.

Still another man, looking like what I expected a butler to look like, opened the front door; yet another took my short coat. Uncertainly I watched it disappear. I followed my B-4 bag up an opulent, winding staircase with a dark brown, glistening bannister. There was a pendant-resplendent chandelier in the center. I followed the bag into what I guessed was to be my bedroom for the night, where we were met by—what would she be called—the chambermaid?

She was a lollapaloosa, dressed like a maid in a French movie, white lace apron and black dress with very short skirt revealing knockout legs. Her décolletage was low, revealing tremendous—I regret to find myself reverting to Air Force slang—but they were tremendous knockers. When I finally got to her face, it was a beaut. She was a stunner.

The stunner opened my bag quickly, smooth action, hung up my Eisenhower jacket and extra pinks, refolded my underwear and shirts and put them in the chest of drawers. My toiletries went to the bathroom, a private one just off the bedroom.

Thinking I might be doing some flying—silly thought—I had brought my A-2 jacket and my flying coveralls. Before she hung them up, she hugged them.

"Bom-bers?"

I nodded. My voice didn't work.

"Is there anything else, Monsieur?"

There was, but I didn't say so. I was afraid to say anything for fear my voice would break. I shook my head.

She smiled, curtsied, and turned to go. I watched her behind wiggle. Obviously she was being supplied nylons from the PX. Just as she got to the door she turned suddenly and caught me staring at her.

Up went the eyebrows. A giggle. "You are an American."

A knock on the door. The ADC.

"Captain Thatcher is ready to see you."

Into my room came a man—I think his name was Thatcher, and I disliked him instantly. He was too pretty.

I talked with him for thirty minutes and changed my mind completely. This was one bright guy.

My job, Captain Thatcher told me, would be to replace the lieutenant colonel who had gone back to Washington, D.C. He was an old-timer. He had been the navigator on one of the B-25's who flew with Jimmy Doolittle off the carriers, bombed Tokyo, and then landed in China.

"I was in training command until six months ago. After I graduated from San Marcos Navigation School, they found out I can do staff work. Before the war I worked for Samuel Goldwyn in Hollywood. Since General Arnold froze promotions except for combat people, I stayed a first lieutenant for almost a year. I hardly ever fly. I barely get my flying in for flight pay. I have never been in a Fortress, Liberator, Mitchell, or even a C-47. I had to learn fast. This is the picture."

And he described it.

For the next two days I swam with the big fish. I never had seen so many stars, so many generals. Colonels carried briefcases into meetings for generals. Back at Thorpe Abbotts that was done by buck sergeants. Everyone went to work in Class As, shined shoes, pink pants, tie, O.D. blouse, brass, ribbons. The 100-mission hat was now G.I. in the whole Air Force.

Even the WAAFs had rank. I could see that they weren't toys. They were all business, obviously treated as competent officers and noncoms. Their high heels made wonderful click-click-click noises on the marble floors of the ornate halls where we held our meetings. Apparently USSTAF Headquarters was in an important French government building. Everywhere there were pillars, high ceilings, massive dark wooden doors that took at least a sergeant to open and close. The only American touches were the round metal space heaters or electric grills fighting the chill. Americans do not like to be cold.

For me the situation was unreal.

When I told the ADC how confused I was, he said, "I don't think you would have to do much here. Captain Thatcher is the one who does the job. All you would have to do here is wear your medals. When big shots from Washington come here you would talk to them about the Bloody Hundredth and your missions, and keep them off General Spaatz's back."

When we met in the War Room to plan and coordinate the four Air Forces' effort for the next month, I saw General Spaatz. He was clearly in charge, but at first he just sat and watched. A brigadier read the orders from Hap Arnold in Washington. Then the assembled company divided the task into four, what the Eighth, Ninth, Twelfth, and Fifteenth would do. Another colonel provided some background information about weather, geopolitics, and strategy. Nothing from General Spaatz.

After about thirty minutes, the group broke up. The representatives from the Ninth and Fifteenth went into a room with some infantry officers. The Eighth and Twelfth went into another room with some French officers and their interpreters. I heard one gen-eral say that they were to "liase," which was what they called it.

Six people stayed in the room with General Spaatz. Captain Thatcher, who was one of them, asked me to stay with them.

A WAC with master sergeant's stripes came into the room and Spaatz stood up and thought for a moment or two.

"All right now," he said, "let's work on need to know."

For the next half hour, with the WAC taking notes, the small group prepared a list of communications and what would be in them. They worked out the directives which would tell all units involved what they were to do. General Spaatz kept asking the men questions. They seemed to know metro, ordnance, aircraft capabilities and requirements, and flight tactics.

I was dazzled at what Captain Thatcher knew. He knew where every bomber and fighter group and every support unit were stationed. He knew the indicated airspeed, the climbing rate, the load capacity of every plane. He knew, without using an E6B, what altitude did to temperature. He knew the strength every unit could muster for a mission.

When the meeting was over, I asked him, "How on earth did you learn all that?"

He shrugged. "It's all on paper somewhere."

I was dazzled by the performance, and dazzled by what went on back at the Coty Mansion.

At the end of the day, the ADC got a command car and gave me a brief tour of Paris, the Eiffel Tower, the Louvre, Trianon, Champs Élysées, Arc de Triomphe, Place de la Concorde, the shops, the cafés, and the fountains. We didn't stop. I didn't get out. Whirlwind tour.

And so back to the Coty Mansion.

I went inside and up to my room. A shower, with the stunner laying out my clothes, anxious to help.

Dinner was "dining in."

I knew the term came from the British, the night at the Officers' Mess when all the officers "dined in," the singles who lived in the BOQ, the Bachelor Officers Quarters, and the marrieds who lived out, with their wives, who—on this night—stayed at home.

"Every night is dining in," said one of the inhabitants.

There were about twenty of us, and I was motioned to take an alternate seat. A real "dining in" would be stag. At this dinner, in every other seat was a French girl.

What a group of women! It was as though someone had gone to an auction and bought only the best. Every one of them was a beauty. All brunettes. All shapely. All well dressed. Each blouse cut low in front, and well filled. Each girl with her own fragrance. Each girl with a smile. Each one anxious to please. Did they have jobs? Were they on salary? Were they there for just that one evening? Were they regulars?

I never knew.

The food was tasty, obviously French cuisine. The conversation was spritely, flirty. Suggestive, nonmilitary. Much of it in French.

After the dinner, drinks in the library, the girls making sure there was something for everyone.

Yvette had attached herself to me.

"Did you know Paris"—she pronounced it "Pa-REE"—"before the war?"

"No."

"An American who has not seen the Folies!"

"I am an American who has never been to Paris before."

She actually said, "Ooh, la la." Then she rolled her eyes and said, "Now you can live."

I talked a while, tried to understand the cosmos of USSTAF, and eventually looked at my watch.

USSTAF worked hard in their Class A's. I had to be at HQ at 0700 hours.

Yvette looked at the huge clock on the wall. "Twenty-two hundred hours. You Americans like to go to bed early." She arched her pretty eyebrows.

I excused myself from the highest ranking officer in the room, nodded to the rest of the assembly, and headed upstairs, Yvette at my side.

We walked down the hall, the rugs so thick that my feet did not feel firm underneath me. Maybe it was the wine.

When I came to my room, I turned and smiled.

"Good night, Yvette. Thank you."

"Good night?" Puzzled.

I turned and went into my room. The stunner had turned down my covers, laid out my pajamas. I thought about the expression on Yvette's face. Had I missed a signal?

In the morning I talked with Captain Thatcher.

"You've got the job if you want it. To be honest, much of our job is that we have to impress people. We have to convince people who don't know what we are talking about. The fact that you were an original member of the Bloody Hundredth who survived, the fact that you flew all the long and hard ones, means that you are what we want. The first guy with the job was Charlie Maas. He was Curtis LeMay's Group Navigator. Then he went to Third Division and finally came up here. He could do the public relations and the military part. Now it takes two men."

When I flew back to Thorpe Abbotts, except for the pilots, a radio operator, and a mechanic, I had a whole C-47 to myself—and plenty of time to think.

I was impressed by what I had seen. Everything clicked, and everything seemed to work. When they planned what Forts were supposed to do, they knew what they should know.

How would it be to be a figurehead and have a job in Paris?

Much of it would be very good. I would get one, maybe two, promotions. I would meet a lot of big shots. I would see Paris. I would have to learn how to handle situations with ladies like Yvette and the stunner.

Before we landed at Thorpe Abbotts, I knew the answer.

USSTAF was not for me.

I did not know how I would succeed at impressing people. I did not know how I could convince people about stuff which I did not understand myself.

I stayed with the 100th where I was pretty sure I was good at what was expected of me.

OPERATION
MANNA-CHOWHOUND

In the final months of the war, we got very good at what we were doing. With the help of our blind bombing apparatus, our air discipline, our superb lead crews—and the fact that the early crews, the original 100th, had done their part in destroying the Luftwaffe—we had many successful, and safe, missions. For every success, we must give credit to the men in our support services, seven on the ground for every one of us in the air, who kept us flying, and encouraged us.

To a degree, we learned to cope intellectually and emotionally with our life as destroyers. Some of us had trouble with our consciences. In long, late-night talks at the WAAF site, we discussed our ambivalent feelings about war, patriotism, and heroism. What was happening to us? Were we machines? Were we avengers?

Had we adjusted too well to the humdrum business of winning the war? We felt strange about how much respect we had for the Luftwaffe. When the field order came in some nights there were occasional references to "the Hun" or "the Krauts," or "the Nazis." The briefing officer always changed the words to "the Germans" and "the Luftwaffe."

I told our little discussion group about how when an ME-109 with the yellow nose of the Abbeville Kids, our most respected—and feared—opposition, flew through our formation, I saw the pilot wave at us.

"What did you do?"

"I waved back."

George Erbe, in peacetime a Hollywood interior designer with Deanna Durbin as a client, told me about Friedrich Nietzsche. "He said that when we grapple with monsters, we must be careful that we do not become monsters ourselves."

I thought about that.

I told our impromptu discussion group how I still felt guilty that I had laughed when Stew Gillison told me about how they got rid of my competition, Leafy Hill, by dumping him out over Germany. I told them about how I felt when one of my navigators came to me and said he could not get a parachute. Instead of staying at their section till the flyers took off, the officers and enlisted men in the equipment section locked up and left, and my navigator couldn't get a chute before a mission.

Enraged, I took the young navigator in my jeep to the parachute shop, kicked the door to splinters, and took a parachute. Then I went to the Officers' Mess, chewed out the supply officer in front of his friends, and ordered him to go back and repair the door. I wasn't sure about this new Harry Crosby.

Our missions were so neat. On our blind bombing missions, we went up over the clouds. Our bombs dropped into the white stuff, and we never saw the cities—or the people—whom we destroyed.

A new chaplain was assigned to us briefly, a lanky, skinny, country sort of guy. He went around the base with a toothpick in his mouth. He insisted that he be taken out to the firing range where aerial gunners practiced with their machine guns. He put his hat on backwards, grabbed a gun, pulled the trigger, and spewed out bullets at the target, all the while singing "Praise the Lord and pass the ammunition."

He was shipped out the next day.

One aircrew gunner kept a gunnysack to collect about fifty pounds of rocks. Every time he went on a mission and wasn't firing a gun, he dropped the rocks out, one at a time, over what he called "Krautland." I remembered again that on his last mission, Frank Valesh had gone around to every station on his plane, picked up the relief jugs, and then dropped them over Germany. On a mission, when I salvoed one of my #10 sacks, filled with the produce of my airsickness, I had always hoped, without thinking much about it, that it would hit someone on the ground.

We learned to live with our notoriety and our reputation by making fun of it—and enjoying the attention it earned us.

On February 9 a new crew came to the base short one member. When the crew got to the assignment station and learned they were to become members of the Bloody 100th, the "hard luck outfit of the whole Air Force," the copilot went over the hill.

When the crew, sans a copilot, went to their new barracks, they found all beds empty. "None of them got back from the mission," they were told.

Big joke. No, the crews didn't come back. Thorpe Abbotts got socked in, landing was below ILS (Instrument Landing System) standards, and the crews were told in advance to land in France. They flew back on the next day, but the veterans had the fun of flakking up the new crews.

In London I met another navigator and learned he was a member of the 390th Group. I told him I was pleased to meet another member of the Thirteenth Wing. He told me, "I am glad to meet a member of the 100th—who is alive."

Our station big band, which included some of my especially good friends, including Irv Waterbury, Danny Shaffer, Rex Baker, Eddie Dolezal, Pappy Daiger, and John Williams, got so good with their Glenn Miller arrangements that they were invited to play all over the ETO, and even put on a show at Piccadilly Circus. Mario Londra, the tenor, sang "When the Lights Come On Again," in a way that would break your heart. More attention for the 100th.

We upped our social life.

Every Wednesday afternoon we had a "tea dance" at the Officers' Club, inviting girls from the surrounding towns. One of our enlisted men's clubs constructed a still to make rotgut whiskey. Some officers in the ordnance section figured out how to make gin in their bathtub. We saved our cookies and candy for the parties we held every other week for all the English kids within ten miles.

On February 3—it seemed so sudden because we

didn't expect it—Rosie went down again. It was his fifty-second mission. He was leading the entire task force over Berlin. The report stated that he was hit just after the I.P, at 25,000 feet, at 1115 hours, with a ground rocket hitting the number one fuel tank. "Fire and dense white smoke were seen coming out of the fuselage and bomb bay." Heading northeast, "the plane flew level for a few moments, while the crew bailed out. It was last seen at 15,000 feet, "burning and beginning to spin."

Gloom on the base, like when the two Buckys went down. An enlisted man in Group Ops told me, "Sir, Major Rosenthal is a legend here. We all feel bad."

Rosie, the Indomitable, was gone.

The 100th hurt.

On February 22, we took on a new way of life. General Spaatz told Jimmy Doolittle that the Eighth was no longer strategic. It was tactical. Our primary mission was to support the ground troops who were fighting their way across Germany. Mostly we were to disrupt rail and highway communication. Now, usually when we went out, we saw what we were hitting.

In a speech to the troops, General Spaatz explained what it meant that we were now a tactical air force instead of strategic. He compared tactical bombing to kicking over a bucket of milk every day. "When you were strategic," he said, "you were killing the cow."

On February 23, out in the Pacific, on the tiny island of Iwo Jima, a small group of U.S. Marines fought their way to the top of a mountain and, on a twenty-foot pipe, raised an American flag. That was a war.

On February 28, we hit the railroad yards in

Kassel and came back to a tea dance in the Officers' Club.

On March 1, wonderful news. We got a phone call from Rosie. "I'm in Russia. Will you save a squadron for me?"

When he landed in his chute, instead of turning west for France and the American armies, he headed east. Soon he was surrounded by soldiers, their rifles aimed menacingly at him.

Rooskies.

Wildly, he waved the American flag, handkerchief size, that was in his escape kit. Not a rifle wavered.

Somehow he convinced them he was Americanski. They shipped him to Moscow, where he had dinner with Ambassador Harriman. The ambassador patched a phone call through to Washington, and then to the embassy in London, and then to Thorpe Abbotts.

On March 8, I navigated a whole planeload of the 100th to Paris, and we enjoyed a three-day pass. I saw the Folies-Bergère.

As the Russians in the east and the British and Americans from the west converged, we had fewer and fewer city targets. On March 18 we went strategic again. Harry Cruver led 1,329 heavies on what was to be the 100th's last mission to Berlin.

April 1 was both Easter Sunday and All Fool's Day. It was also the day we became yet another kind of air force. Since the weather was good for three weeks, we went out every day. Instead of being strategic or tactical, we became part of Operation Manna-Chowhound.

All during the war, we had a custom in the 100th that any ground officer or enlisted man could fly on one combat mission. Many of them, for whatever reason, took advantage of the opportunity. Some of them learned to fire a machine gun and manned one of the waist guns. Some of them sat in the nose and watched what was happening. Some of them took a hefty drink, bundled up in blankets, lay down in the catwalk behind the radio compartment, and tried to sleep during the whole mission.

Suddenly the ground volunteers tripled, quadrupled. Everyone wanted to fly. And the combat crews wanted to fly extra missions.

From our escapees and the Red Cross we heard horror stories about the Dutch and French. The departing Germans took all the food. We heard the Dutch were eating flower bulbs; the French were eating rats and cats. When a starving horse died in his harness, they carved him up on the spot.

Now we began to drop food, medical supplies, and clothing on the formerly occupied countries.

The operation was combination RAF-USAF, but its name symbolized our different ways of looking at things. The RAF called the operation Manna, from the biblical story in the Book of Exodus, referring to the food God dropped from Heaven on Moses and the Jews during their wanderings in the desert. The USAF, with its inclination to mask serious or human acts, called it Chowhound. In toto, the operation used both names. Ergo, Manna-Chowhound.

We were told that the Germans had agreed not to shoot at us as long as we stayed in our briefed corridors across the Zuider Zee and along the corridor on the coast which had always been flak free.

On April 6, nineteen of our planes, flying in single file, dropped thirty-two tons of food and medical supplies on Hilversum near The Hague; another eighteen planes dropped thirty-four tons over Bergen.

An ordnance man in the 350th Squadron, charged with the responsibility of loading the cylinders with food, also inserted his name and a letter. In a very short time he received a response forwarded from Canada. One of the Dutch who profited from the drop sent the note via an RCAF flyer who had been harbored by the Resistance when he was shot down. The letter read, "I am a 19-year-old blond lady, considered to be good looking and shapely. If you wish to correspond after the war, we can do so."

The ordnance man was already married. End of story.

The flyers took their home food packages—usually cans of candy or meat—fashioned parachutes, and dropped them.

Between April 29 and May 7, the 8AF dropped 11,000 tons of food on France and Holland. When the Germans surrendered in Holland, we put every plane we had in the air and dropped every bite of candy, every tin of meat, every extra pair of shoes, all our galoshes, and packs and packs of cigarettes. We went in at 200 feet.

On bombing missions, crews waited to be awakened in the morning before they flew. For Manna-Chowhound, flyers and ground men got up in the morning by themselves and came down to Ops to see if they could have a place on a plane.

"Colonel Sutterlin," I said, "we are supposed to put twenty-one planes up, but we have 280 men who want to go along."

"Put up another flight of three planes. Since they won't be at altitude, they won't need oxygen stations. Let them fly fourteen men per plane."

On one mission I permitted six supernumeraries to go along in one plane.

There were still losses and deaths. Our crews reported a plane from another group which tried to ditch in the Channel. All went well until, just as it stalled in, the left wing went down and hit the water. The plane cartwheeled and broke into bits. Our crew reported no rafts and no crewmen in the water. Our crews dropped marker dyes to help Air Sea Rescue. They threw out their own Mae Wests to help any swimming crewmen.

On April 6, a B-24 tried to make an emergency landing and crashed in the woods east of the base.

One of our planes crashed five miles from the base. A woman saw the burning plane, ran into it and began dragging men out of the fire. The plane blew up, killing her. The 100th passed the hat and raised a fund for her children.

A few miles from us three B-24's collided and blew up.

And we had a new worry.

All during the air war, thanks in part to Axis Sally, who kept making threats about a new secret weapon that was almost ready to face us, we worried about when the Germans would send up jet aircraft.

On April 5, at debriefing, our gunners reported seeing some new planes which had no propellers and left a trail of smoke. We knew they were the ME-262's, and there were three of them. On April 7, our gunners reported two passes by the German jets.

With their high speed, the 262's could make a single pass from the rear. On the first pass the new planes ever made, they destroyed five Third Air Division bombers.

As great as our P-51 Mustangs were, they could do nothing against German jets who could fly 540 miles per hour, almost 200 miles per hour faster than our Little Friends. What our Ninth Air Force fighters could do was hit the planes on the ground, and they strafed and bombed every German airdrome they could find. The bombers of the Eighth went to Peenemünde, where we thought the 262's were produced, or maybe the V-1 and V-2's, and destroyed the factory—at least temporarily. We heard that we made a great dent in jet production, especially since Hitler was more interested in revenge and retaliation on English cities and poured more effort into the V-1 and V-2 buzz bombs than he did into jet aircraft.

Then we began to hear of the *Sonderkommandos*, suicide pilots who were taught to ram head-on into our bombers. Our radio operators heard women's voices exhorting the suicide pilots to remember their "dead wives and children buried in the ruins of our towns."

During these months we were very aware of what was going on in the Pacific—because there was a new American plane out there. We were interested in the B-29, which had been given the flattering name of "Superfort," as though our B-17 had been its forerunner. We had to stretch to fly ten hours; the B-29 could fly sixteen. It had been used in the Pacific, with the first raid being from India, June 5, 1944, with Bangkok as the target. Major General Curtis LeMay, then thirty-eight years old, was put in charge of the Twentieth Bomber Command. This gave us a personal interest in that theater. Now LeMay's B-29's were bombing Tokyo.

Fly, fly, fly. On April 7, to Buchen, in Germany. On April 8, to Czechoslovakia. On April 11, the 100th flew its 300th mission, to Landshut, northeast of Munich, with Colonel Sutterlin as command pilot. He did a good job. On April 11, the Eighth put up 1,300 bombers in perfect weather, bombing marshaling yards, airfields, oil and ordnance storage in Regensburg, which was the last large-scale strategic mission we flew.

On April 12, President Franklin D. Roosevelt died, and, in mourning, we called off our Three-Hundred Mission Week. For many of the men on our base, Franklin Roosevelt was the only president we had known. We were sorry we hadn't finished the war in time for him to know about it.

We knew the new president, Harry Truman. As a senator from Missouri, he chaired the commission which discovered the serious flaw in the B-26 bomber. He had saved the lives of flyers.

On April 13, 14, 15, and 16, we turned to German batteries still holding out on the French coast near Royan, which meant the Allies could not use Bordeaux as a port.

On April 18, I had my twenty-sixth birthday. In contrast to the other flyers, I was an old man. On that day, we sent the 100th to railroad marshaling yards in France and Germany.

I still have the briefing flimsy. Our three call signs were, for the lead squadron, Kidmeat; high squadron, Poobah; low squadron, Rubberband. Jack Staples was command pilot. Ellis was lead crew. Our flare was red-yellow. The wind at ground level was 360 degrees, 25 knots. Taxi time was 0805, T.O. at 0810. The formation was due back at 1730.

It was a day of dirty business: we dropped incendiaries and firebombs, napalm, a jellied form of gas.

On that day, the Eighth Air Force dropped the last of the 696,450 tons we dropped on the Reich during the war. Our crews saw many 262's, and our fighters went after them.

On the next day the 100th went to France, and our division lost six Forts, the last of our Big Gas Birds to be destroyed by German fighters.

On April 20, more attacks on railroad marshaling yards.

On that day, the Soviet and American armies met at the Elbe River and Germany was cut in half. There remained nothing for 8AF bomber groups to hunt. What were we to do?

We had plenty to do. On April 22, we began a week of revels to celebrate our 300th mission.

We accelerated Operation Manna-Chowhound.

On May 1, the 100th went to Walkraiburg. The lead bombardier dropped parachute containers with large white crosses which were to mark where our thirty-seven planes at 400 feet dropped 71.7 tons of supplies. Over The Hague our crews saw Dutch people on rooftops waving American and English flags.

On May 1, the Russians raised their flag over the Reichstag. On that day, our crews flew over Holland at 500 feet and dumped seventy tons of 10-in-1 rations on a racetrack and airfield near The Hague. On May 1, 2, 3, 5, and 6 we dropped more food. Coming back, our crews reported that these were "the pleasantest missions we ever flew."

On the ground, everywhere, people waving.

Somehow they made huge signs in the fields—"Thank you, Americans."

I felt better about Manna-Chowhound than I did about Operation Clarion.

We also flew what were called "revival missions," on which a five-man crew would fly into Germany, land at a Luftwaffe base, pick up as many as forty POWs, and bring them to Paris. The 8AF flew out 8,000 U.S. and 1,500 British. Many of our crews saw friends from the 100th. Most of them had lost forty or fifty pounds.

On May 2, thirty-eight of our planes dropped seventy tons of supplies over Schiphol. Planes went over the drop area in single file, skimming the terrain, pulling up to miss buildings and smokestacks. There was a heavy roar as pilots changed propeller pitch to adjust to altitude.

All the crews took their supplies of fresh fruit, the first oranges they had seen in months, to drop to the Dutch. They could see faces of people waving and praying.

On May 3, the 100th dropped another seventy tons of supplies on Bergen, and the same load on Hilversum. The supplies were in burlap bags, and our flyers saw them explode on the ground.

Reports came back about "happiness hats." During the war, the Resistance and Underground had to hide parachutes since they were evidence of American airmen coming down in the area—and evidence of who had helped them. Now the silk came out, was dyed in vivid colors, and fashioned into hats, scarves, and skirts, so bright in color that we could see them from the air. Now they were proud symbols of who had helped the escapees and evadees.

A ball turret operator told about seeing a very fat woman walking along the road in a "happiness skirt." As the planes roared by, she raised her skirt, with nothing on beneath it.

"Hey, tail gunner," he called on intercom. "Close your eyes. You are too young to see this."

On May 5, Field Marshal Montgomery announced he was to accept German surrender. The Germans in Holland did surrender. On that day twenty-one of our planes dropped thirty-seven tons of food and medical supplies on Bergen. Twenty more planes went again to Hilversum to drop thirty more tons. We dropped seven tons on Baarn. Our crews saw people on the streets of Amsterdam.

Instead of flying formation, the planes again went in single file, flying at thirty-second intervals, and the crews scattered the supplies to real people waiting below. Everywhere they saw Dutch flags and "happiness clothes." The Dutch were obviously deliriously happy. As our planes buzzed by, they waved their flags and jumped up and down. Our planes skimmed housetops at 150 feet, and waved to the people on the streets and in second-floor windows.

With that many planes going out and flying so low, there were bound to be casualties. On almost the last day of the war, our crews reported seeing a 95th plane catch on fire just as it zoomed up after dropping its load of mercy. The pilot tried to ditch in the North Sea, but the plane hit a swell and broke in two.

I went on none of the missions. I never could handle low-level navigation. At that altitude I had to work too fast to take time to use my #10 sacks. At that altitude the bumpiness would have made me so sick I am not sure I could have performed my duties.

But I briefed every navigator, and I exulted at the joy of the young men—really boys—who had stopped bombing cities, and were now saving people.

On May 8, five days after our son Stephen was born, there was a "cessation of hostilities."

Victory in Europe.

Our part of the war was over.

EPILOGUE

✈ And so the heroes went home . . .

In New York Harbor, the greatest show on earth. "Welcome home, Victors!" Thousands of onlookers in boats, at the dockside, on the streets. Fireboats shooting fountains of water into the air.

A huge sign: "YOU DID IT."

I walked across the gangplank. I was home. Safe.

A Pullman ride across half of America.

Chillicothe, Missouri. Jean.

A tiny baby. I was afraid to hold it.

"What if I drop him?"

"You won't, silly."

We bought a '39 Dodge. We loaded Steve, his gear, and our possessions.

Two idyllic weeks in reassignment at Miami Beach, Florida. We were in a posh hotel, converted into an officer's R&R spot. Rest and recuperation. A promo-

tion put in for me before I left Thorpe Abbotts
caught up with me, and I started wearing the leaves
of a lieutenant colonel.

In two weeks I was rested and recuperated.

We started to drive to Ellington Field, in Houston,
Texas. For me to be an instructor? For me to get
ready for B-29's in the Pacific?

Who knew? We were happy, foolishly, ridiculously, deliriously happy.

In August, en route to my next assignment, in
Louisiana, a car passed us on the highway. Honking.
The passengers waving and yelling.

They had a radio and we didn't.

"V-J!" they yelled.

The war was over.

It took a few weeks for me and the Air Force to
separate. Until I received my conversion to civilian
status, I had perfunctory duties checking out trainee
navigators. The head of navigation, impressed by my
medals and rank, sent me up with ten second lieutenant navigators on a Brownsville–Corpus
Christi–Houston triangular mission. Jack Wild, one
of the 100th's great command navigators, was with
me.

"Show them how to do it, Colonel Crosby," said
the Chief of Navigation.

We never got to Brownsville.

I got sick just as we took off. I whipped out my
sack, and did what I always did. I kept doing it.

Then, one by one, the trainee navigators got sick.

For the first time in his Air Force career, Jack Wild
got sick.

I was still using my sacks.

To keep out the fumes of my distress, the pilot and

the copilot drew the curtain between their compartment and mine.

Then they got sick, very sick.

The pilot, in disgust, racked the plane around.

Back we went to Houston. End of mission.

At the Officers' Club, Jean and Jack's wife Doris were waiting for us. They saw us, the trainee navigators, and the two pilots.

"Never before in my life," said Jean, "have I seen people who are pea green."

Maybe I was one of the best command navigators in the world. I was probably one of the best four or five navigators at getting 2,000 planes together and shepherding them to destroy a metropolis.

But this was just about the least marketable skill I could imagine. It wasn't even transferable. I could get two thousand planes together and make a rendezvous on a split-second schedule, but now I learned that by the time I got my wife and baby son to church, the choir was halfway through the opening hymn.

Like every veteran of WWII, I profited as a civilian from what was ready for us stateside. We went home to the grandest reception, the most moving welcome, and the greatest generosity the United States ever offered.

I marched in every parade. Jean, Steve, and I visited our families, and I talked at the Kiwanis, Rotary, and Optimists' Club in both towns. Then we went to Iowa City for me to go back to the university, and I talked at all three clubs there. Everyone was impressed with my medals. I did not tell them that during WWII, 38,500 other DFC's were earned, and awarded.

We profited from the G.I. Bill, one of the grandest pieces of social legislation ever devised. On its generous stipend, I earned an M.A. at the University of Iowa and a Ph.D. from Stanford University. Heavily influenced by my observations during the war that the ability to communicate was all-important, I studied language usage. The mentor for my dissertation, Wallace Stegner, was important in my development. Jean, Steve, and I went back to Iowa City where I became the writing supervisor for the rhetoric program. We bought a home in a pleasant section of town. Because of the G.I. Bill, the interest rate on our mortgage was 3.5 percent.

My first bombardier, Howard Hamilton, the boy from Kansas, also used the G.I. Bill. He got a Ph.D. in electrical engineering from the University of Minnesota. With his wife Gerry, Jean's apartment mate in Chicago, he spent a lot of time advising governments in South America, and became head of the department at the University of Pittsburgh. No one in the 100th would have predicted that.

Many of my friends did not feel their service was over. They stayed in the Air Force. Ev Blakely stayed in. He took graduate work in Spanish studies. He and his wife, Marge, Jean's other Chicago apartment mate, spent several tours in South America. He was the head of the Air ROTC program at Notre Dame during the Vietnam War.

The two Buckys stayed in. Bucky Egan died very early, of cancer. Bucky Cleven had an unusual career. While in the service, he earned an M.B.A, from the Harvard Business School and a Ph.D. in interplanetary physics and became an important figure in computerizing the Pentagon. Wearing quite a different hat, he was a member of the Air Force space program.

Jim Douglass, Ray Miller, Jack Wild, Leonard Bull, Cowboy Roane, Sammy Barr, and many others stayed in. Most of them became colonels.

Six of the 100th became generals. Jack Wallace and Fred Sutterlin made one star. Brigadier generals. Jack Kidd, Tom Jeffrey and Bill Veal got two stars. Major generals. In the Air Force reserve, John Bennett also became a major general and was offered the job in Washington as Under Secretary of the Air Force.

Time magazine had an editorial about the men and women of our age. They called us the Take Charge Generation, with John F. Kennedy as our prototype. I don't know about that. If I were asked to list any one quality which characterized my associates from the 100th it would be their continued dedication to public service.

Bob Rosenthal, "Rosie," went to Germany where he and his wife served during the Nuremberg Trials. For years they both have been active in social and humanitarian causes in New York where he was a very successful lawyer. Cowboy Roane and John Stephenson went into education and became school superintendents. John Brady entered politics and for years was chairman of the town council of Laurel, Maryland. Bucky Elton started a ranch which provided a halfway experience for former convicts. Jean and I also had the bug. Between us we were president of five different PTAs. We were active in many civic affairs. I was a campaign chairman for two Massachusetts congressmen, Father Robert Drinan and Barney Frank, and for the mayor of Newton, Massachusetts, Ted Mann. I was elected a member of the Newton Board of Aldermen.

Along with many of my 100th friends, Jack Kidd and I became strongly antiwar. We both were respectful of all service men and women who accepted the call of duty. I, however, was co-chairman of the first official movement opposing the War in Vietnam. His years in the Air Force convinced Jack Kidd that war is futile and the military inevitably wasteful. He joined a group of other high-ranking military leaders including Admiral Gene La Rocque to form the antimilitary Center for Defense Information. Jack's book, *The Strategic Cooperation Initiative*, argued—before the peace movement became popular—for an end to the arms race, the elimination of nuclear weapons, and a reversal of the degradation of the world environment.

One lesson all of us seem to have learned from our time with the 100th is the value of comradeship. Like many other military organizations, we have stuck together. Like most other WWII units, we have reunions. The average attendance at a reunion of other bomb groups is about two hundred. At the last 100th reunion, chaired by E. A. Cassimatis, my old friend, the navigator whose poker winnings subsidized my wedding and honeymoon, our attendance was over a thousand.

I have learned, however, not to brag that our reunions are bigger than those of the other Eighth Air Force bomb group associations. I made this statement once to a veteran from the 390th, and he said, "Yes, the 100th always were clannish." Then he put me in my place. He reminded me of the reputation we once had. "Yes," he said, "You always did stick together."

A pause, and then, "Except when you flew formation."

I have kept up my old friendships with the comrades I knew at Thorpe Abbotts. At our meetings and through our newsletter, *Splasher Six*, for which I am editor, I have become friends with Jim Scott, Jack

Bryce, John Affleck, Harry Vaughn, Hong Kong Wilson, Leonard Rosenfeld, Bud Buschmeier, Deno Bonnucchi, John Swenson, Carl Thorkelson, Chuck Harris, Charles Hacker, Red Harper, Charles Nekvasil, and others whom I hardly met with the 100th.

We have our very own meeting place. One of our pilots, Dave Tallichet, owns seventy-five restaurants, most of them decorated with historical themes. His Cleveland restaurant, right next to the landing strip of the municipal airport, is called "The 100th Bomb Group," and it's decorated like our Officers' Club. As you enter, you will see a picture of our plane, old *Just a-Snappin'*, 393, coming in for its final landing as we just barely made it back to England after the Bremen mission. The original of the painting, by Mike Deibel, is in the Western Reserve Hall of Fame. In a montage with the painting is a picture of Blakely's crew. Four— Saunders, Nord, Via, and Douglass—are dead. Forkner, Yevich, McClelland, Blake, and I still see each other at reunions, and are in close touch. We have never located "Little Britches," Monroe Thornton.

The Brits, our neighbors back in Diss, Bungay, Dickleburgh, and the other villages, have not forgotten us. Led by Mike and Jean Harvey, Richard and Norma Gibson, Ron and Carol Batley, with the cooperation of landowners David Wigans and Sir Rupert Mann and dozens of other members of the FOTE—the Friends of the Eighth—they resurrected our old control tower, built two more buildings, landscaped the area, collected our memorabilia, and established a museum visited every year by thousands from the U.K., the U.S., and the rest of the world.

At the University of Iowa, I became the writing supervisor of the rhetoric program. We had three more children, April, Jeff, and Rebecca. All four of our children, now grown and happily married, are doing very well, thank you. They have provided us eight grandchildren. Jean and I and the family moved to Newton, Massachussetts. At Boston University I became chairman of the Department of Rhetoric at the College of Basic Studies. We roamed the world, spending summers or sabbaticals in Nova Scotia, Mexico, Alaska, Spain, and western Europe. All of my kids have been around the world; they have toured most of the States.

After I became emeritus I went across the river and became director of the Writing Center for Harvard University.

My ambivalence about the military kept me out of the Reserve, but the Air Force invited me back to help set up the Academy in Colorado Springs. I am very proud of the writing program and the humanities enrichment syllabus we established. I was asked to go to Pakistan where I became the Director of Studies for the Air Force for two years, helping bring about the conversion of a flying school to an accredited institution of higher education.

Through it all, Jean was a superb wife and mother. When we were in Pakistan, she organized a drama group which contributed greatly to the liberation of women. When a brouhaha developed among the cooks and bakers at Risalpur, our base, and disrupted the graduation party for the college, she organized all the Pakistani memsahibs in their filmy, silken saris, and provided an extravagantly successful dinner for the President of Pakistan.

Because of her work with the church, schools, and as an assistant for Congressman Drinan, she became a community leader.

In 1980, we learned she had terminal cancer, with seven months to live. She was, of course, brave, stoic, cheerful. Near the end, she said, "The closer it gets, the less attractive it seems." When she died, 750 people came to her memorial service.

Eventually, I remarried.

Now, on a 150-acre farm in Maine, I am living out my idyll with Mary Alice. When we married I acquired three more children—Haley, Maura, and John. They, too, now are grown. Mary Alice was the director of Buckingham Browne & Nichols lower school; now she teaches in New Hampshire. This is not the winter of my life. It is the harvest.

With Mary Alice and my friends in Lovell and elsewhere, especially those of my vintage, we talk about The War.

Was it worthwhile? When I think of the 100th's casualties, 732 killed, and another 1,040 who went through the ordeal of being shot down, who became POWs, evadees, or internees, I doubt whether any war can be good. I visit the Military Cemetery near Cambridge, England, and see all those stars and crosses arranged in a semicircle like a silent choir. I wonder what poets, what statesmen, what inventors, what husbands, what fathers, never were permitted to play their part in a contribution toward human well-being.

Since I cannot forget my own shortcomings during the war, the times I was off course or missed rendezvous and we got hit by flak or fighter, the fact that my first crew was shot down and I wasn't, the navigators who were killed when I assigned them to an ill-fated crew—and the cities and people I destroyed—I have trouble assessing my own contribution. I do have one evaluation, and it came as a surprise to me.

In 1946, just before he became Chief of Staff of the Air Force, Major General Curtis E. LeMay was asked to list the outstanding people who served under him. In his response to Major General F. L. Anderson, on 7 March 1946, he wrote,

I am submitting the names of thirty-two (32) officers, nineteen (19) of which served under me in the European Theater of Operations and thirteen (13) of which served under me in the Pacific. I have carefully screened the outstanding officers which have served under me and believe each of these submitted comes within the category which you defined as being particularily outstanding in combat.

I was one of the nineteen in the ETO. About me, General LeMay wrote:

Major Harry H. Crosby, 0-731272, outstanding officer, both from combat and training standpoint, has a superior record in combat leadership and in devising training methods beneficial to the 3rd Air Division, 8th Air Force.

I don't know who the other eighteen men were, but I feel that I was among select company. Apparently General LeMay forgave me for not bombing Bonn.

Was it a good war? Did we have to fight it? Studs Terkel, when he writes about "The Last Good War," says that it was, and we did.

Did aerial bombardment do any good? Did it hasten the victory? John Kenneth Galbraith has written that "strategic bombardment produced no significant results in Europe during World War II." Other historians have disagreed. Professor David MacIsaac has proven, to me conclusively, that along with other contributions—our diversions when we were sent "to go after the sub pens, to split forces in North Africa, to support the invasion, and to get the V-1 and V-2"— we "succeeded in our primary mission, to stop German war production." After a survey of Luftwaffe officers for *American Heritage*, Carl Sulzberger found agreement with one German flying officer that "there is no doubt that the Americans harmed us most. The Russians were negligible as far as the home front was concerned, and we could have stood the British attacks on our cities. But the American devastation of our airfields, factories, and oil depots made it impossible for us to keep going."

Was the 100th famous or notorious? Our legends have grown. An article by Kenneth Kinney in *American Legion Magazine* tells what happens among veterans when one of them "says he was in the 100th Bomb Group. The respect for this man will fairly permeate the air. For the rest of the men realize they are conversing with a museum piece—an ex-pilot, bombardier, navigator, or gunner who flew with the 100th and lived to tell about it." The article concludes, "So if a guy tells you he flew with the 100th, be nice to him. He deserves it."

I have learned to live with ambiguity. I remember the cities we destroyed, and the German poets and inventors we stilled, but I remember the time when we went to the edge, when we put our lives on the line, for a cause that we believed to be just. I remember my friends, those who made it through and those who did not. I remember the tragedies, and the horror, but I remember the laughter.

I have read many books about the war, trying to get straight on what happened. There are many good ones, especially those by Roger Freeman, Ed Jablonski, Martin Caidin, Ian Hawkins, Richard LeStrange, and Martin Middlebrook. I wonder how they tell the story so well when they weren't there.

One of the excellent books, *One Last Look*, by Rex Alan Smith, has a paragraph I have read and reread.

> *No American or East Anglian can think seriously about B-17's today without feeling the tug of their great purpose and destiny. They were the two-fisted tin cans that tore the roof off a deranged empire. When they swarmed over occupied Europe, people blessed them. One day, when several hundred of them roared across Holland, a little girl cried out in fear. Her father put his arm around her, took her hand, and looked up. "Listen to it, Helene," he told her. "It's the music of angels."*

Was it worth it? Those years? Those lives? That destruction?

I still don't know.

But I do know that I, too, heard the angels.

★ INDEX ★

Harry H. Crosby (B.A. and M.A. University of Iowa; Ph.D., Stanford University) was Writing Supervisor of the Rhetoric Program at the University of Iowa, Chairman of the Department of Rhetoric at Boston University, and Director of the Writing Center at Harvard University. He helped establish the original curriculum of the Air Force Academy in the 1950s and was Director of Studies of the Pakistan Air Force College in 1960-62.

Now retired, he and his wife live on a tree farm in Maine, where he edits the 100th Bomb Group newsletter, *Splasher Six*, and is active in local politics and civic affairs.